Honour, Violence and Emotions in History

Honour, Violence and Emotions in History

Edited by
Carolyn Strange, Robert Cribb
and Christopher E. Forth

Bloomsbury Academic
An imprint of Bloomsbury Publishing Plc

BLOOMSBURY
LONDON · NEW DELHI · NEW YORK · SYDNEY

Bloomsbury Academic

An imprint of Bloomsbury Publishing Plc

50 Bedford Square	1385 Broadway
London	New York
WC1B 3DP	NY 10018
UK	USA

www.bloomsbury.com

BLOOMSBURY and the Diana logo are trademarks of Bloomsbury Publishing Plc

First published 2014

Paperback edition published 2015

British Library Cataloguing-in-Publication Data
A catalogue record for this book is available from the British Library.

ISBN: HB: 978-1-4725-1947-4
PB: 978-1-4725-1946-7
ePDF: 978-1-4725-1948-1
ePub: 978-1-4725-1949-8

Library of Congress Cataloging-in-Publication Data
A catalog record for this book is available from the Library of Congress.

Typeset by Integra Software Services Pvt. Ltd
Printed and bound in Great Britain

CONTENTS

ILLUSTRATIONS

ACKNOWLEDGEMENTS

The inspiration for this volume was an interdisciplinary conference, titled 'Honour Killing across Culture and Time', held at the Australian National University in 2011. Karen Downing, the chief administrator of the conference, and Joshua Wodak, the technical co-ordinator, made the administration of the event a success. On reflection, it became apparent that there was scope to produce a squarely historical collection that would focus on the distinctiveness of the past. Thus, we are grateful to our contributors who responded to our call for submissions and we appreciate their willingness to incorporate the insights of historians of emotion into the study of honour-based violence. We are also grateful for the constructive criticism offered by the press's anonymous reviewers.

The editorial staff at Bloomsbury have been a pleasure to deal with. We worked first with Claire Lipscomb and Frances Arnold, and our move to our astute editor, Emily Drewe, was smooth. Each has provided prompt and expert support, and Emma Goode has ferried us through the choppy waters of production and permission issues with skill and tact. Robyn Curtis wrestled the manuscript into submission-ready copy in good time and spirit.

The image on the book's cover ('Anxiety') is graciously provided by artist Ida Våg. We are grateful for her permission to use her arresting work.

We also appreciate the support and critical insight provided by colleagues who assisted us at the early and late stages of the manuscript's production, particularly Anne-Marie Kilday, Michael J. Casimir and Barbara Rosenwein.

Finally, we acknowledge the financial support of the Australian Research Council.

Carolyn Strange
Robert Cribb
Christopher E. Forth

1

Historical perspectives on honour, violence and emotion

Carolyn Strange and Robert Cribb

From the vantage point of the early twenty-first century, connecting the words 'honour' and 'violence' conjures up two images: the assault and murder of girls and women thought to have cast family honour into question; and the duel, an outmoded ritual of masculine confrontation. The first is a grave political and legal issue that persists in many parts of world, whereas the latter – knights locked in mortal combat or gentlemen squaring off over points of honour – appears to be a phenomenon of the Western past. Psychologist Steven Pinker attributes the decline of duelling in the West not to the laws that criminalized it, but to its growing disrepute: 'honor is a bubble that can be inflated by some parts of human nature, such as the drive for prestige and the entrenchment of norms, and popped by others, such as a sense of humour'.[1] In other words, duelling persisted in Europe and North America until it was undone by disdain, contempt and ridicule. In contrast to Pinker, whose objective is to chart the diminution of violent tendencies over human history, anthropologists and historians have delved deeply into the norms that have supported the violent defence of honour in diverse political, social and cultural contexts. This body of research has focused on the ways in which cultural codes have informed individual behaviour, particularly codes associated with gender, class, religion, ethnicity, age and marital status. From the Ancient World to the islands of urban impoverishment in world capitals, we now have a wide array of scripts and rituals associated with violent encounters over notions of honour.[2] However, the subject of emotion and its relation to codes of behaviour has yet to be interrogated systematically in these studies. In view of the emotion-laden terms in which clashes over honour have been articulated historically, an intriguing question arises: what role has emotion played in the history of honour-associated violence? This question is the instigation for this volume.

A rich vein of literature on codes of honour and on violence inflicted in its name emerged in the 1980s, when social historians, drawing on earlier anthropological and sociological studies of the dynamics of honour, produced landmark studies of duelling in England, Western, Northern and Southern Europe, and the United States.[3] This research highlighted honour's profound association with masculinity and demonstrated that males, overwhelmingly, have been the chief antagonists in violence inflicted in its name. Whether in German military academies of the early-twentieth century, where young officers were tutored into responding to ripostes, or in the village squares of early modern Spain or Italy, where men of lower ranks knew which dishonouring words or gestures had the potential to spark a knife fight, historians have studied honour disputes to illuminate the ways in which social and economic hierarchies were cross-cut by other status markers defined through character traits and behaviour. Although the emphasis placed on particular qualities (such as bravery or honesty) has varied over time and between societies, legal and medical records confirm that failure to uphold such characteristics, or even the insinuation of failure, could spark physical attacks, often lethal. To ward off the unpalatable prospect of losing respect or feeling shame, men have turned to violence (albeit not invariably, and rarely after the turn of the twentieth century, except in remote and loosely governed pockets of the world). Duelling and other rituals of violence associated with honour have gone in and out of fashion in different jurisdictions and the social locus of these customs has also shifted over time. For instance, in France the duel declined as a noble male practice, only to be taken up by bourgeois men in the nineteenth century, eager to adopt their betters' touchiness as a sign of refinement. More recent literature stresses that men at all levels of society valued public standing and were prepared to resort to violence – often in ritualized brawls – in order to recover respect.[4] But, as with aristocratic duelling, this plebeian form of honour's violent defence eventually declined in response to increasingly disfavourable public opinion, which eroded the capacity of violence to restore respect.

Ironically, historical analysis of the demise of duelling in Western history commonly points to the suppression of aggressive emotions without first establishing how emotion figured in the history of honour-based violence. Despite the fact that texts associated with duels and honour-related brawls are often suffused in emotion – such as words of anger, shame, fear, pride and grief in letters and diaries and in public accounts – the dynamics of the duel are depicted principally through codes of masculinity in connection with youth, class and regional codes. This approach illuminates what made individuals act with violence in confrontations over honour, but it does not probe how historical actors felt about honour, nor the relation between their feelings and their sense of honour's meanings.[5] The measures that drove duelling and brawling from the social landscape were legal, ethical and moral, but the emotional registers of those measures are unclear in studies of the rise and fall of duelling. Instead, the foundational literature on honour-based violence attributes its decline to the 'taming' of emotions.[6] When it comes to the study of honour-based violence, the realm of emotional experience has thus far taken second place to social and political factors, which in some contexts encouraged the violent defence of honour, while in others, it has provided the means and encouragement for the peaceful resolution of differences, whether through litigation or pledges.[7]

This approach to emotion is most mechanistic in the work of historians who work within the framework of Norbert Elias' interpretation of civilizing processes. Elias (1897–1990) drew on a vast array of European etiquette manuals and literature that set standards of politeness, and he plotted them in relationship to changes in state formation, especially the growing monopolization of violence. These political and social changes altered the psychological make-up of 'Western man', rendering him more capable of controlling his impulses (everything from spitting to doing violence) by the modern era.[8] Written in 1939 and influenced deeply by Freudian analysis of personality development, Elias's masterwork continues to inspire historians intrigued by the steep drop in the rate of recorded homicides, from a high point in the late medieval period to the comparatively peaceful nineteenth century, after which it has remained low and relatively stable in European countries (though not in the United States).[9] According to Pieter Spierenburg, the key trigger for this shift is the transition in the meanings held for honour over this long period. Prior to the 1800s, honour was a bodily oriented concept for Western Europeans. Medieval and early modern man, left on his own to defend his property, took pride in his capacity to defend his reputation and the standing of his family, and he made ready use violence to deter rivals and to maintain his status claims. Trespass against the 'ideal sphere' of his body (a notion traceable back to Freud), even a symbolic affront such as knocking off a hat, risked an impulsively violent response, unrestrained by challengers' or victims' thoughts of possible consequences.[10] Gradually, and in tandem with the rise of centralizing powers in modern monarchies and new republics, the notion of honour became 'spiritualized' and democratized, Spierenburg argues, since anyone deemed to be trustworthy, comradely, honest and generous could now be considered worthy of honour.[11] Under the subtitle, 'Ritual, Masculinity and Impulse', he states that 'impulse is always a matter of degree....to get angry and aggressive, you first had to have a reason, however suddenly found'.[12] Some medievalists have questioned the assumption that people of the distant European past were impulsively violent by showing that public rituals, particularly customs associated with honour, channelled individuals' 'free-floating' violent passions far earlier than Elias had recognized.[13] But criticism of this nature leaves the Eliasian concept of 'impulse' unchallenged, since the terms of the debate remain the same: whenever, and wherever, violent impulses are least controlled, the idea of honour provides a 'reason' for violence.

There are two problems with this explanatory framework, and the contributors to this volume tackle both of them. The first concerns the misconceived notion of emotion as 'impulses' or irrational forces, an understanding that persists in spite of the substantial scientific and historiographical advances in the study of the subject since the 2000s. The concept of bodily impulses leaves the analysis of emotion somewhere back in the late nineteenth century, when physical scientists defined it as a form of nervous energy that acted upon the body. In 1884, neuropsychologist William James described emotions as 'visceral stirrings', in which the brain and the mind were second to 'organic excitement'.[14] Whereas previous metaphysical writers had spoken of 'affections' and 'sentiment', words that had bridged thinking and feeling, nineteenth-century researchers secularized the psychology of emotion, leaving a 'simple and sharp dichotomy between cognition and emotion'.[15] Over the ensuing century, cognitive psychologists, such as Robert C. Solomon, and anthropologists of emotion, notably Michelle Zimbalist Rosaldo and Catherine A. Lutz, broke down the dichotomy between feeling and meaning-making, instead stressing the social and cultural situatedness of emotions and the capacity of emotions to influence behaviour and social relations. The historians who pioneered the study of emotion, notably Barbara H. Rosenwein and William H. Reddy, further advanced this understanding by showing that a human phenomenon subject to cross-cultural variability can also be historicized. However physical the capacity for emotion may be, and however physiological the sensation of emotion (apparent, increasingly, through brain imaging), emotions are processed feelings, sensed, experienced and expressed distinctly through historically situated language and modes of expression. Thus, to posit that 'free-floating' impulses ignited violence in the name of honour until Europeans 'tamed' those impulses rests on the assumption that emotion comes in just two varieties: expressed or repressed. According to Elias and his adherents, the sources of control – the state monopolization of violence, combined with social, religious and educational edicts – intensified over time until modern Westerners searched for esteem and respect through virtue, not violence. Yet it is hardly likely that a phenomenon as complex and historically contingent as emotion can be pinned down so neatly. Under what circumstances, and among which groups, is the expression of particular emotions validated? Which emotions are considered salient by individuals and the groups with whom they affiliate? And specifically, what emotions attach to honour, making it something worth killing and dying for? By addressing these questions, the contributors to this volume adopt an understanding of emotion that foregrounds its communicative and social nature.

The second problem concerns the Western-centric orientation of the historiography in which studies of duelling in the European and North America past have come to stand for the history of honour-related violence. Studies of Western history have certainly identified and examined social and cultural variations in patterns of violence; however, they do so primarily in terms of region – such as the greater propensity towards honour-related violence among Mediterranean men as opposed to Northern Europeans, or the so-called Southern code of honour in the United States, distinct from the culture of the comparatively law-oriented North.[16] Similarly, Western historical research has delineated scripts of honour that have marked the behaviour of different classes and cohorts of men, but little cross-cultural analysis has occurred. Because the foundational sources focus on the West, evidence from a small number of countries sets the standard against which 'other' histories of honour-based violence, in Asia or Africa, for example, fall into the category of 'difference'.[17] The historical and regional diversity of the West suggests that examining other parts of the world will reveal further diversity.[18] Until historians' insights into the mechanisms of honour, its gendered character and its emotional dynamics are applied outside Europe and North American, they should be considered contingent, not universal, and specific to Western, largely Christian history, rather than held up as definitive explanations of the links between honour, violence and emotion. Thus, prior to Eiko Ikegami's groundbreaking analysis of honorific Samurai culture, Western-trained researchers searched for functional equivalents of Western, Christian values, rather than examining Japanese cultural idioms through their historic roots.[19] To widen the scope of analysis calls for the study of polities in which, for instance, Confucian understandings of honour and normative emotional configurations have prevailed; and it also suggests that practices such as 'running amok' or widow suicide be interpreted alongside the history of duelling. In these respects, this collection approaches the emotional dimensions of honour-associated violence anthropologically as well as historically, seeking threads of connection while anticipating cultural variation, rather than starting from a Western point of reference, against which exceptions to patterns are defined.[20] Calls for a similar agenda have also been voiced in recent debates over the shortcomings of the historiography of emotion, a field forged and still dominated by historians of Europe. Eugenia Lean, a historian of China, as well as Ikegami, is among a new cohort of scholars whose research signals that the West can no longer stand as the normative space for understanding emotions.[21]

In keeping with the objective to unsettle Western-centric chronologies and readings of emotion's past, this volume charts new historiographical territory by interrogating the historical links between honour, violence and emotion in a range of social, cultural, political and economic contexts over the past four centuries. It presents nine case studies that encompass colonial South African and Australian history, South American history, Korean and Chinese history, British history, and Northern and Western European history. Accordingly, the chapters are organized chronologically, without the conventional temporal subsections that impose European periodization. Read as a collection, the contributions show how ideas about honour and ascriptions of its significance transcend culture and time; at the same time each chapter highlights how the actions and words that constitute disrespect and the repertoire of responses considered appropriate and inappropriate have varied greatly, far more so than between 'the West and the rest'. Using texts that include gallows broadsides, court transcripts, jokes, love letters, suicide notes, paintings and editorials, the authors examine how honour has been imagined and represented, and how emotions, as constructs and performances, have been attached to concepts of honour, especially in cases where anxiety over reputation and status has led to violence. Each chapter explores how individuals and groups negotiated demands for emotional expressiveness against demands for emotional discipline and reticence. Together, the contributors expose and analyse how emotions have shaped, and have been shaped by, specific social, cultural, political, economic and religious factors that impinged on the uses and agents of violence.

* * *

Recent analyses of emotion as a brain function have greatly advanced earlier efforts to analyse the concept scientifically, and leading historians of emotion have welcomed growing neurobiological evidence that affirms the significance of their research focus.[22] Monique Scheer, for instance, notes that affective neuroscience and studies inspired by Extended Mind Theory reinforce historians' assertion that 'emotions must necessarily have a history, as they each link cognitive-emotional processing to elements that themselves are subject to historical change and cultural specificity'.[23] Historians have a unique role to play in this multidisciplinary field of inquiry, especially since historical analysis counters the tendency, evident in some neurobiological and genetic studies, towards presentism, or the assumption that our contemporary understanding of emotions held in the past and will likely hold in the future.[24] Empirical research is needed to unearth the range of behaviours associated with particular emotions, and in analysing the varied ways in which individual feelings (in this case, concerning honour) have been conjured and given meaning over time. As the chapters in this volume confirm, emotions are not just felt individually or controlled externally, like the build-up of steam pressure capped by a gasket: they are constituted through collective values and institutions, which shape their forms of expression and evaluation over time, between and within societies, and in relation to class, gender, ethnicity and age – to all the other significant categories that historians call upon to understand the past.[25]

Lucien Febvre was an early advocate of research that would lead historians to capture the ways in which emotions connect individuals to groups, and expression to action. In 1941 he wrote that emotions 'very quickly acquire the power to set in train all those concerned, by means of a sort of imitative contagion'.[26] In other words, even if emotions are experienced by individuals, their social recognition hinges on shared interpretations and expectations, which in turn shape emotions. Through this process individuals appreciate how they 'should' feel, as well as how to make sense of others' emotions. As a human phenomenon lodged in historical and social context, emotion resists universal classification into categories, whether broad and general such as 'anger' or more narrowly drawn, such as 'nostalgia'. For this reason some historians suggest that 'it might be better to stick with the complexity, fuzziness, and over inclusivity of "emotion" rather than to retreat still further from the world of everyday concerns into new scientific jargons'.[27] Equally, leading scholars caution against subscribing to the common-sense hydraulic understanding of emotion.[28] This inapt perspective reinforces the supposed divide between emotion and reason, which William H. Reddy resolves through his notion of emotion as 'effortful pursuit of expression'.[29] Individuals' and communities' emotions are processed sensations, perceived and expressed through language and culture; they are appraisals which may or may not be conscious or articulated.[30] Thus, what Eliasian scholarship describes as the sociogenetic suppression of impulse is better understood as varied and changing forms of self-management, which do not lead, inexorably, towards the declining use of violence, nor arise, exclusively, from the example of elites.[31]

Historians have always written about feelings and passions, particularly in relation to interpersonal violence, but it was not until the 1980s that emotion became a distinct category of historical analysis, requiring new questions and interpretive frameworks, though not necessarily new sources. Pioneering work by Peter and Carol Stearns, followed by the signal contributions of Reddy and Rosenwein, produced an explosion of forums, journals and research centres that have carved out a new field of scholarship since the early 2000s.[32] Topics ranging from intimate friendship to political rhetoric have now been placed within the compass of this scholarship, and historians have debated which methods and analytical frameworks are best suited to historicize such a palpable yet elusive aspect of human experience.[33] Examining the emotional dimensions of honour-based violence complements this broader enterprise by subjecting the lingering concept of expression-suppression to scrutiny.

Approaching emotion in historical perspective lifts the phenomenon from the realm of human nature to an understanding of its changing social nature. That is to say, the emotions that we readily recognize – anger, sorrow, joy, regret, malice and so forth – are not products of the neurobiological evolution of humankind, on a par, for example, with viviparity. Despite their physiological basis and status as a common biological given among humans, they have evolved alongside and, as part of human culture, have taken on multiple forms in different historical contexts.[34] In her analysis of fear, often described as a 'primal' emotion, historian Joanna Bourke argues that emotions are not 'reports of inner states'; instead, they work as a means of mediating 'between the individual and the social'.[35] The social dynamics of emotion are captured best in Rosenwein's concept of 'emotional communities' – collectivities 'whose modes of emotional expression' and whose 'values and ideas' shaped individual behaviour and its judgement, a crucial factor in acts and appraisals of violence in association with honour.[36] By applying this notion, historians of emotion have analysed the ways in which emotion figures within different social groups in a single society, and not just in different historical periods. This growing corpus of research concretizes Rosaldo's insight that 'feeling is forever given shape through thought and … thought is laden with emotional meaning'. To the extent that emotion is 'schooled by public cultural discourse', which varies from social group to social group, it also varies over time.[37]

Thus, the historians in this collection approach emotion as a distinct and enduring dimension of human cognition about the individual and her or his place in society, not as irrational impulses, increasingly suppressed by the modern rational world. First, the volume explores honour-based violence on a canvas within and beyond Europe. Rather than studying emotional diversity as manifest in different classes and times exclusively within Western history, it incorporates case studies that examine the emotions invoked, expressed and judged in honour-based violence, both self-inflicted and in acts of violence against others. In addition, the chapters cover a wide span of time, from the sixteenth century to the present. Second, the authors highlight the place of emotion in acts of physical harm and verbal assault, as well as their social and legal judgements and cultural representations. In doing so we connect individuals to their 'emotional communities', and we account for shifting performances and patterns of honour-related violence through reference to political, economic, social and intellectual transitions without subscribing to an evolutionary or teleological account of change.[38] Finally, by challenging the Western-centric orientation of the historiography of emotions, this volume underlines the need for further research that explores common humanity in balance with historical specificity.[39]

* * *

Georg Simmel, one of the founders of modern sociology, was the first social scientist to analyse honour and its links to violence.[40] Writing in 1898, a time when fatal duels still occurred in the German officer class, Simmel described honour as a mechanism of 'social maintenance', a 'social requisite' that commands the behaviour of an individual in relation to his social circle.[41] Although he identified a close coherence between individual and social interest, and acknowledged that honour was an ideal 'preferred to life', Simmel did not integrate emotion into his theorization. After Simmel, anthropologists took the lead in the mid-twentieth century, as they attempted to outline the social structures of honour and to unlock the cultural codes that convey its meanings regarding the use of violence in its defence. Julian Pitt-Rivers moved outside of his own society to study the ways in which Mediterranean peoples defined honour. Based on his ethnographies he defined honour as 'a sentiment, a manifestation of this sentiment in conduct, and the evaluation of this conduct by others'.[42] J. G. Peristiany, Pitt-Rivers' collaborator, hinted at the significance of emotion when he wrote that 'honor is too intimate a sentiment to submit to definition: it must be felt ... ' (adding that 'it cannot be analysed except by the anthropologist').[43] Disciplinary hubris aside, their work was most concerned to decipher the 'logic' of honour among contemporary Mediterranean, Basque and Islamic peoples, and they proposed that similar logics had once been at play in Europe, where similar motivations and ritualistic violence had been manifest. Broadly speaking, they argued that codes of honour function as rules of behaviour that uphold social relations and keep them stable. As powerful norms, honour codes prescribe forms of behaviour as strictly as, or even more strictly than, any form of law. According to this foundational anthropological reading, codes of honour override emotion, because they are formularistic: a word or gesture that registers as an affront to the honour of another requires a prescribed response, including violence. The emotion of the two (or more) parties in this transaction is secondary to its social meaning. For these ethnographers, sentiments, not emotions, are called into play when honour is at stake.[44]

Pierre Bourdieu, who worked in North Africa during the Algerian War, advanced the analysis of honour's emotional qualities over the course of his career. Through his initial study of the Islamic Kabyle people he defined honour as a constellation of thought and feeling that, under defined circumstances, motivates and authorizes violence.[45] Bourdieu approached honour as he did love, defining it as a complex sentiment and a 'common and intimate code', through which emotions were connected through cultural logics.[46] However, his later theorization of 'habitus' replaced the concept of a biological–cultural divide (and with it the primitive–civilized binary) with the notion of disposition or the social nature of the seemingly natural. By the 1970s, he applied this understanding to explain how a sense of honour becomes embedded mentally and bodily, conducting, 'without being in any way the product of obedience to rules', individuals' emotions in association with fundamental values. The 'conducts of honour', Bourdieu concluded, are 'the product of a more or less conscious pursuit of the accumulation of symbolic capital'.[47]

For the purposes of this collection, we plot honour and emotion in relation to violence across a wide temporal and geographic terrain, and we adopt a capacious understanding of honour, drawing on anthropological theory and the historiography of honour-based violence, as well as recent methodological advances in the study of emotion. Honour, a cultural attribution related to specific clusters of 'values and idealised norms', has always pivoted on the importance of respect paid and respect due, both to individuals and to the groups to which they belong.[48] It is dependent on and generative of the desire for esteem in the eyes of others whose opinion matters – generally oriented along a horizontal axis of status, but occasionally played out through vertical social relations.[49] Honour is an individual quality, but it also connects individuals to families, clans, communities, professions and ethnic and religious groups.[50] Consequently, its potency derives from a web of social understandings about obligations and duties.[51] The anticipation of respect is linked historically with the right to personal integrity, meaning the right to be free of unwarranted interference with one's person. All assertions of honour, as anthropologist Frank Henderson Stewart underlines, are 'rights claims' to status and respect.[52] Such claims spring less from a concern over material loss or personal inconvenience than from anxiety over an individual's sense of personal integrity, as defined by social context and social values.[53] Thus, honour's internal and external dimensions encompass emotion and thought.

* * *

The chapters in this collection illuminate the necessity to ground theorizations of honour in the emotional worlds of individuals, the complexities of their interpersonal and social relations, as well as the political, legal, economic and cultural contexts in which they made choices about how to respond to dishonour, or how to assert a claim to honour. For instance, in late eighteenth-century Cape Town, intentional rudeness could be communicated by the racially loaded term *Caffer*, and also by words such as 'scoundrel' or 'louse'. Such words, particularly if uttered in public, had the capacity to erode personal integrity and social standing. Dishonour could also be challenged by apparently trivial gestures, such as a failure to greet (as Eliza Ferguson discusses in her chapter on a spurned woman who shoots her cold-hearted ex-lover). Jungwon Kim's study of widow suicide in late nineteenth-century Korea shows that integrity's infringement, even in the absence of wounding words or physical assault, could be fatal. The right to be free of suspicion of dishonourable conduct is equally significant to personal integrity, something that women have struggled to assert, as Dana Rabin's chapter on infanticide trial accounts from eighteenth- and nineteenth-century Britain illustrates. Anxiety over personal integrity and susceptibility to fear or shame arising from dishonourable association varies markedly, however, from society to society, and whenever individuals and communities sense profound insecurity. Such perceptions were often amplified in times of economic and political crisis, whether in the impoverished backlands of nineteenth-century Brazil or in China, where tens of thousands of loyalists to the fallen Ming dynasty sacrificed their lives in the mid-seventeenth century.[54]

The significance of honour is most pronounced, as Anton Blok described, when men fret over their status and measure it against other 'men in groups'.[55] Nevertheless, there is much that remains to be understood concerning the ways in which such groups form and transform, and the norms that govern the resort to violence as well as its aversion. The historiography of honour-oriented violence, like popular portrayals of duelling, is tilted overwhelmingly towards men's history.[56] Ethnographic and criminological research similarly focuses on the interweaving of masculine codes and codes of honour, giving sense to violence that would otherwise appear to be senseless.[57] In 1993 Robert N. Nye stated that 'honor is a masculine concept. It has traditionally regulated relations among men, summed up the prevailing ideals of manliness, and marked the boundaries of masculine comportment'.[58] In this volume, he shows how men who aspired to honourability were called upon to uphold rising standards of ethics over the nineteenth and twentieth centuries, offsetting masculine legal and political privileges. Hierarchies of masculinity and conflicting codes of honour and respectability within societies have recently attracted closer attention by historians. Contributors Penny Russell and Nigel Worden show that in early colonial Australia and in the Dutch Cape Colony in the late eighteenth century, sailors, ex-slaves and convicts had their own sense of honour and their own means, often violent, to assert it. When power-holding men in authority judged the brawling and homicides committed by the lower orders, they weighed the possible range of responses to such violence against their competing concerns for order: colonial authorities found ways to work towards the reparation of social harmony, often violating their own ideals of honour, and never, predictably, in ways that fostered the 'civilisation' of inferiors.

The authors of this volume contribute to the growing sophistication of the analysis of gender by examining women's involvement in honour-related violence and the associated vocabularies of women's emotions. The historiographical neglect of these subjects arises, in part, from the assumption that men have honour, which may be lost but can be recovered, whereas women have virtue, which, once lost, can never be restored.[59] To the extent that feminine virtue is connected with chastity (both virginity prior to marriage and sexual faithfulness within marriage, extending to widowhood in many cultures), there is considerable historical evidence that bears out this claim, although research on acephalous societies and cultures in which women are not subject to strict patriarchal governance shows that women have developed an independent women's code of honour.[60] Yet even in these contexts, masculine honour has not generally rested on sexual purity; instead, where male-oriented cultures of honour have predominated, the sexual restraint of women has played a significant role in men's and family honour, an investment often protected and strictly policed by senior women.[61] Allegations of cuckoldry and aspersions cast against the chastity of a man's wife or female kin were weapons for those seeking to dishonour him (themes Jonas Liliequist explores in the context of early modern Sweden). Yet, women have responded to such gender asymmetries in a variety of ways, including the use of violence. Dana Rabin's study of tracts that depict the deeds of women convicted for infanticide highlights the readiness of their authors to document a wide range of emotions expressed at trial and on the gallows – not just shame and contrition, but anger against philandering husbands and resentment against moral judgement. In this context, innocent infants and unwilling mothers both paid with their lives for dishonour. Sexual honour was also at stake in the case of Marie Bière, an unwed mother charged with the attempted murder of her paramour in fin-de-siècle Paris. As Eliza Ferguson shows, Bière's acquittal was a gesture of chivalry on the part of the male jurors and judge; more than this, it provided an inroad for subsequent legal reform, which forced sexually profligate men to acknowledge their offspring and bear responsibility for them. In a far more turbulent period of history, that is, during the fall of the Ming dynasty, female as well as male warriors avenged the deaths of their loyalist fathers, which would have been dishonourable had they not, as daughters, acted out the prime Confucian virtue of filiality. Alison Bailey, drawing on this evidence, concludes that 'moral martyrdom was not the only road for women to take'.

Suicidal behaviour comes squarely within this collection's focus on honour-related violence, again, providing a corrective to the overwhelming historiographical attention on violence focused towards others – knife fights in village squares, trial by combat, pistols at dawn. Little of this scholarship has highlighted the degree to which self-destructiveness is implicated in the violent enactment of honour codes, for instance, in duels where combatants are aware that either or both parties might perish in a battle prompted by a disrespectful provocation. When it comes to self-killing, an act Durkheim associated with weak or fractured ties of social integration, individual understandings of honour are often apparent, deeply connected to shared values and patterns of cognition, though not always in concordance with them.[62] In late Chosŏn Korea (the nineteenth and early twentieth century), women who conformed outwardly to Confucian concepts of chaste widowhood harboured emotions that never appeared in public endorsements of their suicides, as Jungwon Kim reveals in her analysis of suicide notes. As one woman lamented privately, 'Who would ever know my thoughts inside? Where can I write down the layers and layers of resentment that rankle in my heart?' Although studies of suicide allow for deeper analysis of shame, an emotion strongly associated with honour and violence, the sensitive reading of textual evidence can illuminate the association of self-harm with dispiriting social and political conditions. Thus, when the Manchu conquerors ordered all Han Chinese males to shave their heads and wear a queue, a symbol of their humiliation, many Ming loyalists refused, fully aware that they risked execution. Later chroniclers honoured them for their fortitude.

By examining honour, violence and emotion in an unprecedented range of societies and regions, this volume's contributors help to exorcize this 'hyperreal ghost of Europe' in the historiography.[63] As the historiography of emotion matures, leading historians have begun to question the European orientation of historical research and the reliance upon Western histories of emotion as the benchmark against which research of similar phenomena in Asian and African history might be interpreted. As long as it does, an evolutionary and implicitly racist notion remains unchallenged, that certain categories of people, including premodern people, the poor, 'primitives' and 'Orientals', are particularly susceptible to emotion.[64] No historian of emotion claims that a Western-centric approach is adequate, yet very few have undertaken the detailed study required to disturb prevailing periodizations and analyses. For instance, the introduction to a 2013 special journal issue on suicide sketched the practice's history from the Greco-Roman period through the medieval period and the Enlightenment up to the present. The introduction's authors suggest that 'much work remains to be done in order to evaluate the collision of Western values with non-Western civilizations', but their acknowledgement did not alter their analysis of suicide's history or periodization.[65] A growing body of research has established that 'feeling rules' have governed violent actions and shaped sentiments of honour in ways that have evoked emotion distinctly over time.[66] Barbara H. Rosenwein puts the challenge of conducting transhistorical and cross-cultural research succinctly: '*every* culture has its rules for feelings and behavior; *every* culture thus exerts certain restraints while favoring emotional expression'.[67] This volume endorses and responds to Rosenwein's call.[68]

***

It is honour's emotional dimensions that make its stories so compelling, both for historical actors and for historians of violence. Shame, pride, guilt, joy, anger, humiliation, fear – these are the emotions that appear repeatedly in depictions of honour-related violence. Yet the configuration of emotions involved in honour-related violence defies definitive categorization, for individuals as well for societies.[69] When historical research moves across time and space this defiance becomes clearest.[70] The idea of the Mediterranean as an 'honour-shame' culture, supposedly rooted in an ancient 'tradition', has recently been questioned. The norms that Pitt-Rivers and his colleagues observed were not evident in ancient Greece. Furthermore, Aristotle did not identify sexual misconduct of female family members as a source of masculine shame.[71] These norms emerged historically, rather than simply surviving from a notionally primitive past. Whose emotions are authorized or valorized in accounting for violence, and whose are discounted or dismissed? And what are the circumstances and settings within which stories of honour-related violence narrated? Longitudinal studies looking to trace how violence was suppressed do not seek to answer such questions. In contrast, historians interrogating emotions and intentions read overlapping texts closely to probe honour's multiple emotional registers. In Daniel Lord Smail's words, it is the 'intimate knowledge made available through a case study' that allows the historian to illuminate how emotional worlds vary 'from one culture to the next and across time'.[72]

The chapters in this collection deal entirely with the dead, centuries dead in most cases, and each contributor works creatively with what remains in the historical record, both intimate utterances and public statements. Historians rarely encounter our subjects in person, and even when we do we can never speak with scientific certainty about the emotions our subjects feel or express.[73] By drawing on a wide range of sources, not just the prescriptive literature that early historians of emotion relied upon, historians can advance the study of emotion by posing questions that can be answered with the full range of extant evidence.[74] Textual traces are all we have to construe our subjects' motives and their decisions to enact violence against particular targets, and attending to silences is just as important as identifying word choices that articulate emotions.[75] For instance, by reading the personal diaries and published writings of American founders for indications of their emotional dispositions and sensitivities, Joanne B. Freeman was able to recast prior interpretations of the value Revolutionary leaders placed on honour. In 'a note on method' she explains how she sought out and analysed patterns of expression in official and private correspondence, from which she determined her subjects' core beliefs and 'intuitive level of thought'.[76] Similarly, the contributors to this volume apply the conceptual models introduced by historians of emotion, starting with William M. Reddy's notion that emotions come into being through a process of translation into utterances – words, principally, but also visual art and music – through which individuals communicate meaningfully to themselves and to others.[77]

To track the emotions associated with honour-related violence, each author makes the most of such utterances, by searching for terms that appear to indicate emotion, without pre-supposing what those words might be, and without presuming that the meaning of such terms is fixed. Only through deep, contextual reading of texts can historians construe the norms and values of particular communities.[78] Through her subtle analysis of the discordant ways in which colonial officials and a local indigenous community read the murder of an Aboriginal boy, killed by convicts in 1826, Penny Russell examines the various arenas within which 'competing cultural understandings emerged of right and wrong, compassion and self-interest, justice and revenge'. The variability of emotional 'expressions, practices, and control methods', even 'within the same linguistic and/or ethnic context', is clearly evident in the texts that recounted the crime of infanticide.[79] As Dana Rabin shows, eighteenth-century broadsides were not flat prescriptive tales; instead, their gaps and contradictions suggest ambivalence over what constituted a 'good execution', particularly when women refused to express the anticipated emotion of shame. Different strategies were at play in Sweden. There, as Jonas Liliequist discusses, playwrights' use of satire and ridicule to call the cult of aristocratic duelling into question in the early eighteenth century proved a more potent attack on the often-deadly practice than were the monarchy's edicts. Despite the long association of codes of honour with the authorization of violence, Robert N. Nye argues, concepts of insult, offence, dignity and respect travelled from early modern duelling manuals, to professional organization codes of the nineteenth century, and more recently to the democratization of honour in the form of statutes governing offences such as hate speech and in declarations of human rights.

When historical research carefully attends to the subtle emotional lexica of honour, the temptation to characterize one period or another as a time of restraint, or to paint one culture or another as oriented towards guilt or shame, breaks down. For example, in the late eighteenth century, Southeast Asian slaves in the Cape Colony, who brought with them an acute awareness of self-worth and vulnerability to shame, occasionally ran *amok*. The meaning of the word, first used to describe Malay warriors' frenzied and savage disregard for personal safety in battle, changed in the context of exile. In the South African slave community, the typical amok-runner became the individual male who faced the grim prospect of life without honour.[80] At the same time, stereotypes of ethnic and racial dispositions to violence can be dislodged by connecting emotional dispositions to demographic and economic circumstances, rather than by relying solely on lexical evidence. Martha Santos' chapter re-examines the idea that the 'macho' culture of the Brazilian *sertanejos* inclined poor freemen towards explosive violence and exaggerated sentiments of honour. Contemporary portrayals overlooked the specific socio-economic conditions that prevailed in the arid backlands, but historians need not follow. Santos shows how worsening droughts and shifts in staple crop markets over the mid-nineteenth century marginalized young male workers and increased their willingness to use violence to retain respect.

Rather than approach emotion as something to be isolated and defined, this volume considers its place in stories of violence, enacted and narrated through specific understandings of honour.[81] These constellations of meanings, feelings and actions cannot be placed neatly into 'Western' and 'other' history, as the contributions, read in concert, illustrate.[82] Through this collection we join other scholars working towards a practice of history that 'seeks global connections and pioneers a sustained dialogue between historians specializing in the history of particular continents'. The point of researching the history of emotion, ultimately, is not to evaluate whether historical subjects' expressions were sincere or feigned, and certainly it is not to pronounce them as irrational or sensible; instead, the object is to discern the shared values and emotions that made actions, including violent encounters over honour, appear both logical and essential. Of all forms of violence, perhaps the most storied is violence in association with honour, and this collection, spanning centuries and continents, moves us closer towards an appreciation of the shared and distinctive features of this phenomenon of enduring significance.[83]

Notes

1 Steven Pinker, *The Better Angels of our Nature: Why Violence Has Declined* (New York: Viking, 2011), 23. Pinker quips that the duel is more likely in the twenty-first century to call to mind 'Bugs Bunny and Yosemite Sam than "men of honor"'. See also Kwame Anthony Appiah, *The Honor Code: How Moral Revolutions Happen* (New York: W.W. Norton, 2011).

2 David Konstan, *The Emotions of the Ancient Greeks: Studies in Aristotle and Classical Literature* (Toronto: University of Toronto Press, 2006). Robert Muchembled notes that honour-related violence is especially rife among male youth in European history and in contemporary Europe. Muchembled, *A History of Violence from the End of the Middle Ages to the Present*, trans. Jean Birrell (Cambridge: Polity, 2012).

3 Bertram Wyatt-Brown, *Honor and Violence in the Old South* (New York: Oxford University Press, 1986); Victor Gordon Kiernan, *The Duel in European History: Honour and the Reign of Aristocracy* (Oxford: Oxford University Press, 1988); François Bellacois, *The Duel: Its Rise and Fall in Early Modern France* (New Haven: Yale University Press, 1990); Robert N. Nye, *Masculinity and Male Codes of Honor in Modern France* (Berkeley: University of California Press, 1993); Kevin McAleer, *Dueling: The Cult of Honor in Fin-de-Siècle Germany* (Princeton: Princeton University Press, 1994); Ute Frevert, *Men of Honour: A Social and Cultural History of the Duel*, trans. Anthony Williams (London: Wiley, 1995); Robert B. Shoemaker, 'The Taming of the Duel: Masculinity, Honour and Ritual Violence in London, 1660–1800', *Historical Journal*, 45 (2002): 525–45; Steven C. Hughes, *Politics of the Sword: Dueling, Honor, and Masculinity in Modern Italy* (Columbus, OH: Ohio State University Press, 2007); Scott K. Taylor, *Honor and Violence in Golden Age Spain* (New Haven: Yale University Press, 2008).

4 See Nigel Worden, ed., *Cape Town Between East and West: Social Identities in a Dutch Colonial Town* (Johannesburg and Hilversum: Verloren, 2012); J. Carter Wood, *Violence and Crime in Nineteenth-century England: The Shadow of Our Refinement* (London: Routledge, 2004); and Thomas Gallant, 'Honor, Masculinity, and Ritual Knife Fighting in. Nineteenth-Century Greece', *American Historical Review*, 105, 2 (January 2000): 359–82.

5 For exceptions, see Pablo Piccato, *City of Suspects: Crime in Mexico City, 1900–1931* (Durham, NC: Duke University Press, 2001), and Eiko Ikegami, *The Taming of the Samurai: Honorific Individualism and the Making of Modern Japan* (Cambridge: Harvard University Press, 1995).

6 The taming metaphor, implying wildness or irrationality, typically includes the notion of emotions brought under 'control'. See, for instance, Shoemaker, 'The Taming of the Duel', 541–2.

7 On the peace-making customs of a society conventionally associated with brutal violence, see William Ian Miller, *Bloodtaking and Peacemaking: Feud, Law, and Society in Saga Iceland* (Chicago: University of Chicago Press, 1990).

8 Norbert Elias, *The Civilizing Process: The History of Manners and State Formation and Civilization* (Oxford: Blackwell, 1994), xix. See also Norbert

Elias, *On Civilization, Power, and Knowledge*, ed. and intro. Stephen Mennell and Johan Goudsblom (Chicago: Chicago University Press, 1998).

9 Pieter Spierenburg, 'Violence and the Civilizing Process: Does It Work?', *Crime, History & Societies*, 5, 2 (2001): 87–105.

10 This Freudian term was adopted by Anton Blok to explain the physicality of honour. See Blok, 'The Narcissism of Minor Differences', *European Journal of Social Theory*, 1, 1 (1998): 33–56, 36, 41. For Blok's application of the concept in European history, see Anton Blok, *Honour and Violence* (Cambridge: Polity, 2001).

11 Pieter Spierenburg, 'Introduction', in *Men and Violence: Gender, Honor and Rituals in Modern Europe and America*, ed. Pieter Spierenburg (Columbus: Ohio State University Press, 1998), 4–7.

12 Pieter Spierenburg, *A History of Murder: Personal Violence in Europe from the Middle Ages to the Present* (Cambridge: Polity, 2008), 36. Although Jonathan Fletcher incorporates the Bourdieusian concept of habitus, he concurs that in the modern West, fears previously inspired by others 'are lessened without disappearing, while inner fears increase; the balance between the two types of fears tips in favour of the latter'. Fletcher, *Violence and Civilization: An Introduction to the Work of Norbert Elias* (Cambridge: Polity Press, 1997), 28.

13 See, for instance, Claude Gauvard, *'De grace especial': Crime, État et Société en France à la fin du Moyen-Âge Paris, 2 Vols.* (Paris: Publications de la Sorbonne, 1991). 'Free-floating' is Spierenburg's term for unrestrained emotions. 'Violence and the Civilizing Process', 96.

14 William James, 'What Is an Emotion?', *Mind*, 9 (1884): 188–205, 194, 195.

15 Thomas Dixon, *From Passions to Emotions: The Creation of a Secular Psychological Category* (Cambridge: Cambridge University Press, 2003), 17, 227.

16 Michael Casimir and Joanne Jung, '"Honor and Dishonor": Connotations of a Socio-symbolic Category in Cross-Cultural Perspective', in *Emotions as Bio-Cultural Processes*, ed. Birgitt Röttger-Rössler and Hans J. Markowitsch (New York: Springer, 2009): 229–80, 230–31.

17 For instance, Monique Scheer notes that anthropologists have discovered 'striking different emotion concepts in non-Western cultures'. Scheer, 'Are Emotions a Kind of Practice (and Is That What Makes Them Have a History)? A Bourdieuian Approach to Understanding Emotion', *History and Theory*, 51 (May 2012): 193–220, 195.

18 Elizabeth S. Cohen, 'Honor and Gender in the Streets of Early Modern Rome', *Journal of Interdisciplinary History*, 22, 4 (1992): 597–625, 599.

19 Ikegami, *The Taming of the Samurai*, 9–10. Ikegami refers here to the work of anthropologist Ruth Benedict and sociologist Robert N. Bellah, published in the mid-twentieth century.

20 Eiko Ikegami, 'Emotions', in *A Concise Companion to History*, ed. Ulinka Rublack (Oxford: Oxford University Press, 2011): 233–53, 337.

21 Eugenia Lean, 'AHR Conversation: The Historical Study of Emotions', *American Historical Review* (December 2012): 1487–531, 1527. Ikegami

offers a comprehensive critique of the notion of shame cultures (Eastern) versus guilt cultures (Western) which endures in Eurocentric approaches to emotion. Ikegami, 'Emotions', 343–6.

22   Ute Frevert, 'Forum: History of Emotions', *German History*, 28, 1 (2010): 67–80, 79; Jan Plamper, 'The History of Emotions: An Interview with William Reddy, Barbara H. Rosenwein, and Peter N. Stearns', *History and Theory*, 49 (May, 2010): 237–65, 261. For a study that challenges the 'affect-cognition' distinction, see Seth Duncan and Lisa F. Barrett, 'Affect as a Form of Cognition: A Neurobiological Analysis', *Cognition and Emotion*, 21 (2007): 1184–211. For recent developments in neuroscience, see the 2012 special issue of *Brain Sciences*, titled, 'The Brain Knows More Than It Admits: The Control of Cognition and Emotion by Non-Conscious Processes', http://www.mdpi.com/journal/brainsci/special_issues/contr_cognit_emot (accessed 20 February 2013).

23   Scheer, 'Are Emotions a Kind of Practice', 196. Scheer also draws on Bourdieu's concept of 'habitus' and on cognitive psychology and neuroscience.

24   Barbara H. Rosenwein, 'Problems and Methods in the History of Emotions', *Passions in Context: Journal of the History and Philosophy of the Emotions* 1 (2010): 1–33, http://www.passionsincontext.de/index.php?id=557 (accessed 12 February 2013), 2–3.

25   Ikegami, 'Emotions', 342.

26   Lucien Febvre, 'Sensibility and History: How to Reconstitute the Emotional Life of the Past', in *A New Kind of History: From the Writings of Febvre*, ed. Peter Burke and trans. K. Folia (New York: Harper & Row Publishers, 1973 [1941]), 12–26, 14. For a recent turn towards the analysis of 'affective assemblages', see Margaret Wetherell, *Affect and Emotion: A New Social Science Understanding* (London: Sage, 2012), 140–60.

27   Alan Confino, 'Forum: History of Emotions', 80; Thomas Dixon, ' "Emotion": The History of a Keyword in Crisis', *Emotion Review*, 4, 4 (2012): 338–44, 343, 338. Dixon adds that the concept has been in a constant state of definitional crisis since its adoption as a psychological term in the late nineteenth century (338).

28   On the cognitive and emotional implications of metaphor, see David E. Leary, *Metaphors in the History of Psychology* (Cambridge: Cambridge University Press, 1994). For an early cognitive critique of the hydraulic model, see Robert C. Solomon, *The Passions* (New York: Doubleday, 1976), 140.

29   William H. Reddy, *The Navigation of Feeling: A Framework for the History of Emotions* (Cambridge: Cambridge University Press, 2001), 115. For Reddy, self-management both modifies feeling and pursues feeling to modify behaviour.

30   Robert C. Solomon, 'Thoughts and Feelings: What Is a "Cognitive Theory" of the Emotions, and Does It Neglect Affectivity?', *Royal Institute of Philosophy Supplement*, 52, 2 (2003): 1–18, 2, 11, 12. Solomon defines emotions as complexes of 'judgments', though he suggested that some feelings are perceived, or construed.

31   William H. Reddy's formative work is integral to this approach. See in particular his *The Navigation of Feeling*. Like Rosenwein and Frevert, he argues that neuroscientific research supports his insights, drawn from historical sources.

32 The following are the most significant centres for the study of emotion as of 2013: Amsterdam Centre for Cross-Disciplinary Emotion and Sensory Studies (The Netherlands); ARC Centre of Excellence for the History of Emotions (Perth, Australia); History of Emotions Research Centre (Max Planck Institut, Berlin); Languages of Emotion (Freie Universität, Berlin); Emotion and Motion (Zentrum für Literatur und Kulturforschung, Berlin); Cultural History of Emotions in Premodernity Network; EMMA: Les Émotions au Moyen Age – Research Program on Emotions in the Middle Ages (France); Centre for the History of the Emotions (Queen Mary, University of London); Manchester Centre for Emotion and Value; ISRE – International Society for Research on Emotion; and Concordia Sensoria Research Team (CONSERT) (Montreal, Canada).

33 Peter N. Stearns and Carol Z. Stearns, 'Emotionology: Clarifying the History of Emotions and Emotional Standards', *American Historical Review*, 90, 4 (October 1985): 813–36; Barbara H. Rosenwein, ed. *Anger's Past: The Social Use of Emotions in the Middle Ages* (Ithaca: Cornell University Press, 1998); William M. Reddy, *The Invisible Code: Honor and Sentiment in Postrevolutionary France, 1815–1848* (Berkeley: University of California Press, 1997). For an historiographical review of the field's development and directions, see Plamper, 'The History of Emotions'.

34 Michael J. Casimir, '"Honor and Dishonor" and the Quest for Emotional Equivalents', in *Emotions as Bio-Cultural Processes*, ed. Birgitt Röttger-Rössler and Hans J. Markowitsch: 281–316, 282.

35 Joanna Bourke, 'Fear and Anxiety: Writing about Emotion in Modern History', *History Workshop Journal*, 55,1 (Spring 2003): 111–33, 124. For a neuroscientific formulation of this concept, see Antonio Damasio, *Descartes' Error: Emotion, Reason, and the Human Brain* (New York: Penguin, 2005 [1994]): 146–8.

36 Barbara H. Rosenwein, 'Worrying about Emotions in History', *American Historical Review*, 107 (2002): 821–45, 842. Rosenwein credits post-1980s anthropological theory for the development of her thinking in this regard. See her 'Theories of Change in the History of Emotions', in *A History of Emotions, 1200–1800*, ed. Jonas Liliequist (London: Pickering and Chatto, 2012), 7–20, 13.

37 Michelle Z. Rosaldo, 'Toward an Anthropology of Self and Feeling', in *Culture Theory: Essays on Mind, Self, and Emotion*, ed. Richard A. Shwerder and Robert A. LeVine (Cambridge: Cambridge University Press, 1984), 139–57, 143, 141. Catherine A. Lutz's work has been equally influential. See her *Unnatural Emotions: Everyday Sentiments on a Micronesian Atoll and Their Challenge to Western Theory* (Chicago: University of Chicago Press, 1988).

38 For a critique of this tendency in the work of Elias and scholars who apply his thought to the history of honour-related violence, see Gerd Schwerhoff, 'Criminalized Violence and the Process of Civilisation – A Reappraisal', *Crime, History & Societies*, 6, 2 (2002): 103–26, 119–20.

39 In contrast, Elias defined his project in opposition to historical approaches, which identify 'only constant transformation, without penetrating to the order underlying this transformation and to the laws governing the formation of historical structures'. Elias, *The Civilizing Process*, xv.

40 See also Hans Speier, 'Honor and Social Structure', *Social Research*, 2, 1 (1935): 74–97. The foundational anthropological work is Julian Pitt-Rivers, 'Honour and Shame', in *Honour and Shame*, ed. Jean G. Peristiany (London: Weidenfeld and Nicholson, 1966), 19–77.

41 Georg Simmel, 'The Persistence of Social Groups: I', *American Journal of Sociology*, 3 (1897): 662–98, 680, 683.

42 Julian Pitt-Rivers, 'Honor', *International Encyclopedia of the Social Sciences. 2nd ed., Volume 6* (New York: Macmillan, 1968), 503–11, 503.

43 Jean G. Peristiany and Julian Pitt-Rivers, *Honor and Grace in Anthropology* (Cambridge: Cambridge University Press, 1991), 4.

44 Referring back to their earlier work, Peristiany and Pitt-Rivers stated in 1991 that they were content 'to confine our investigation to the role of concepts of honour and shame in ordering society'. Peristiany and Pitt-Rivers, *Honor and Grace in Anthropology*, 6.

45 Pierre Bourdieu, 'The Sentiment of Honour in Kabyle Society', in *Honour and Shame*, ed. Jean G. Peristiany (London: Weidenfeld and Nicholson, 1966), 191–241.

46 Bourdieu, 'The Sentiment of Honour', 231. In this initial analysis of how honour 'works', he does not refer to emotion; instead he refers to logic, formula and dictates. Bourdieu, 'The Sentiment of Honour', 213, 214.

47 Pierre Bourdieu, *Outline of a Theory of Practice*, trans. Richard Nice (Stanford: Stanford University Press, 1990), 53, 16. Bourdieu further signalled his move away from a structuralist approach in his chapter title, 'From the "rules" of honour to the sense of honour'.

48 David D. Gilmore, 'Introduction: The Shame of Dishonor', in *Honor and Shame and the Unity of the Mediterranean*, ed. David D. Gilmore (Washington, D.C.: A Special Publication of the American Anthropological Association, 1987, no. 22), 2–18, 5.

49 Frank Henderson Stewart, *Honor* (Chicago: University of Chicago Press, 1994), 54–63. For applications of this 'axis' concept outside of European history, see John Ilifee, *Honour in African History* (Cambridge: Cambridge University Press, 2005), and Ikegami, *The Taming of the Samurai*.

50 On the changing compass of honour's referents, see Geoffrey Best, *Honour among Men and Nations: The Transformation of an Idea* (Toronto: University of Toronto Press, 1982).

51 Bourdieu conceived this web through his concept of 'habitus'. For the impact of Bourdieu's thought on the study of emotion, see Deborah Reed-Danahay, *Locating Bourdieu* (Bloomington: Indiana University Press, 2004), 99–128.

52 Stewart, *Honor*, 5–6; 15–16.

53 Bettina Schmidt and Ingo Schroeder, ed., *Anthropology of Violence and Conflict* (London: Routledge, 2001). See especially the chapter by Glenn Bowman, 'The Violence in Identity', 25–46.

54 The association of honour-based violence with social dislocation and economic competition in contemporary society is explored in *'Honour' Killing and Violence: Advances in International Policy and Practice*, ed. Aisha Gill, Carolyn Strange and Karl Roberts (London: Palgrave Macmillan, 2014).

55 Blok, *Honour and Violence*, 111–12.

56 These works also contributed to an historiographical appreciation of masculinity's constructed nature. See Christopher E. Forth, *Masculinity and the Modern West* (London: Palgrave MacMillan, 2008): 117–22.

57 See especially David D. Gilmore, *Manhood in the Making: Cultural Concepts of Masculinity* (New Haven: Yale University Press, 1990).

58 Nye, *Masculinity*, vii. Here Nye draws directly on Bourdieu and Elias. Bourdieu's 'La Domination Masculine' was first published in 1990, and then in book form in 1998.

59 Ute Frevert defines honour as a male prerogative exclusively. Frevert, *Emotions in History*, 67–8. Michael J. Casimir and Susanne Jung suggest that the masculinist character of honour is, in part, an artefact of masculinist research practices. Casimir and Jung, 'Honor and Dishonor', 259.

60 Casimir and Jung, 'Honor and Dishonour', 257.

61 Lyman L. Johnson and Sonya Lipsett-Rivera, 'Introduction', in *The Faces of Honor: Sex, Shame and Violence in Colonial Latin America*, ed. Lyman L. Johnson and Sonya Lipsett-Rivera (Albuquerque: University of New Mexico Press, 1998): 1–17, 12.

62 Emile Durkheim, *Le Suicide* (1897). For an excellent re-assessment of the Durkheimian legacy, see Maria Teresa Brancaccio, Eric J. Engstrom and David Lederer, 'The Politics of Suicide: Historical Perspectives on Suicidology before Durkheim. An Introduction', *Journal of Social History*, 46, 3 (Spring 2013): 607–19.

63 Eugenia Lean and Julie Livingston, an historian working at the crossroads of anthropology and medicine, agreed on this point. 'AHR Conversation', 1527. William Reddy countered that his and others' achievements in historicizing emotion has helped to undo assumptions of European rational superiority over non-Westerners, 1521–2.

64 For precursor to Febvre's image of the past as a time of hot emotion, see Johan Huizinga, *The Waning of the Middle Ages: A Study of the Forms of Life, Thoughts and Art in France and the Netherlands in the XIVth and XVth Centuries*, trans. Frederick J. Hopman (London: Edward Arnold, 1924). For the notion that Western civilization will eventually spread to Africa and the Orient, see Norbert Elias, *The Civilizing Process: Sociogenetic and Psychogenetic* (Oxford: Blackwell, 2000), 386, 404, 544, n. 4.

65 Brancaccio et al., 'The Politics of Suicide', 609.

66 Arlie Russell Hochschild, 'Emotion Work, Feeling Rules, and Social Structure', *American Journal of Sociology*, 85, 3 (November 1979): 551–75.

67 Barbara H. Rosenwein, 'Worrying about Emotions', 837. Elias did, however, acknowledge that 'in both "primitive" and "civilized" peoples, there are socially induced prohibitions and restrictions, together with their psychological counterparts, socially induced anxieties, pleasure and displeasure, distaste and delight'. Elias, *The Civilizing Process*, 135.

68 Eiko Ikegami's work is a model in this regard. See her 'Shame and the Samurai: Institutions, Trustworthiness, and Autonomy in the Elite Honor Culture', *Social Research*, 70, 4 (2003): 2351–77, 2351. See also Ikegami, 'Emotions', 345–6.

69 Catherine A. Lutz and Geoffrey M. White, 'The Anthropology of Emotions', *Annual Review of Anthropology*, 15 (1986): 405–36.

70 For an analysis of honour and emotion in second-century B.C.E. China, see Stephen W. Durrant, *The Cloudy Mirror: Tension and Conflict in the Writing of Sima Qian* (New York: SUNY Press, 1995).

71 Konstan, *The Emotions*, 302–3, n. 44. For the Ancient Greeks, shame arose 'not at the contemplation of loss of honour in the abstract, but from specific acts or events that bring about disgrace'. Konstan, *The Emotions*, 101.

72 Daniel Lord Smail, *The Consumption of Justice: Emotions, Publicity, and Legal Culture in Marseille, 1264–1423* (Ithaca: Cornell, 2003), 244.

73 As Julie Livingston argues, oral histories provide a no clearer guide than historic texts to 'real' experience. See her *Debility and the Moral Imagination in Botswana* (African Systems of Thought Series) (Bloomington and Indianapolis: Indiana University Press, 2001).

74 Confino, 'Forum: History of Emotions', 71.

75 Rosenwein, 'Problems and Methods', 17.

76 Joanne B. Freeman, *Affairs of Honor: National Politics in the New Republic* (New Haven: Yale University Press, 2001), 289–90; 292. Freeman stresses the utility of reading for 'judgment' words.

77 In a recent interview on the state of the art in the history of emotions, Reddy defines emotional expression as 'an attempt to call up the emotion that is expressed; it is an attempt to feel what one says one feels'. Plamper, 'The History of Emotions', 240.

78 Rosenwein, 'Passions in Context', 12–14. On the need to look for unexpected connections in emotions talk, see Martha Nussbaum, *Upheavals of Thought: the Intelligence of Emotions* (Cambridge: Cambridge University Press, 2003), 156. Like many theorists of emotion, she draws on the work of anthropologist Catherine A. Lutz.

79 Ikegami, 'Emotions', 356. Ikegami adds that 'classes, genders and other social categories' also account for variance within periods and societies.

80 John Spores, *Running Amok: An Historical Inquiry* (Athens: Ohio University Press, 1988).

81 Rosaldo, 'Toward an Anthropology of Self and Feeling', 139–57, 145.

82 Ulinka Rublack, 'Preface' in *A Concise Companion to History*, ed. Ulinka Rublack (Oxford: Oxford University Press, 2011), xi–xxvi, xii–xiii.

83 For contemporary studies of honour-based violence in the recent past, see Tor Aase, ed., *Tournaments of Power: Honor and Revenge in the Contemporary World* (Aldershot: Ashgate Publications, 2002).

2

The severed head speaks: Death, revenge, moral heroism and martyrdom in sixteenth to seventeenth-century China[1]

C. D. Alison Bailey

This chapter explores questions of moral heroism and martyrdom in the late Ming (1368–1644) to the early Qing (1644–1911) dynasties in China, with a particular focus on the late sixteenth to early seventeenth centuries. This period saw a brief but highly significant philosophical and cultural shift away from the traditional Neo-Confucianist state orthodoxy's stress on rational or moderate conduct (shaped by regularized, communally oriented ritual action) towards a heightened emphasis on individualism and the expression of genuine feeling. This emotional turn, appearing at a time of great political turmoil, social disruption, imperial weakness and invasion by hostile Northerners (the Manchus, who founded the Qing dynasty), was short-lived; however, its influence was immense. Contemporary and later commentators characterized this new valorization of emotion as introducing either a period of cultural florescence or a time of social disorder that led, ultimately, to the fall of the Ming dynasty.[2] Emotional intensity characterized this period and also underpinned Ming loyalist resistance to the Qing, which persisted long after the older dynasty was displaced.[3]

By focussing on individual feelings, this chapter charts new ground, highlighting the ways in which the intertwined strands of honour, violence and emotion combined in this crucial period of history to shape the responses and actions of people caught up in the tragic events that led up to and followed the conquest of Ming dynasty China by the Manchus in 1644. In particular, it examines the changing political value of the emotional, political and ritual roles played by revenge and the rhetoric surrounding revenge, righteous anger, grief and honourable death (both through suicide and resistance) in the name of the parallel Confucian virtues of filial reverence to one's parents (*xiao*) and loyalty to one's ruler (*zhong*).[4] This chapter will also show how the physical and metaphorical severed head became a symbol of power, vengeance, defiance and filial mourning through its use by contemporary actors and chroniclers to 'speak' for the dead.[5]

Confucianism, as the state orthodoxy of the Ming dynasty, made the linked practices of filial reverence and mourning ritual central both to the expression and regulation of emotion and to the cosmological and political ordering of state and society. Emotions that elsewhere might be considered private, such as grief over a parent's death, were part of a state-sponsored mechanism for the regulation of feeling into correct channels. While parents lived, a filial child showed gratitude through reverence and obedience; when parents died, they were honoured by a child's grief expressed through correct ritual mourning practices. Ancestor worship was the linchpin of Confucian society: an individual's duty was to honour his family line (or her husband's, in the case of a woman) through morally freighted acts that brought glory to their ancestors. The ideally virtuous family was a microcosm for the ideal state: the emperor who regulated himself and his family ruled by example and was given the same reverence by his subjects as that accorded to a father. Filial piety and loyalty to the ruler were essential bonds ensuring the maintenance of social, political and cosmological harmony. As Eugenia Lean suggests, 'the Confucian tradition and its vibrant cultural history offered ... an entirely different epistemological context from which to interrogate how we in the West think about the very category of emotion'.[6] In the Confucian philosophical framework for conceptions of the self, human nature and feeling are articulated through an explicit homology between the family and the state that shapes discourses of personal and political relationships and obligations. Thus, the cultural and historical contexts of emotion, the particular 'salience'[7] of a 'ubiquitous but as yet barely examined category of experience',[8] provide comparative indices for what has been recognized as a 'key category of historical analysis'.[9]

The homology between state and the family and the essential bonds of filial piety and loyalty maintained an almost unbroken powerful hold on state discourses and practices shaping imperial China until modern times. However, in the sixteenth and seventeenth centuries a new philosophical shift altered perceptions of political and personal usages of emotion. While not questioning the fundamental links between family and state, the Wang Yangming (1472–1529) School, an influential strand of the Neo-Confucianist dominant ideology, had a profound effect on beliefs and practices, particularly on traditional concepts of the self, encouraging a new individualism that had the potential to undermine social cohesion. Wang's ideas instigated what came to be known as the cult of *qing* (a polysemic term encompassing passion, true feeling, sentiment, genuine emotion).[10] Most discussions of the role of *qing* in late imperial Chinese culture have focussed on the emotion of love,[11] but this new trend in Confucian thought was also relevant to the emotions of grief and righteous anger, which gave rise to both rhetorical and extreme physical acts of violence. The contrast between the enthusiasm of the Wang School for unrestrained, genuine passion and the traditional valorization of proper, contained expression of feeling was paralleled by an opposition between the school's acceptance of the validity of righteous anger and conservative fears of dangerously excessive emotion leading to chaos. The Wang Yangming School, and particularly Wang's more radical, unorthodox followers, emphasized the importance of authenticity in individualistic feeling and its expression (a theme Eliza Ferguson also traces in her chapter). Significantly, it confronted the traditional Confucian emphasis on emotional restraint. The school's call for a more egalitarian vision of the individual's capacity to attain a form of divine state or sagehood, more commonly associated in standard Confucian thought with ancient divine moral exemplars, was partly responsible for a fraught political environment.

In late Ming dynasty China, these elite emotional communities[12] contested for power and ideological dominance.[13] As Nicole Eustace points out, the ways in which patterns of emotional expression are manifested can tell us a great deal about power relations.[14] This is certainly true in the case of the late Ming era, when emotion, its expression and its regulation became critical forces in shaping discourses on the failure of the Ming imperium to withstand social and cultural disorder on a massive scale. In addition to the emergence of local associations and cross-regional political factions, which offered a threat to centralized state power, class barriers were breaking down through greater access to education and the rise of an influential merchant class whose aspirations caused anxiety among the scholar-gentry. Social unrest, despotic or weak emperors and reduced access to traditional official positions for members of the literati added to a sense of looming crisis that culminated in conquest by the non-Han Chinese Manchu Qing dynasty in 1644.[15]

Confucianism, filial duty and emotion

Confucianism conceived the individual in terms of a web of hierarchical relationships known as the Five Relationships (*wu lun*): ruler and subject, father and son, older and younger brother, husband and wife, and friend and friend (the only nonhierarchical linkage). The analogy between father and emperor was central to political discourse: a filial son was, ipso facto, a loyal subject to his ruler-father, the emperor. This foundational doubling of the two 'fundamental bonds of Confucian ritualism' – filial piety (*xiao*) and loyalty (*zhong*) – made systematic 'an identification between loyalty and filial devotion'.[16] These relations were founded in emotion: mutual feelings of obligation and affective ties of reverence and respect of junior to senior underlined each constitutive role. From the earliest times, however, Confucian doctrine regarded both excess emotion and the absence of emotion as inimical to harmony, rational moderation and good social order. In regulating the Five Relationships, therefore, Confucian scholars prescribed standard forms of behaviour which were meant both to encourage and to channel and control the public expression of emotions. Ritual conduct was widely recognized as the key to social stability. The early Confucian thinker Xunzi (312–230 BCE) identified moral education and ritual practice, both ceremonial and habitual, as the effective means for disciplining feeling. This doctrine led, as Anthony Yu suggests, to the situation in which a human subject, as understood in Confucian discourses, was 'only constituted by the social bodies of family and state.... Kinship and political structures, therefore, will define the normative location of subjectivity, its expression and operation to be guided by rites that are invented to serve those structures'.[17] In short, although emotion might be expressed publicly – Confucianism never dictated a stoical purging of emotion – this expression should only take place through standard, ritualized means.

Accordingly, mourning rituals for parents were far more than an expression of personal distress; until very late in imperial times they were also an affirmation of the proper hierarchical structure of society. Thus there was general recognition that the loss of one's parents aroused natural grief, the expression of which was 'morally obligatory'.[18] Xunzi was unambiguous on this point: 'A man will love his parents endlessly until he dies... if all of a sudden one's revered parents perish but he who attends their burial is neither grieving nor reverent, then he is no better than a beast.'[19] Yet Xunzi and the majority of later writers identified the ritual practices associated with mourning parents as important in containing emotion (*qing*). In elite mourning practice in the Ming the elder son would mourn his father for three years, ideally living in a simple hut by the grave, wearing hemp clothing and eschewing official service and pleasures such as sex and good food. Conservative Confucian commentators did consider publicly expressed grief for the death of parents to be excessive if it extended beyond the first three days of ritual mourning. Overwhelmingly, though, emotions of grief were considered salutary as long as rites served as normative means to shape them to ensure their correct and moderate expression.

This view of mourning changed in the latter part of the Ming period. From early in the sixteenth century, important cultural figures, influenced by the Wang Yangming School, urged that the genuine expression of individual emotions ought to take precedence over formalistic ritual regulation of feeling. This approach arose out of a broader philosophical willingness to credit the individual mind – emotions and all – with the capacity to distinguish between good and evil in order to create a moral society. Under the influence of Wang's School, what had previously been considered to be excess grief became a badge of honour, manifesting as an illness known as *huiji*, 'ruining emaciation' whereby bones begin to protrude on the chief mourner's face. In the words of the late Ming writer Wei Yong (fl. seventeenth century), '*Qing* [emotion] is that for which the living could die and because of which the dead could be resurrected. This is why filial sons, men of righteousness and chaste women are all people rich in *qing*.'[20] Imperial commendation or official recognition was given in some cases of death from grief.[21] There was considerable ambivalence about such expressions of unfettered emotion even at the height of the cult of *qing*. Conventional thinkers continued to regard such ostentatious expressions of emotion as selfish. They also found the late Ming practice of widow suicide and the chastity cult (again often given imperial sanction) to be extreme conduct shaped by unregulated feeling.[22]

As Imperial commendation suggests, the Wang School's confidence that the mind's emotions could be trusted soon turned into an alternative set of ritual expectations. Chinese practice did not simply urge particular kinds of behaviour: it consistently identified outstanding individuals who had lived up to – or exceeded – what society might expect of them. In particular, it valued the choices made between life and death when faced with extreme moral dilemmas. Depending on circumstances, either choice might be the commendable one; the challenge was to choose in extreme circumstances. As the great Han dynasty historian Sima Qian (ca. 145–86 BCE) suggests, this choice was central to the way in which one was viewed by posterity: it validated one's life and integrity.[23] Public recognition of unusual virtuous conduct brought honour to oneself but also, and more importantly, to one's ancestors. The record of such conduct was inscribed in texts which spread widely among Chinese elites who sought in turn to learn the best ways to achieve posthumous recognition. Thus Anne McLaren points to examples of wives who did *not* commit suicide to join their politically martyred husbands because it was their duty (as articulated by their husbands) to stay alive, to raise their sons to serve the ancestral altars and to continue the bloodline, thereby following an equally honourable path to moral heroism or 'exemplary virtue: political rectitude in the case of the husband and chaste widowhood in her own'.[24]

The case of a late Ming filial avenger, Wang Shiming (fl. ca.1577), from the eastern province of Zhejiang suggests the significant role that violence played in the working out of this new approach to emotion. When Wang's father was beaten to death by a fellow clansman, Wang chose to avenge his father's death, first by the ritual killing of his enemy, then by taking his own life, rather than pursuing more pragmatic legal redress. In this instance his wife, Madam Yu, followed him by committing suicide.[25] Wang's dramatic public acts, both his self-sacrifice and vengeance, became subjects of numerous accounts by both fiction writers and historians before and after the fall of the Ming dynasty.[26] Chroniclers noted that Wang Shiming followed ancient precedent when he decapitated the man who had murdered his father and presented the head at his father's spirit tablet. He refused to allow an autopsy of his father's body because, although it might have saved his own life by proving his father's murder, it represented an unconscionable act of corporeal desecration no filial son could permit. Wang's revenge was slow in the making (six years), not undertaken in the heat of the moment, and as such it was considered the act of a gentleman or *junzi*, rather than that of a petty 'small man' whose vengeful anger, according to common parlance, is shaped by squalid motives rather than a moral response to injustice.

Wang's act of revenge and his subsequent surrender to the authorities, followed by suicide, brought him considerable public sympathy from members of the local elite in Zhejiang and beyond. Officials called upon to judge him were reluctant to do so, and his later chroniclers produced at least ten different historical and fictional accounts of his dramatic action. The public sympathy and political debate engendered by Wang Shiming's vengeance and suicide were common in cases of filial revenge – an indication of the central significance of filial piety in Chinese culture. However, the taking of a life was a serious matter in Chinese law, an anomaly that has led Michael Dalby to describe filial revenge as a 'very special crime'.[27] In China, as in parts of the West, legal thinkers have faced a dilemma when anxious to commend moral exemplars while condemning those who abrogate the state's role by taking the law into their own hands. There was considerable ambivalence among jurists and rulers on how to handle revenge cases, with discussions on honouring the natural feelings and moral imperatives of filial children vying with the state's need to avoid vendettas and punish homicides. Over time, as Dalby has shown, the legal parameters for justifiable revenge narrowed considerably, but public sympathy and popular support remained strongly in favour of the aggrieved avenger.[28] However, in the case of male filial avengers in particular, it was a constant expectation that revenge should be followed by the avenger's death – either by suicide or, more rarely, execution.[29] Wang Shiming followed this inexorable path willingly, to public acclamation.

It is quite possible, given the timing of his actions, that contemporaries considered Wang's martyrdom in the cause of filial piety in the light of Chief Grand Secretary Zhang Juzheng's (1525–1582) shameful failure to return home to mourn his father for three years, on the grounds of state necessity. Wang Shiming's chroniclers, seeking to find models of heroism at a time when the perceived and real chaos and decadence of the late Ming seemed to offer few positive exemplars, used his story to illustrate core virtues in action. Wang's wilful, self-conscious and stubborn martyrdom for the sake of ancient moral precedent perhaps struck a chord in his recorders' minds. Wai-yee Li has commented on the late Ming delight in self-invention and dramatic, heroic gestures.[30] Chroniclers who admired this filial piety depict Wang Shiming and his wife as self-consciously embracing their roles as cultural heroes. An identical performative quality of self-consciousness in action can be found in the myriad accounts of the deaths of Ming loyalist martyrs. The same stubborn assertion of will (*zhi*) and conscious choice to die for deeply embedded cultural principles of loyalty and filial gratitude to one's emperor-father are detailed time and time again.

Elite Chinese responses to the political disorder of the late Ming and to conquest by the alien Qing were profoundly shaped by strongly felt emotions of righteous anger and grief. The cult of *qing* seems to have encouraged many to court honourable martyrdom as a concrete expression of morally infused true feeling, thereby bringing glory to their family lines. Filial sons, chaste widows, widow suicides and loyal subjects (and their wives and daughters) found their way into literature and the biographical sections of local and national historical texts as moral exemplars listed under such typologies as 'Filial and Righteous', 'Exemplary Chaste Women' and 'Loyal and Righteous'. These categories established official, public affirmation of gendered acts of morally principled (or honourable) conduct designed to provide posterity with models of correct behaviour. Rather than simply types, these descriptions of honourable personhood inspired countless people to act out prescribed roles in life and, more importantly, in death, which became dramatically apparent in the 1620s under the influence of the Wang Yangming School.

The Donglin faction and the rise of martyrdom

In 1628, the Chongzhen emperor (r. 1627–1644) ordered the public interrogation of a group of eunuchs and prison guards who were accused of persecuting members of what was then known as the Donglin political faction. The interrogation represented a reversal of fortunes of a kind that was not uncommon in Chinese imperial courts. The Donglin faction, once influential, had fallen out of favour and its leaders were tortured and killed. Now the same fate was about to befall those who had persecuted the Donglin leaders. Such interrogations were often a semipublic event, allowing those who attended to hear the direct testimony of accused criminals and see the tortures inflicted on them. On this occasion, the proceedings were disrupted when two men burst from the crowd and began to stab the accused with sharp awls. They injured some of the accused before being overpowered, but they were permitted to remain on the scene to watch the final stages of the interrogation, in which the accused were beaten to death.[31]

The perpetrators of the disruption, Huang Zongxi (1610–1695), the future Ming loyalist and philosophical historian, and Zhou Yanzuo, were both sons of leaders of the Donglin political faction (Huang Zunsu and Zhou Zongjian) who had perished in the earlier purge. According to ancient precedent in China, a grieving son had the right to avenge his father's unjust death at the hands of corrupt officials in times of disorder when the state had failed to act.[32] As the *Li Ji* had stated, 'One should not live under the same Heaven with the enemy who has slain one's father.'[33] In this case, however, the state's stern intention towards the persecutors of the Donglin leaders was unmistakable. There was no doubt that the accused would be killed with state approval after their interrogation. Huang and Zhou, however, risked their own lives by intervening in the formal judicial process for the sake of vengeance. This act of abrogation did not incur the wrath of the Chongzhen emperor (r. 1627–1644); instead their moral heroism was perceived as laudable, partly due to ancient precedent but even more because of the contemporary ideological climate that newly privileged authenticity in emotions. To a significant extent, this climate was a product of the actions of the Donglin faction members themselves.

The Donglin group had called for a radical Confucian-oriented renovation of moral leadership in order to resolve the internal and external crises facing late Ming dynasty China. Linked to, but not completely aligned with, the Wang Yangming School, the Donglin faction advocated an activist form of Confucianism that they characterized as loyalist.[34] The scandal caused by Zhang Juzheng's perceived lack of filial piety – his failure to return home to mourn his father – and the Wanli emperor's (r. 1572–1620) tacit or active encouragement of this attitude have been considered one of the major factors that created the climate that allowed factional groups such as the Donglin to vehemently criticize the government. Bitter, destructive quarrels were the order of the day, leading, in the eyes of many, directly to the collapse of the Ming dynasty.[35] Fuelled by an absolutist belief in the righteousness of their cause and brooking no criticism, Donglin partisans sought to place their adherents in positions of influence at court and in officialdom. Their passionate convictions and uncompromising moral advocacy brought them equally passionate enemies, not least the powerful eunuch Wei Zhongxian. In 1624 the outspoken Donglin leader Yang Lian defiantly presented to the court the 'single most famous censorial memorial of Ming times and perhaps of all Chinese history',[36] denouncing the 24 crimes of Wei Zhongxian.

Couched in 'passionately indignant' language,[37] the memorial is a paradigmatic example of the rhetoric of Donglin righteous anger. In a different context, Stephen D. White points to the 'quasi-juridical' scripted public displays of anger by medieval nobles as being more than an emotional response to political acts, what Barbara Rosenwein characterizes as a 'constructive use of wrath' or 'anger in control'.[38] Yang Lian's memorial to his emperor utilized the accepted legal channels of remonstrance by an official against imperial misconduct; however, several colleagues, in complete agreement with his contempt for Wei Zhongxian, nonetheless felt he had gone too far and counselled him to moderate his language. This he did not do.

Yang Lian's scorching critique of a weak and absent ruler betrayed extreme emotion and demanded an extreme response. He knew he was risking punishment but he remained defiant: 'I know full well this will fail … but I've … mounted the tiger … I will sacrifice myself in the name of righteousness.'[39] To underscore his sincerity he challenged the emperor to behead him if removing Wei from power did not have the required effect. Yang's self-prophesied martyrdom was not long in coming. Wei instigated a brutal campaign to destroy the faction's major spokesmen known as the 'Six Gentleman' and seven of their close colleagues, including Huang Zunsu and Zhou Zhongjian.[40] Yang himself was arrested with five others and tortured so horribly that he cried for mercy to no avail and was murdered alongside his less outspoken colleagues in prison.[41] The horrifying torture-murders of the 13 Donglin members in imperial prisons and the repression of adherents elsewhere by imperial representatives caused demonstrations and a public outcry, including from some who decried factionalism as a symptom of Ming decline. The case of the Donglin martyrs was widely seen at the time as a major symbol of growing state disorder largely created by the Chongzhen emperor's predecessor, the weak, child-like Tianqi emperor (r. 1620–1627), who had granted his notorious eunuch-intimate Wei Zhongxian unprecedented freedom to act without restraint. Public and textual emotional responses to the terrible suffering endured by the Donglin martyrs had a profound impact, for revenge was not long in coming: the newly installed Chongzhen emperor, after some deliberation, allowed a violent, sweeping purge of the torturers and their instigators.[42]

Huang and Zhou's decision to risk martyrdom at a time when their fathers had been exonerated and their murderers punished was a reflection of the extreme emotional temper of the times. Their desire to act upon their grief by avenging their martyred fathers' deaths was shaped by the prevailing ethos of moral righteousness influenced by the Wang School's stress on passionate authenticity of feeling. Their act fully embodied the emotions driving their fathers' stubbornly defiant assertion of the absolute rightness of the Donglin cause despite the inherent dangers of that defiance. The sons hoped to honour and emulate their fathers through their act of filial piety.[43]

Seventeenth-century historian Chen Ding suggests that the legacy of moral righteousness promoted by Donglin supporters in the wake of their martyrdom was in fact to change China by creating a 'spiritual revolution', in which thousands of men and women willingly committed suicide or died resisting the fall of the Ming dynasty in the next few decades.[44] Less than two decades later the Chongzhen emperor's suicide and fall of the Ming dynasty would evoke extraordinary gestures of loyalty through mass suicides that share the ardent compulsion to recklessness found in the Donglin party and their supporters, demonstrating the awful culmination of the power of intense emotions. Wang Shiming's anguished grief and calculatedly ritualistic act of revenge found echoes in the public and often carefully staged suicides by later Ming loyalists responding to the suicide of their emperor and fall of the dynasty. The conscious theatricality of seventeenth-century loyalist deaths conformed to dramatic convention. As Frederic Wakeman writes, 'the genre par excellence of the martyr is drama, where the private is made public at once'.[45]

The Donglin faction did indeed play a significant role in creating the impetus towards moral heroism, which is so much a part of the romantic and violent history of Ming loyalism. Ming martyrs actively embraced an ethos that encouraged righteous death, often despite the misgivings many felt about the imperial family itself. Their deaths seem to have been more for the sake of an honourable ideal than personal loyalty, but the rhetoric surrounding those deaths deployed the emotional language of filial duty to the ruler as father, of mourning and of revenge. Nevertheless, Chen's 'spiritual revolution' seems to have been an intensely felt but short-lived phenomenon, closely tied to the emotional tenor of the times as adumbrated through the cult of *qing* (emotion) and fading away once the Manchu Qing government consolidated its power and Ming loyalism transformed into resigned pragmatism.[46]

The public attempt by the two aspiring avengers, Huang Zongxi and Zhou Yanzuo, to kill their fathers' murderers could have been read as a critique of the Chongzhen emperor's failure to act expeditiously despite his role in punishing those responsible for the martyrdom of Donglin supporters. Instead, it seems to have been forgiven and condoned. Their anger and grief at the murders of their fathers were fully accepted as the natural feelings of filial sons. Similarly, the emperor's complaisance was perhaps due to the powerful linkage between filial piety and loyalty to the state, whereby rulers and subjects are bound by mutual obligation.[47] These mutual bonds of filial piety and loyalty, given new valency through the prevailing late Ming emphasis on the salience of emotion, played a profound role in shaping the responses of innumerable martyrs to the Ming cause when it fell in 1644 to the combined depredations of rebellions, natural disasters and Manchu invasion. Huang Zongxi, for example, perhaps in gratitude to his ill-fated 'emperor-father' (*junfu*), the Chongzhen emperor, became an active Ming loyalist until the even more imperative demands of filial piety – protecting his aging mother from harm at the hands of the Manchus – led him to abandon a life of martial resistance for one of scholarly engagement in 1649.

Huang Zongxi was not alone in trying to find a balance between the conflicting dictates of moral duty. Public and private loyalties were intertwined in complex ways, creating dilemmas for many individuals at the fall of the Ming, torn between the choice of righteous death, repaying their ruler's 'benevolence' or living on for a variety of reasons. It must be stressed that there were many who did not choose to die, either for motives of expediency, preferring pragmatic accommodation with the conquerors, or for complex reasons ranging from conflicts between filial duty and loyalty or a desire to fulfil unfinished tasks (this last motive often claimed by historians feeling driven to record the tragic events of the time).[48] Others chose a form of symbolic suicide by becoming monks or hermits, consciously withdrawing from their family line and so ensuring they would not dishonour their ancestors by serving the conquering dynasty in an official capacity.[49] Nonetheless, tens of thousands chose loyal resistance, and many thousands merchant and trading class that benefited from urban expansion and the development of trade opportunities after the middle of the eighteenth century, and who also invested in the banks and manufacturing. Moreover, Young found that the main source of start-up capital for micro-enterprise in rural Scotland between 1840 and 1914 was savings from previous wage employment.[15] Indeed, referring to the UK, Crouzet argues that about 50 per cent of the founders of large industrial undertakings between 1750 and 1850 came from the working class or lower middle class, and less than 10 per cent of entrepreneurs were descended from a landed family.[16] Even if a significant contribution was eventually made by the Scottish banks, parsimony, it seems, was indeed at least as important as great wealth for the financing of rapid industrial growth in the nineteenth century.

In nineteenth-century Scotland, the links between coal-mining, iron and steel, heavy engineering and shipbuilding meant a rather dense inter-industry connectivity, even if the whole was driven by a somewhat fickle export demand. Chapter 6 makes it clear that by the early twentieth century there was a rather widespread view that Scotland's manufacturing sector was too much oriented towards iron, steel, shipbuilding and other heavy engineering industries, all of which were highly dependent on export demand, and too little oriented towards a rapidly growing domestic consumer demand for automobiles, etc. The two world wars were said to have saved these industries temporarily, but after the Second World War another hegemonic view emerged along the same lines, when shipbuilding, railway engines and other heavy industries faced increasing international competition from the USA, Germany and Japan. After a brief period of focus on 'indigenous industry' by the new Scottish Development Agency in the 1960s, support for the traditional industries faltered in the 1970s and was effectively ended by the Thatcher government in the 1980s. The focus switched to what Arthur Lewis called 'industrialisation by invitation', especially on inward investment by US multinationals in office machinery and light manufacturing. These multinationals preferred a non-unionised labour force, and reinforced Thatcher's anti-union policies and legislation in the 1980s. While other comparable countries managed to expand shipbuilding and heavy engineering, particularly Germany and Japan, and adopt new techniques, Scotland failed to do so, and the efforts to turn things around look, in retrospect, rather half-hearted.

The discovery of North Sea oil in the late 1960s and its exploitation in the 1970s provided little or no succour to Scotland's indigenous industries, as it came at a time when the relevant industrial base was weak and failing. Downstream and upstream activities mainly benefited US multinationals, while tax revenues accrued to the Westminster government and were used by it to bolster the Thatcher neoliberal project, prosecute international aggression and bolster re-election prospects. For these reasons, Norman Smith calls his book on the subject *The Sea of Lost Opportunity*,[17] while Christopher Harvie titled his earlier book *Fool's Gold*.[18]

In short, the UK was following neo-liberal, free-trade approaches to everything, especially so from the 1970s, and failing to take the necessary action to retain and adapt its traditional and formerly highly successful skills and industries. It also became highly dependent on inward flows of investment, especially from the USA, both for oil development and for manufacturing generally, with the result that much of the value-added leaked out from Scotland, something that Adam Smith would surely not have supported.

Norway's approach to industrialisation, natural resource ownership, and oil specifically, was quite different from that of the UK, and by extension Scotland. First of all, Norway's industrialisation was based largely on hydro-electric power which was a dispersed resource seen to belong to communities rather than individuals, unlike coal which was a privately owned geographically concentrated resource in Scotland, mostly in the hands of the large landowners. Foreign investment in hydro power and related manufacturing was controlled by the Concession Laws which not only secured reversion of the hydro-power dams and related infrastructure to the municipalities and counties after a period of years, but also insisted that manufacturing should go hand-in-hand with the development of the hydro power. This manufacturing included the smelting of metal ores and the manufacturing of fertilisers and other chemicals, which required cheap energy. After twenty-five or thirty years, then, we see many years when the surpluses from hydro-electric generation largely accrued either to the State electricity companies or to the local authorities who were able to use them for local development purposes. This is still the case in many Norwegian counties and municipalities today, more than a century after the first Concession Laws were passed and despite the 'neo-liberal turn' in the 1980s and 1990s when local authorities were encouraged to sell off such assets, and some did.

The approach to hydro power was also followed with the development of North Sea oil, where ownership has remained in national, and to a very large extent government, hands. It is a largely state-owned company – Statoil – that owns the oil and exploits it. The revenues for the most part go into a Sovereign Oil Fund today worth more than £6 billion, or roughly £100,000 per citizen.[19] This helps to avoid 'Dutch disease' – or the super-inflation of the exchange rate – common in natural resource-rich economies. Just as important, it represents a fund to draw on when the oil is no longer there or exploitation ceases for other reasons. In addition, it is largely Norwegian companies that supply the oil industry, meaning that the revenues from oil have a much larger local economic impact than they do in Scotland.

Although Norway has also made mistakes, especially in the period since 1980,[20] the headline is that it has taken much greater care to ensure that it and its people benefit from its hydro-electric and oil resources than Scotland has been able to do, or the UK has been willing or inclined to do. This has not been because Norway led Scotland in traditional skills or enterprise relating to hydro or oil – indeed, the reverse is certainly the case with oil – but is because independence from Denmark in 1814 allowed it to develop better economic policies, rooted in a more democratic and participatory polity.

POLITICS AND POLICY-MAKING

In his critique of the prevailing hegemonic idea that free trade and movement of capital is inevitably 'good' for development, Dieter Senghaas points out that 'it has hardly ever been questioned whether, during its initial development stages in the nineteenth and early twentieth centuries, Europe itself had developed in such a way. And rarely have the repercussions of free trade in different societies been properly examined.'[21] Senghaas points out that Norway did not follow a conventional development path. It remained poor in the nineteenth century, when it was still exporting timber and fish, and its main export earner was in fact the Norwegian- owned merchant fleet, Norway having the third-largest tonnage after Britain and the US in 1860. To Senghaas, it was the coming of hydro-electric power and attendant industries, together with the State regulation of that process, which made the difference. Norway was able to 'disassociate itself' from the international economy, to use Senghaas' terms. Meanwhile, Britain was in a liberal period, having abolished the corn laws in the mid-nineteenth century, and of course having preferential trade arrangements with the British Empire, then at its apex.

Norway protected its land and natural resources from foreign exploitation and speculation, whereas Britain had a consistently 'open door' policy for most of the period in question. True, the coal industry was nationalised between 1947 and 1994 and Scottish hydro-electricity between 1943 and 1991, but in the case of coal this did not happen at a formative stage of industrial development,[22] while in the case of hydro power in Scotland the process of nationalisation was extremely centralised in its approach, leaving no surpluses for the local communities that they could deploy on their own account, but certainly leading to a large extension of electric power to rural households. What it did do was allow the electrification of most of the 50 per cent of homes in the Highlands and Islands that lacked electricity in 1950 during the following twenty years.

The choices made by Norway were made by it autonomously and against the hegemonic thinking of the time. They were made because of specific histori-cal, political and social conditions in Norway. Britain, on the other hand, was a major part of the hegemony, and it faced a different set of conditions. This is why Senghaas rejects both 'world systems' and 'core–periphery' theories that imply that the development of a core must necessarily be at the expense of a periphery, in a kind of zero-sum game.[23] Of course, core–periphery processes may occur, but only where the core exercises some kind of control over the periphery. As Chapter 3 makes clear, Denmark was a weak 'core' for Norway, and a non-existent one after 1814, while England was a much stronger core for Scotland, especially after the middle of the eighteenth century. The defining moment for Norway was indeed 1814, as within the Norway–Sweden Union of Crowns, Sweden started as more of an equal partner that became progressively weaker until the dissolution of the Union in 1905. While Scotland became more of a dependent periphery within Britain and the UK, Norway became increasingly independent within a framework of loose Nordic cooperation (see also Chapter 10).

Norway's choices were made in a political system that had been relatively democratic – certainly in comparison to Scotland – since 1814, due to the widespread and relatively even ownership of land on the one hand, and the related urban–rural alliance. Not only was the proportion of the enfranchised population significantly higher in Norway after 1814 than in Scotland even after the 1833 Reform Bill but, as we can see in Chapter 3, the grip of the old regime on Scotland's polity was very much stronger at the beginning of the nineteenth century and remained much stronger thereafter. Moreover, the rural–urban alliance, formed mainly in the nineteenth century, was strengthened in the crises of the twentieth century and underpinned the development of social democracy, a strong welfare state and a model of development that became known as a distinctive model.

Norway is one of the 'mixed economy' countries that, deliberately or otherwise, followed Karl Polanyi's (1944/2001) analysis of the failure of market liberalism, the hegemonic idea emerging from Britain's leading role in the world economy during the nineteenth century. In particular, the idea that the market is embedded in society and its institutions is one that is perhaps best exemplified by the Norwegian approach. This idea is precisely the opposite of that of neo-liberals who believe that society, if it exists at all, is or should be embedded in the market. While 'dislocation', as Polanyi calls it,[24] was common in Scotland in the nineteenth and twentieth centuries, it was far less so in Norway, at least until after the Second World War.

In his conclusions, Senghaas stresses three imperatives of development policy, mainly aimed at the 'third world' but founded on his analysis of the European development experience, and therefore relevant to our analysis. The first is the imperative of dissociation from the global regime, as only in this way can the necessary self-centredness that leads to an inward-orientated accumulation process be stimulated. The second imperative is socio-economic restructuring in a way that leads to what he calls 'building up of coherent accumulation structures' which, although he refers particularly to Freidrich List, is also – despite List–Smith disagreements – derived from Adam Smith. The third is both about the international division of labour and, perhaps more importantly, about the building up of sub-regional, regional and continental infrastructures and institutions that can counter the hegemony, wherever that is located. With regard to the first imperative, Norway dissociated itself in the early twentieth century by means of the Concession Acts. With regard to the second, the policy of location, ownership and linking of hydro-power plants and related industrial activities, as well as the structure of landownership and protection of that structure from external forces, was critical. With regard to the third, the development of Nordic cooperation, starting indeed in the medieval period but reinforced in the nineteenth and twentieth centuries, and the notion of the Nordic Model as a distinctive approach to development, political life and human welfare in the twentieth century are a clear example (see also Chapters 3 and 10).

By contrast, Scotland was politically unable to follow such a prescription after the Union of 1707, and its dependence on the central and increasingly central-ised government in Westminster increased, especially after the middle of the nineteenth century, with the only concession to Scottish governance up until devolution in 1999 being the establishment of an administrative presence in the form of a Scottish Secretary in 1885 and later a Scottish Office, both as part of the Westminster government (see Chapter 3).

CONSENSUS POLITICS

The political conditions facing Scotland since the Union have meant, for the most part, subordination to an increasingly centralised Westminster government, which was elected on a very limited and quite unrepresentative franchise in the nineteenth century, and which remained unrepresentative of Scottish voters even after the extension of the franchise for most of the twentieth and early twenty-first centuries. This lack of democratic representativeness was compounded by the bi-cameral system in the UK, with an unelected second chamber in the form of the House of Lords that, for most of the period under study, was peopled with the representatives of Britain's 'ancien régime', notably the upper echelons of the landed classes and members of the religious and legal elite.[25] Even in those rare periods when over half of the Scottish voters voted for the same party or coali-tion that won the UK elections under the first-past-the-post system, they had to contend with a House of Lords that was for the most part on the opposite side of the political spectrum.

As Tom Devine[26] has argued, the British Reform Bill of 1832 was hardly radical, and even less radical from a Scottish point of view where the franchise covered an even smaller proportion of the male population. Democracy was seen by the British elite as a threat, and the Reform Bill was aimed at preserving as much of the traditional landed power as possible. The legislation also allowed the corrupt practices amounting to 'vote-stuffing' to continue.[27] The failure of the Bill led to the rise of Chartism as a response to the failure to extend the franchise to the working class. Chartism failed as a political force in the later nineteenth century, but it did deepen and enlarge the Scottish radical tradition, already established in the 1790s.[28] It is also worth noting, in the context of our earlier discussion of land-ownership, that the Chartist Land Plan outlined a 'vision of smallholding colonies and agricultural self-sufficiency as an alternative to industrial capitalism'.[29] Nineteenth-century Scottish political ideas were anti-landowner rather than anti-capitalist, and contained strong elements of Scottish nationalism.[30]

Prime Minister Gladstone, a Liberal who was also popular in Scotland, won the UK elections in 1868 and in the same year the franchise was extended to the skilled working classes. There followed a period of Liberal dominance in both Scottish and UK politics which essentially lasted until 1914, albeit in an increasingly fragile political environment, and with some coalitions in the latter period. Although it could not be argued that Scotland as a whole was disenfranchised in this period, the period of Liberal dominance in Scottish politics is seen by Nairn as one of profound crisis for Scottish nationhood.[31] However, as Devine points out, this was also a period when Scots were prominent if not dominant in the Empire project, in industry and industrial inventions, in banking and in literature and academia.[32] Gladstone's government, with the help of the Crofters' Party, initiated the Napier Commission's enquiry into the condition of crofters and cottars that led to an important 'land reform' in terms of the granting of security of tenure to crofters, rent controls and other rights and protections in response to the abuses of the Highland Clearances, as discussed in Chapter 1. Those voters in general supporting land reform, home rule for Scotland and extension of the franchise voted Liberal in this period, and to a large extent this led to an alliance that cut across class boundaries.[33]

The Liberal hegemony collapsed after the First World War when, helped by the extension of the franchise in 1918, Labour gained a third of the votes in the elections of that year. However, the 'first-past-the post' system meant that only eight Labour MPs were sent to Westminster. The Irish Catholic vote moved from Liberal to Labour after the Irish Partition in 1920. Liberals lost votes because they provided neither promised land nor promised housing 'fit for heroes' to soldiers and sailors returning from the war. In the 1922 election, Labour became the largest party in Scotland for the first time with 32 per cent of the votes and 29 MPs in the UK parliament. However, Labour's fortunes were also to be affected by the Russian Revolution and the economic crises of the inter-war period, both of which polarised politics nationally and caused the middle classes to move to the right, a shift that Conservative Prime Minister Baldwin took advantage of, and which simultaneously deepened the marginalisation of the Liberals. Nevertheless, Baldwin's popular Conservative government of 1935 only polled 42 per cent of the Scottish vote. From then on, and up to the present day, Scottish voters have only once cast more than 50 per cent of their votes for the government in power in Westminster.

One can only conclude that because of the nature of the franchise – the first-past-the-post electoral system, different voting patterns between Scotland and the rest of the UK, and the existence of a second chamber dominated for most of the period in question by the landed elite – Scottish people have been in a very real sense disenfranchised by the British political system for most of the period between the Union of 1707 and the present day. The main exception seems to have been the period of Liberal hegemony between 1868 and 1914. It was perhaps in that period above all that we can see the glimmers of a kind of alliance between small farmers, working class and middle class that led to social democracy and consensus politics in the Nordic countries, but which ended in polarised and conflictual politics in the UK and Scotland in the twentieth century (see also Chapter 3).

In Norway, as Knut Heidar argues, people's political power was transformed by the new Constitution of 1814 when the vote was given to all owners of land and some tenants as well.[34] Because of the wide distribution of landownership, this meant that 45 per cent of males over the age of 25 were eligible to vote. However, the power of the parliament was for the time being restricted due to the Union Monarchy with Sweden: 'From about 1850 onward the liberal intelligentsia in the cities increasingly joined forces with the peasant groups in parliament in order to make government more responsive to parliament – at the expense of the old class of state officials.' In 1884, this coalition of forces came to power and secured a parliamentary form of relationship with the executive. All men were given the vote in 1898, and in 1913 this was extended to all women. Meanwhile, local government had been championed by the peasants in the 1830s and elected representative municipalities were established in 1837. Heidar argues that the local political autonomy created in 1837 was extremely important for later democratisation.[35] As Chapters 3 and 5 make clear, Norway created a local democracy that had and has very substantial powers and financing, as well as much greater representation and higher voter participation, than was or is the case in Scotland. This was the means by which the peasants successfully resisted centralised planning, centralisation, transfer of fishing rights to capitalist interests, and promoted concession laws and other progressive measures in the field of natural resources and land.[36]

Up to 1928, government oscillated between Liberals and Conservatives, although the Liberals were the 'natural party of government' in this period.[37] Labour benefited from universal male suffrage in 1898 and more so from the introduction of proportional representation in 1921, winning an eighteen-day control of government in 1928, and a more solid – if minority government – control in 1935 with support from the rural centre party, which gave it a thirty-year control of power broken only by the war period. This Labour government was a social democratic government, despite its history as a member of the Komintern[38] between 1919 and 1923, and it became the hegemonic party in Norwegian politics until the mid-1960s. During the entire period from 1950 to 1980, the Labour party was out of office for less than eight years. Heider states that

Social progress was founded on more or less continuous economic growth during this period. The state gave priority to industrial development, and a strong belief in progress, as such, permeated society. Planning was a central instrument in state economic policies, and sectors like agriculture, fishing, and transportation were all strongly state regulated. The social democratic order was also marked by a belief in a strong state. Primary public goals were full employment, social equality, and a high level of welfare. Accordingly, redistribution of resources was a major objective, and it was considered the responsibility of the state to provide free education and free health care and to look after important cultural institutions. In short, markets were to be guided, private solutions were eschewed, and the chances for 'opting out' were restricted.[39]

CONCLUSION

This chapter is titled *towards* a theory of divergent development, and so does not purport to be *the* theory of divergent development between Norway and Scotland. It is of course a matter of judgement whether any person likes the outcome better in Norway or, *vice versa*, in Scotland. I have used a Classical approach to the issue, married with Polanyi's approach which involves an economy embedded in society rather than the opposite. And I believe that this approach is the best one for explaining long-run divergence between two countries following, of their own volition or in a dependent manner, essentially different paths. I understand differences in the initial condition of land ownership and distribution to be central to these divergences, not just for their own sake but because they had an impact on political values and beliefs, as well as alliances and, ultimately, coalitions. These values and beliefs and political conditions in turn underpinned the dissociation from the global hegemony of free markets and capital movements at a critical juncture of history, notably the start of modern industrialisation on the strength of hydro-power resources at the end of the nineteenth century. They also underpinned the development of a more generous and universal welfare state in the twentieth century and the later development of North Sea oil. Taken together, I find much more of a 'Smithian' model of development in Norway than in Scotland.[40] However, perhaps it should be called a 'Smith-Polanyi' model because of the incorporation – whether by design or otherwise – of Polanyi's specific considerations relating to false commodities, land, people and money.

The dominant political cleavages in a rapidly industrialising Scotland in the nineteenth century were between workers and sections of the middle class, and the landed interests that were so much against the extension of democracy; and between the Protestant and (migrant Irish) Catholic working-class factions. The most powerful and enduring alliance was between the skilled workers and the urban middle classes that created the Liberal hegemony against large landowners and in favour of home rule, but ultimately fracturing into polarised Labour and Conservative regimes dominated by the Westminster government. In Norway, the dominant cleavages of the nineteenth century were first, between the towns formerly privileged by monarchs and the rural areas; second, between farm workers and their employers; and third, between workers and capitalists. The most powerful and enduring alliance was that between small family peasant farmers, many of whom were also small fishermen, and the growing working class, which led to the social democratic and consensual political system still enduring today. This was reinforced by early extension of the effective franchise and adoption of proportional representation. The two very different political systems that emerged help us to understand the different political choices made in Norway and in (but mostly for) Scotland in the modern period.

Does this comparative development 'story' have any more general theoretical pointers? We think it does. For one thing, the cases of Norway and Scotland do not support generalised 'stages' theories[41] that imply, for example, that an 'agrarian revolution' involving in particular the dispossession of peasants need precede an industrial revolution. For another, the cases demonstrate that peripheries are not doomed to remain dependent and poor, trapped in a vicious cycle. Yet again, there is no support from the Norwegian case for the notion that the development of market capitalism needs to precede 'social development' (the 'Sen-Bhagwati argument'), since 'trickle-down' from the development of capitalism will finance the development of education, health and other social supports. No doubt one could find many more examples but suffice to say here that it is important to examine the particulars of each case – Norway has its own very particular history, even distinct from the other Scandinavian and Nordic countries.

The story nevertheless has some pointers for both Scotland and Norway. Should Scottish people vote for independence, its new policy-makers can certainly find considerable support for the creation of a new political system, with multiple parties and proportional representation, and a much stronger local democracy to give those living in the very different parts of Scotland a real voice and powers to tailor policies to their needs and aspirations, and resist hegemonic ideas from the centre. New political leaders, parties and democratic elements can also drop the current obsession with the neo-liberal development path reflected by the policies of the main UK parties over the past thirty-five years, and emanating from the USA. They can, and hopefully will, open their eyes to other alternative development paths towards a more 'human' economy and society.[42] In this they will desirably be informed by the experience of the Nordic countries which have a robust alternative 'model', albeit one that has been formed in specific national political, social and economic conditions. To follow an alternative path, more like the Nordic social democratic path, Scotland will need solid alliances to counter the England–US axis, and these are also most likely to come from the Nordic countries, which already have a history of alliances between themselves in the Nordic Council of Ministers and the Nordic Council, to name but two. But opportunities will also arise in the EU, where Scotland would be in a position to play a more positive role than the remainder of the UK.

The issue of landownership and more generally the distribution of wealth and income also needs to be tackled in an independent Scotland, as do the related issues of control over land transactions and land value taxation. The very distorted distribution of wealth and income today in the UK has distorted democracy and disenfranchised the poorer section of society.

The role of the State will be critical in these and other matters, but to exercise that role properly the State must be legitimate and seen to be so. Politicians and the executive must be scrupulously just and fair, open and honest. Anything less should not be tolerated. People must trust the State and its institutions. The strengthening of social democracy must include the thoroughgoing reform of local government, including devolution of power, responsibility and taxation, and democratisation of the Non-Departmental Public Bodies (NDPBs) that dominate so many areas formerly under local government responsibility, including housing, water and sewage, recreation and the environment, flood protection, tourism, culture and economic development.

Notes

1. Smith [1776] 1910, Book III: 344.
2. Ibid.: 345.
3. Smith [1776] 1910, Book III: 351.
4. By and large this was also the view of the Scottish working class and liberal bourgeoisie in the nineteenth century, who supported a liberal trade regime, the notion of the 'good employer', with whom they were allied against the old regime of the landed aristocracy. See also Chapter 6.
5. Smith [1776] 1910, Book V: 400.
6. Smith [1776] 1910, Book II: 301.
7. Ibid.: 312.
8. We understand 'enclosures' to imply the individualisation of formerly common or collective property and other use rights such as the hunting of game, fishing, collecting of firewood and mushrooms, access and rights of way and the winning of peat for heating and cooking. We understand clearances to imply the removal of farmers, crofters or cottars from the land on which they had customary use for farming, etc.
9. Nor did it happen in Japan or, much later, in Italy.
10. See, for example, Binswanger et al. (1995) and Falkinger and Grossman (2012).
11. It is true that Norwegian industrialisation after 1847 adopted 'infant-industry' protection of the kind recommended by List (1789–1846), who opposed Smith on this point, at least for a period. However, later in the nineteenth century Norway adopted free trade, although infant-industry protection was reintroduced for the development of the oil industry in the 1970s (see Chapter 6).
12. Arrighi, 2007: 359–64.
13. W. A. Lewis (1954), *Economic Development with Unlimited Supplies of Labour*, The Manchester School, May.
14. Smith [1776] 1910, Book II: 301.
15. Young, 1995.
16. Crouzet, 1985: 77.
17. Smith, 2011.
18. Harvie, 1994.
19. The Fund is now called the 'Government Pension Fund Global'.
20. This is not the place to list Norway's mistakes, but they include losing control of hydro power and Norske Hydro, and they currently include various privatisation projects in the public sphere, as well as proposals for local government reorganisation. Other mistakes are mentioned in Chapters 7 and 10 in particular.
21. Senghaas, 1985: 6.
22. At which time the British political system was firmly in the hands of the old regime (see also Chapters 1, 3 and 6).

23. Senghaas, 1985: 154–5. Senghaas here refers to a debate between T. C. Smout, the Scottish historian, and Immanuel Wallerstein, leader of the World Systems approach. One of the present authors (Bryden) also debated a core–periphery approach to Scottish development with Smout in an ESRC seminar in Edinburgh University on 21 March 1980. See also Seers et al. (1979) and Bryden's contribution in that volume. An unpublished postscript to that contribution was presented by Bryden at the Edinburgh seminar.

24. Some call this 'disembedding', a term not in fact used by Polanyi himself. By 'dislocation' Polanyi was referring to the commercialisation of those things such as land and people or even food that were formerly part of social institutions and 'places'. Polanyi [1944] 2001, Chapter 15.

25. In his John McEwen lecture, Bryden analysed Andy Wightman's data to show that over half of the top 100 landowners were also hereditary peers with the right to sit in the House of Lords (Bryden, 1996: 6, n4). Because of this, the popular cause of land reform in Scotland did not become politically feasible until after devolution in 1999, when Scotland took back control over its own land law. Also present were the bishops of the Church of England and the Law Lords. See also Wightman, 1996:142.

26. Devine, 1999: 274.

27. Ibid.: 274.

28. Devine, 1999: 280.

29. Ibid.: 280.

30. Knox, 1999: 169.

31. Nairn, 1977.

32. Devine, 1999: 289–98.

33. Knox, 1999: 163–74.

34. Heidar, 2001: 18. See also Chapter 3.

35. Ibid.: 19.

36. Brox, 2006: 33–42.

37. Heidar, 2001: 24.

38. The Moscow-based communist international organisation calling for armed uprising by the working classes. See also Heidar (2001) and Chapter 3 in this volume.

39. Heidar, 2001: 25.

40. See also Arrighi (2007). Arrighi explores Adam Smith's model as applied to China.

41. For example, those of either Marx, whose system in *Das Kapital* vol. 1, Chapter 24 depends so heavily on the enclosure movement in England, or Rostow's *Stages of Economic Growth* (1960). However, Gerschenkron (1962), who had a stage theory of his own, allows that it is neither necessary nor sufficient to have 'preconditions' for takeoff as well as the fact that each country need not go through the same set of stages.

42. For a discussion of 'Human Economy', see for example Hart et al. (2010).

CHAPTER 3

Cousins Divided? Development in and of Political Institutions in Scotland and Norway since 1814

Nik. Brandal and Øivind Bratberg

ABSTRACT

Scotland and Norway started the nineteenth century as political cousins with seemingly similar structural features with regard to the political unions in which they took part. Yet from that point onwards their national development diverged. Norway turned out to become a rapidly developing, consensus-oriented and egalitarian nation-state, where democratisation ran parallel with the pursuit of national autonomy. Its Scottish cousin, meanwhile, remained embedded in the Union of Great Britain. It was characterised by adversarial politics and sharp social inequalities and saw its national aspirations run awry. How and why two countries with a shared point of departure evolved into entities that differ so profoundly today provides the puzzle for this chapter. We assess the perceived similarity between Scotland and Norway at the start of the period, analyse the differences in the social and political models today and trace the factors that may account for how the gap appeared. Finally, we consider the implications for an independent Scotland with this historical backdrop.

INTRODUCTION

The *longue durée* of Scottish and Norwegian history gives ample reason to place the two under the same light of scrutiny. Both nations were unified as seaward empire-nations in the Middle Ages, only to move towards peripheral status under a stronger neighbouring centre during the phase of accelerated nation-building from the sixteenth century onwards. They both turned Protestant in the Reformation and concentrated heavy responsibility for cultural development and education in their State Churches. Both Norwegians and Scots, furthermore, maintained – even during the peak periods of political integration under the dominant external centre – distinctive legal traditions and institutions as well as urban corporations with some independence in their external trade relations. Finally, in cultural terms, both countries harboured progressive rural movements with the potential to forge links with an emerging industrial working class.

In the run-up to the referendum on Scottish independence in 2014 an argument has been made – especially by proponents for independence – that Scotland should regenerate its relations across the North Sea. However, as we will argue in this chapter, in social and political terms Scotland and Norway have diverged widely from a seemingly similar structural position, thus complicating any claim to familiarity today. From the starting point of 1814, Norway turned out to become a rapidly developing, consensus-oriented and egalitarian nation-state, with a social model that emerged from the parallel pursuit of democratisation and national autonomy. Its Scottish cousin, meanwhile, remained embedded in the Union of Great Britain. This was characterised by adversarial politics and sharp social inequalities and saw its national aspirations run awry.

How and why two countries with a shared point of departure developed along such different trajectories is one of the main questions that we will try to answer in this chapter. However, while the historical similarities are certainly glaring, it is also essential not to overstate these commonalities, and as the Norwegian political scientist Stein Rokkan has pointed out, significant differences in historical backdrop between Scotland and Norway extend from external geopolitics to internal territorial structure.[1] Even so, we will argue that the shared historical outlook of Scotland and Norway offers a useful point of departure for analysing the subsequent evolution in both countries.

In this chapter the analysis will focus on the political development in the two countries in order to assess the perceived similarity between Scotland and Norway at the start of the period, analyse the differences in the political and social model today and trace the factors that may account for how the gap appeared. In proffering not only the political but also the *social* model our argument is that patterns of political mobilisation in key phases of the two nations' histories have had a lasting impact on features such as welfare state development, labour market relations, social mobility and redistribution. While these aspects are only superficially treated in this chapter, they are part and parcel of any analysis of why and to what extent Scotland and Norway diverge politically – beyond the obvious difference in political institutions. We will return to this point in a brief concluding section to consider the potential implications for an independent Scotland on the historical backdrop that we sketch.

The analysis is informed by historical institutionalism, according to which the legacy of earlier institutional decisions impinges on current processes, reducing the scope for entrepreneurship and magnifying the significance of discrete choices in the past. Essential to this approach to politics is the concept of path dependence. What it suggests is that historical development follows a branching structure; decisions at critical junctures earn a momentous significance over time, thus making it increasingly difficult to diverge from a selected path to which vested interests and formal and informal rules are attached.[2] Analytically, the concept is particularly apt where the goal is to explain an outcome or structure where a casual reading suggests that history matters but with an insufficient grasp of how or why.

Path dependence thus appears as a particularly fruitful approach to make sense of a development characterised by 'contingency at the front end and some degree of determinism at the back end'.[3] This is precisely the striking feature for an informed observer of the social model attached to both the Norwegian and the Scottish polities. Significantly, path dependence need not translate into a vision of standstill and stasis between rare transformative events. Clearly, moments where the form and shape of political institutions are subject to full reordering are extremely rare. However, even in times of apparent stability there is scope for incremental adaptation to changes in the environment as well as for actors to fight their own turf. As argued by Wolfgang Streeck and Kathleen Thelen, 'political institutions are the object of ongoing skirmishes as actors try to achieve advantage by interpreting or redirecting institutions in pursuit of their goals'.[4] In the current chapter we will apply this broader view of path dependence to analyse the development in and of political institutions in Scotland and Norway since 1814.

CRITICAL JUNCTURE 1: A CONSTITUTIONAL MOMENT?

Path-breaker by Constitutional Design – Norway

The outcome of the Napoleonic Wars for Norway was radical in form and consequence. Externally, the consequences were mitigated by the fact that union with a foreign power was sustained, as Sweden was handed what Denmark was forced to relinquish at the Treaty of Kiel. Beyond the façade of great-power rivalry, however, Norway moved at one stroke from subservience to the enlightened rule of a monarch to a constitutional monarchy with an elected parliament at its heart.

Thus, if there was ever such a thing as a defining moment in the political history of a nation, for Norway it was the year 1814. Within just over seven months, Norway seceded from Denmark and was given to Sweden on 14 January, declared its independence in defiance of the major European powers and adopted a radical new constitution based on popular sovereignty on 17 May, and fought a short war with Sweden over the summer, ending in an armistice on 14 August. In its wake, the Norwegian Parliament voted in support of a Personal Union with Sweden on 20 October and elected the Swedish King Charles XIII as the King of Norway on 4 November. We will examine some of the key events and their consequences for later political developments in Norway.

Merely four weeks after the Treaty of Kiel,[5] a Meeting of Notables convened on 16 February to deal with its consequences for Norway.[6] The meeting had been called as a last-gasp attempt of retaining Danish sovereignty over Norway by the Danish Lord Lieutenant, the heir presumptive to the Danish throne, Prince Christian Frederick. However, it soon became clear that while the delegates were unanimous in their resistance to subjugation by Sweden, the principle of popular sovereignty was equally present among them. From this followed that if Christian Frederick should ascend the throne, it would have to be in a manner seen as democratic. At the conclusion the twenty-one Notables agreed to arrange for the election of a Norwegian Constituent Assembly that was to convene two months later, on 10 April, to draw up a separate constitution for Norway and elect a new Norwegian king.[7]

As such, the events in Norway in the spring of 1814 were a textbook example of negotiated elite-based pacted transition from authoritarian rule in the Linz-Schmitter tradition.[8] This was then followed by a mobilisation from below, in which all church parishes were firstly to swear an oath of loyalty to Norwegian independence, and then designate a number of electors to participate in electing representatives for the Constituent Assembly. Furthermore, military units were to elect two representatives directly, of whom one was an officer and one a representative for enlisted men. There were no clear restrictions on who had the right to participate in the vote, but the representatives selected for the electoral college and the Constituent Assembly were to be over the age of twenty-five and either public servants, burghers, freeholding farmers or leaseholding farmers on large properties, restrictions which were later to be found in the voting rules of the Norwegian Constitution. The assembly that gathered at Eidsvoll on 10 April 1814 could thus be seen as electives of the Norwegian people and represented a broad stratum of Norwegian society.[9] A committee charged with submitting a draft set out fundamental precepts which would underpin all subsequent work on the Constitution: that Norway was to be a free, independent and indivisible realm; the King was to have executive power, an elected national assembly was to have the power to pass laws and grant funds, and independent courts were to pass judgement; freedom of the press and freedom of religion were guaranteed.[10] After six weeks of deliberations, the assembly voted to approve a new Constitution and elected Christian Frederick as the Norwegian King on 17 May.

Norwegian independence was however short-lived, as a few military skirmishes between Norwegian and Swedish troops ended with an armistice at the Convention of Moss on 14 August.[11] Here, Christian Frederick agreed to relinquish claims to the Norwegian Crown if Sweden would accept the democratic Norwegian Constitution and a loose personal union. As such, the Treaty of Kiel was thus tacitly subdued and both the principle and substance of the Norwegian Constitution were accepted. Furthermore, Norway retained its own parliament and separate institutions, except for a common king and Foreign Service.[12] This was confirmed by the Norwegian Parliament, and the conclusion of the year 1814 was thus that Norway was not to be treated as a Swedish conquest but rather as an equal party in a union of two independent states.[13]

The short-term consequences were that culturally Norway remained a part of Denmark, while politically it became a part of Sweden. Meanwhile, with regard to trade and commercial interests it remained in all but name a part of the British Empire, due to the extensive merchant fleet and heavy emphasis on overseas trade with territories under British control. To the budding elites in Norway, the multifaceted relationship with its neighbours meant that the pursuit of national autonomy was never an all-or-nothing exercise against a dominant neighbour. Moreover, it left a significant space for triangulation, which was cleverly used in the first half of the nineteenth century.[14] In the longer term, by far the most important result of 1814 was the establishment of institutions which, according to the Norwegian historian Øystein Sørensen, would serve as hegemonic nation-building projects: the Norwegian Parliament (the *Storting*) and the Constitution.[15] Furthermore, as we will see in the following, the successful outcome of the mobilisation from below became a lesson learned for the political system.[16]

Significantly, while establishing the framework for a liberal democracy, the franchise established by the Constitution was exceptionally broad from a European perspective, as the right to vote was extended to about 40 per cent of all men over the age of twenty-five. This number decreased in the following decades since the number of cottars, proletarians, clerks and functionaries increased and the number of landowners dropped as a part of the population. By 1880 the number of eligible voters had thus dropped to 30 per cent of all men over the age of twenty-five, and in 1884 this led to the franchise being extended on the basis of taxable income. In 1898 it was extended to all adult males, and over the following years women were gradually included until the franchise encompassed all adults in 1913.[17]

While the breadth of the franchise constituted a promising point of departure for political mobilisation, it was aided by the local government reform of 1837 which introduced elected local councils with considerable political clout. Furthermore, the reform provided a democratic education for the electorate, especially in the peripheries, as thousands of farmers, burghers and others who would otherwise not have been involved in politics were given access to a political education, which in turn led many of them to seek higher office.[18] A latent centre/periphery cleavage was thereby given time and space to mature. The mobilisation from below – grounded in the assumedly 'national' culture of independent farmers – would be crucial for the parallel development towards a broadening of democracy (particularly by making the government accountable to the *Storting* in 1884) and national independence, finally obtained in 1905. Here, the budding alliance between the politics and culture of the periphery on the one hand and urban radicals on the other was crucial in transforming the political system towards a broadening of democracy on egalitarian grounds.

also be a way of socializing among equals in an assumed jocular mode and frolicsome tone. Thus, raillery represented a grey area in which the line between friendly teasing and aggression could easily be blurred, on purpose or by misinterpretation, and turn into a balancing act on a knife edge.[16]

Duelling before the law and the monopolization of violence

A significant early prohibition against duels was issued in 1590, though it was restricted to the king's servants. The question was raised in more general terms by Queen Christina in a request submitted to the Diet in 1649, about 'putting an end to fights and duels involving vicious youth as well as their foolish elders, often deliberately and for the mere sake of vain inclination'.[17] In their answer, the nobility gave a slightly different characterization of the actual situation. Since duels and fights 'are most often provoked by disrespectful and unseemly words uttered in a rash mood, the offended party is forced to respond in kind to defend his good reputation and honour which are valued equally with life itself by every honest man'.[18] The argument was twofold: first, aristocrats claimed that duels were not of a strictly deliberate character but arose in the course of an argument and defence of one's honour. Second, defending one's honour was equal to self-defence. However, some provocations and challenges clearly arose out of pure mischief, and in such cases the nobility claimed that the 'innocent' party should not be considered on equal legal footing with the 'criminal'. In contrast, the clergy defined duelling as a deliberate sin that called for capital punishment according to the Old Testament. This 'life for a life' biblical admonition was also explicitly stated in an addition to the first printed edition of the National Law Code, published in 1608. The supplement, usually referred to as 'God's Law', contained extracts from the Mosaic Law and was structured in accordance with the Ten Commandments 'to be observed in capital cases and other serious crime'.[19] However, it was not until 1662 and after the queen's abdication that the first antiduelling ordinance was issued.

The introduction of legislation against duels had two objectives: to avoid God's anger and vengeance upon the nation for not upholding his commandments; and to prevent damage to the fatherland, due to the untimely loss of competent soldiers and military officers.[20] No distinction was made between challenger and respondent as long as a fight had taken place, which meant that neither party could claim self-defence. Furthermore, the ordinance stipulated that challenger could still be punished, even if the challenge failed to elicit a response. Heavy fines were levied for the first offence and lifelong banishment for the second. It was at the same time made clear that these regulations applied only to the nobility and military officers.

Challenges and fights among common people could be (and continued to be) adjudicated and punished according to the letter of the law.

The nobility protested against the ordinance, not the least because it prescribed the dishonourable burial of dead duellists, an indignity that placed them on equal footing with suicides and infamous malefactors, but surviving duellists were subjected to fines and monetary compensation.[21] In a petition for retrial the Noble Estate argued that 'the point of honour could never be comparable to a sum of money. Foreigners would smile if they heard that someone was so *afraid* that he let himself be insulted for a small sum of money rather than pay a fine'.[22] In the opinion of nobles, following the regulation appeared to make law-abiding individuals appear cowardly, a dilemma that came to a head in the case of Conrad Gyllenstierna.

Conrad Gyllenstierna, frustrated duellist

In 1669 Lars Johansson, a student and poet who called himself Lasse Lucidor, composed a wedding poem to mark the wedding of County Governor Baron Conrad Gyllenstierna, member of the Swedish high nobility, to Märta Christina Ulfsparre.[23] The poem Lucidor had taken upon himself to write and distribute at the wedding ceremonial was not well received by the honoree, however. An incomplete official title in the addressing of the poem immediately caught Gyllenstierna's attention and suspicion. All the customary playful allusions to the tribulations of courtship were now scrutinized word for word by the touchy governor, who considered the poem to be libellous, an oblique attack on his own honour and that of his wife. Despite protesting his innocent intent, Lucidor was reported by the governor to the royal court for having printed and distributed a libel (a serious offence against both Swedish law and Royal Ordinances), and he was duly remanded to await trial. The case was referred to the Stockholm Council Court, which found that the poem could not be considered libellous, but fined Lucidor in any case, for breaking His Majesty's prohibition of unsolicited tributes at aristocratic functions. Gyllenstierna called for a tougher sentence in an appeal to the Royal Court, but Lucidor was released on bail until a final settlement was made. In the meantime, Conrad's brother, Christoffer, subsequently petitioned the Crown to return Lucidor to custody as a 'vagrant', and the court granted his request.

By characterizing Lucidor as a vagrant and invoking the law and Royal charters, Christoffer Gyllenstierna tried to frame the incident as a criminal case, not as a conflict involving the honour of two equal parties. Simultaneously, Conrad Gyllenstierna sought the true instigator of the defamatory content among his noble peers. The Baron had recently been involved in a serious argument with Count Wilhelm Douglas, which ended in a settlement instead of a duel, and references to this earlier incident were now read into the text of Lucidor's poem. In one verse, he recounts how the suitor, in a fit of jealousy, 'draws his sword' after a 'young man' had had the presumption to address his bride-to-be. Gyllenstierna took this to suggest that Douglas had been Gyllenstierna's rival for the affections of Märta Christina, perhaps even something much worse (the word 'cuckold' does indeed appear later in the poem). However, the real disparagement lay in the verses that followed, in which the suitor is said to challenge his rival to a duel 'if his boots stop shaking long enough'. The suitor can at least take comfort in the fact that if a settlement is agreed upon, he may continue to court his beloved as if nothing untoward had happened. These allegations were meant to be seen as an amusing account of a failed suitor, in contrast to the virtuous and successful protagonist of the poem, but Gyllenstierna read it the other way around – as an insinuation that he had withdrawn from a duel and agreed to settle due to cowardice.

The capacity for third parties to intervene, to avert violence and also to avoid prosecution for violence unfolded in the next phase of the affair. Gyllenstierna's brother Christoffer, representing the plaintiff in court, claimed that the duel had in fact been stopped by the intercession of the Field Marshal, who had negotiated a settlement. This was in accordance with the antiduelling ordinance of 1662, but judging from the discussions in the estate of the nobility, the settlement was less than satisfactory. This ambivalence was in all probability strengthened by Christoffer Gyllenstierna's long association with the so-called 'Square', an assemblage of young noblemen who were hunting and riding companions of the future King Charles XI in his adolescent years. Known for its breakneck rides, adventurous hunts and dangerous brawls, the Square and similar coteries, like 'Les goinfrès' (the rakes), included some of the most notorious duellists of the day. In one instance, two of the brothers Wachtmeister, acting as seconds, had enjoyed a duel with greatest enthusiasm, letting the combatants come together four times until one of them was fatally wounded.[24] For these young aristocrats duelling seems to have been more like a game or sport with life at stake. Conrad Gyllenstierna thus had good reason to be frustrated.

Uncertain that the settlement with Count Douglas had restored his honour in the eyes of his peers, the Baron suspected a new attack behind the perceived insinuations; however, this time it involved an attack by proxy that could neither be directly confronted nor settled. What remained for Gyllenstierna was to seek satisfaction in court and to demand both a harsh penalty for the purported middleman and a public burning of the poem as a pasquil. Yet his efforts failed. After more than six months in custody, Lucidor was acquitted and released with a warning. Ironically, the trial meant that the very same libellous connotations that were in all probability the sole construction of Gyllenstierna's own suspicious reading were brought to the attention of a wider public and they continued to hound him and his descendants for decades in their attempts to stop further circulation and publication.[25]

The question remains as to how Lucidor came to break with convention by causing offense. He, if anyone, should have been keenly aware of the seriousness of dispensing with formal titles. As the grandson of a recently ennobled admiral, he had been provided the opportunity to study, first in Uppsala and then in Greifswald and Leipzig Universities. The German ones, in particular, were infamous for their institutionalized bullying, violent behaviour and endless duelling. Lucidor seems to have indulged in student life with a passion and his name often recurs in the disciplinary records of the university board.[26] Lucidor was ultimately expelled back home to Sweden, where he quickly acquired a reputation for his poetic talent, greatly enhanced by the Gyllenstierna trial. However, he did not enjoy his fame for long. Well versed in the rhetoric of honour culture, Lucidor ended up as one of its victims. In 1674, he was stabbed in a tavern in Stockholm during a duel that appears to have followed the typical pattern of escalating provocation.[27] In the end, Lucidor and Gyllenstierna were kindred spirits, immersed in an emotional regime which did not permit perceived insults to be ignored and demanded its subjects to always be on their guard. A century later, nobles who found themselves in similar situations were not subjected to the same social pressure of immediate response, due to a shift in logic that aligned violent challenges and responses with unseemly and unmanly self-indulgence.

The discrediting of duels as expressions of overbearing wilfulness and false honour

A first critical treatise on duelling was published in 1674, which argued from a mainly Christian dogmatic point of view. Another and more decisive step was taken in 1682 with a new ordinance issued by King Charles XI (1655–1697) as part of his establishment of royal autocracy and reorganization of the army. Charles was invested in discrediting duelling and the most straightforward way of doing this was to question its purported honourable, noble and manly character. In this policy the concept of virtue played a central role. Originating from classical Greek and Roman concepts of moral excellence, virtue became increasingly important in early modern moral ideals and teachings, both in its classical and Christianized versions. The aristocracy fostered and claimed the classical virtues of fortitude (courage, heroic virtue) and magnanimity (high-mindedness), while the Aristotelian concept and politics of the household became the ethical basis for a good societal order and an ideological legitimization of state power.[28] At the same time, Christian virtues in the form of moral duties 'toward God, oneself and one and all' were taught with growing zeal in Lutheran catechisms and emphasized in conduct books. With the possible exception of more radical Stoic versions, what these different ethics had in common was a social logic according to which virtue was: first, guided by explicit rules and values to be followed in daily practice; second, learned and cultivated through education and practice; and third, directed towards a cause higher than selfish interests. In the last aspect virtue was typically contrasted with the free reign of passions.[29]

Virtue was thus a most useful moral category for both disciplinary campaigns from above and for encouraging self-improvement and refinement among new social groups striving for recognition and status. The latter was especially important among aristocrats, since the proportion of ennobled persons increased rapidly in step with growing demand for competent bureaucrats and military officers. For these new groups, ranked as the lowest in the Estate of Nobility and strongly supportive of the royal autocracy, virtue and social rank became a question of personal merit, not ancestry.[30]

With virtue as a rhetorical weapon, duelling was newly branded as 'willful excess', which sprang from a 'vicious disposition', rather than 'virtue and honesty'. The latter qualities comprised the 'hallmark of true nobility'.[31] In contrast, duellists were depicted as 'overbearing', a term frequently used in legal practice for denoting malice aforethought, not in rational terms but as an emotional disposition associated with excess and unprovoked violence.[32] The honour gained by issuing a challenge and causing 'the unchristian demise of an acquaintance and countryman, friend and brother' was 'false and vain', wrote the former Royal Chaplain Simon Isogaeus in his 1717 treatise on war and duels, and the same applied to the man who accepted the challenge.[33] Although the latter was difficult for members of the nobility to accept, the king and authors of anti-duelling tracts insisted upon it. Duelling critic Rudolph Clingel wrote that calumny and name-calling heap more shame upon the mocker than the mocked and that fearing the slander of a disreputable man was nothing short of madness. Greater honour, he pointed out, is accrued by ignoring such foolishness and showing strength of character by refusing to be provoked.[34]

Simultaneously, the courage of notorious duellists was called into question. In a discussion by the Privy Council in 1669, the chancellor stated that there was 'no real courage' in 'often stepping up' to duel, only 'license and contempt toward the authorities'.[35] It is common knowledge, wrote Isogeaus, that combatants and duellists who are 'overbearing' and 'boastful' at home could be 'pitiful wretches' when the hour is at hand and duty calls on the battlefield.[36] Audacity alone should not be mistaken for courage. It was not battle itself but the reason for battle that made a man courageous. 'Courage without righteousness' should not be extolled but rather decried as 'madness and fury', and exaggerated daring could be the sign of desperation and foolhardiness.[37]

The royal view of duelling painted it, literally, as an act of wilfulness and egotism, as is evident in a series of roof paintings in the royal castle commissioned by Charles XI. One of them (Figure 3.1) shows Royal

FIGURE 3.1 'L'Autorité Royale', Roofpainting in the Gallery of Charles XI, The Royal Castle, c. 1699 Stockholm © The Royal Court, Sweden. Photo Nino Monastra.

Authority (l'Autorité Royale) sitting on a throne with Justice to her right, trampling two dead duellists under her foot. In the background Prudence gazes into her mirror and confirms the wisdom and foresight of the royal policy, carefully documented by a scribe.[38] The nakedness of the dead duellists strengthens at the same time the impression of an infamous death, stripped of all pretence to honour.

The idealization of Gothic heroes as paragons of virtue: Gothic heroes in the service of Crown and country

The paintings in Stockholm's castle were addressed to a circle of the Swedish nobility and foreign royal and noble guests, but the royal policy against duels was also part of a broader mobilization of national patriotism, underway from the early years of the century, with the aim to discipline conscripted peasants and proud aristocrats into loyal soldiers and officers fighting for king and fatherland. Sweden was at war almost continuously during the seventeenth century, and Swedish monarchs consciously cultivated the belief in their heroic leadership of a just cause. Gustavus Adolphus (1594–1632) appeared in Lutheran propaganda as the 'Lion from the North', and he also presented himself as a representative of the ancient Goths, the forefathers of the Swedes, according to the prevailing conception of Swedish patriotism.[39] Swedish war propaganda drafted the mythic Gothic heroes of old as ideals of virtuous manliness in the service of the Crown and country.[40] In Johannes Messenius's 1612 play *Queen Signill*, for instance, renowned Gothic champion Starkotter is portrayed as the archetypal Swedish warrior: 'From infancy it has been my desire to go to war and ride into battle, the more enemies I downed, the broader my heart did smile.' The career of Starkotter is bloody, but his simple, almost ascetic lifestyle is emphasized. He never loses his temper or lifts his sword without just cause. 'The virtue and honour of the Goths would I teach you through my heroic deeds.'[41]

With reference to the Goths and the doctrine of just war, personal honour and manliness could be mobilized for a higher purpose in the name of king and country. Fighting the king's wars was held up as a duty and principle of virtue. In his militant propaganda verse of 1624, Petrus Rudbeckius has a father and his 15-year-old son, Starke, ready themselves for war. His mother's agonized protestation that he is too young and frail are dismissed by the father as 'nonsense'. The son is quick to agree: 'I wish to go to war, to learn its way, if God my life does spare, a man I then will be.' Staying behind is acceptable for those who 'spin, weave and sew', Starke explains, while his father upbraids his wife for encouraging their son to become a 'layabout' instead of a 'full-grown and honest man'.[42] It was on the field of battle, in the self-sacrificing struggle in the name of God and country, that true courage was to be shown, and it was here that manliness and true honour were to be won – in sharp contrast to the dubious fate of the duellist. In the popular ballad about duellist Sveno Johannis Lind, the character bemoans his wasted valour. He who once was trusted to ride out and fight for his country 'like a hero' now stands before a firing squad for murder, all for the sake of a few hasty words that he thought had wounded his honour. 'Evil is that custom, of no value, no good, to urge and challenge, to duel with a sword', warns the cautionary verse.[43] In the same way, the clergy fulminated in their field sermons over the men's bad habit of challenging each other 'over a word, or for a trifle', which they branded an 'accursed sin'.[44] Against this stood the idealized image of the king himself, killed in action on the battlefield of Lützen in 1632. In a memorial sermon by Archbishop Rudbeckius it was said that Gustavus Adolphus had fallen 'not as a rash and overbearing man who takes action without due cause or risks his life for a trifling matter, but as a steadfast, deliberate and fearless Christian knight and confessor'.[45] Such were the qualities of a man of true virtue and manliness. At the same time *glory* rather than honour became the promised reward for courage and manliness. In the above-mentioned paintings, the Nobility was especially addressed by the motto, *Animo dat gloria vires* – 'Glory gives strength to the soul.' In other words, glory makes sacrifices in the king's war and the request for loyalty easier to bear through the promise of reward.[46] While horizontal honour could only be defended, lost or restored, glory was connected to ambition and could as such not only be earned but also bestowed by a king. The double-sided process of anti-duelling policy and mobilization of patriotism contributed in this way to the breakdown of horizontal honour codes.

During the eighteenth century a new state-administered system of vertical honour and rank developed, in which honour could be both bestowed as a merit, in the form of medals and panegyrics, and withdrawn as a loss of civic rights for longer or shorter periods. This vertical honour was at the same time 'democratized'. The feats of great men of public service were no longer preserved and extolled as the sole examples to posterity: common farmers and merchants too could be awarded medals for distinguished service to their country.[47]

Vanity and affectation as the opposite of virtue and manliness

In contrast to the virtuous were men who 'stayed at home', branded as unmanly cowards. In Messenius's play, *Queen Signill* (1612), Starkotter is confronted with the spoiled aristocratic brat, Mama's Boy. The character has never even been near a battlefield. On the contrary, he sat comfily in his mother's lap until he was nineteen and today still rushes 'without trousers' to the 'women's cottage' to have breakfast with the maids. He has never been further than the front yard and even there only with a rope tied securely around his waist to make sure he returned safely to mommy again. Starkotter doubts he is a man at all, or that Gothic blood runs in his veins. Mama's Boy is so terrified by Starkotter's address that he immediately wants to crawl under 'mother dear's' skirts. But he is not only frightened and pathetic; he is also extremely vain. His friend Flattermuch extols his amber cheeks and pale and curly hair and exclaims, 'Thou art a doll of a Knight.' The theme of vanity and cowardice was further developed in a ballet dedicated to King Charles XI, in which six Goths appear on stage reciting satirical verses about the French 'pétites-maîtres' with their powdered curls and 'womanly manners'. In spite of their big words and arrogance they are milksops at war.[48] A new rhetorical figure of unmanliness appears on the public scene – the fop, petit-maître or 'spark' (*sprätthök*) who dresses in the latest fashions, who can barely tear his gaze from his reflection in the mirror and who fills his days with reckless extravagance and vain pretention typically associated with a 'weakly and womanly nature' (Figure 3.2).[49]

FIGURE 3.2 *Unknown artist, 'Sprethök/Spradebassen/A Spark'. National Library of Sweden, Maps and Pictures, Pl. AF 50: 18b.*

Once the matter of vanity had been introduced, an even more radical charge could be levelled at both challenger and respondent. In anti-duelling pamphlets of the seventeenth and eighteenth century, the causes of duels were described, increasingly, as petty and insignificant – a careless word tossed out during a game of cards, a 'stolen' token of affection from a sweetheart, a man cutting in front of one who outranks him socially.[50] Vanity and ostentation, rather than principles of virtue and true honour, were presented as the driving forces behind the duel, according to its critics. Clingel writes about those who with 'vain bluster' might 'rush off to duel', and Isogaeus relates how a military commander puts an end to duelling by only allowing combatants to engage each other on a bridge after dark. Without an audience to bear witness to this display of purported masculine bravado, he contended, the desire to challenge and respond quickly lost its attraction.[51]

Duellists' claims of honour were not only questioned but also parodied through the rhetorical figure of the spark, who acted angrily and impetuously. In eighteenth-century moral satires of conceited sparks and swaggerers this satirical edge grew sharper. In the periodical *Sedolärande Mercurius*, one could read about sparks gathering in coffee houses 'kissing one another, embarrassing one another, smacking one another with their walking sticks "par manière de conversation", and boasting about their brawls, whore-chasing and other rakeries'.[52] Swearing, whistling and noisy, the spark constituted an obtrusive, touchy and ridiculous figure ready to draw his rapier at the most insignificant trifle. Grounded in a forced and overdone mannerism of preferably French origin, his affectations and false pretentions were easy to see through and made him appear both annoying and laughable.

While the vainglorious spark usually appeared as 'frenchified', his ostentatious colleague, the 'boastful poltroon', was often labelled with German eponyms. In the 1782 play *Donnerpamp*, he actually speaks a mixture of German and Swedish, which is very much intended for comical effect.[53] The figure of the boastful poltroon evolved from the recurrent accusation that duellists were 'brave at home' but cowards in war.[54] *Geheimenschreck* is also the German-Swedish eponym of one of the protagonists in the 1789 comedy *The Rivals*, who is confronted with the courtier Ehrencastrat in rivalry for the fair Miss Gustava Bergcrona. As their names attest, neither of these rivals embodies true manhood and should be seen, instead, as personifications of the affected spark and boastful poltroon. Lieutenant Geheimenschreck is clearly the instigator, but while Ehrencastrat is driven by arrogance to respond in spite of his rather weak and feeble appearance, Geheimenschreck's challenges and threatening words are just empty talk. The duel turns into a ridiculous spectacle of failed mannerism with the antagonists standing against each other with swords drawn but frozen in fear.[55]

The emergence of these satirical stereotypes reflected the rise of virtue as the dominating concept for social ambition in eighteenth-century Sweden.

Thus, as part of a general revision of the national law code, new penalties were imposed against duelling in 1738, endorsing His Royal Highness Frederick I's wish that not only the nobility but his loyal subjects, in general, 'hold true virtue to be their most prized possession'. To prove their courage and manliness, men should defend the nation rather than 'indulge themselves in bickering and discord spurred by vindictiveness and a baseless and Godless illusion', which would only lead to their worldly and eternal downfall.[56]

In civil life virtue implied an emotionology very different from the assertiveness and raillery in a duelling culture. Both Aristotle and early modern conduct book authors assumed that virtue was something to be learned and practiced in the active life of social intercourse. However, this presupposed an ability and a willingness to adapt oneself to others. In direct opposition to the rhetoric of duelling, critics advised young men against taking umbrage or prosecuting every word and deed uttered, 'for revenge is a paltry, pitiable source of pleasure'. Reaching for one's sword at the mere hint of a slight is condemned in the same tract of 1700, in which the author depicts the sentiments associated with honour as 'madness'. A young man should instead deflect any provocation with the explicit motivation that 'he does not wish to become outraged'.[57] Similar messages were printed in the mid-eighteenth century as flyers featuring a list of the rules of virtue and decorum, suitable for framing:

> Should someone's words offend,
> Be conciliatory, and polite;
> All discord you forfend,
> When friendship puts it right.[58]

By this period a good-tempered sociability was considered a natural basis and school of virtue. Friendship was held to be especially morally refining, 'since he who desires to be loved by a friend must himself be capable of loving'.[59] But virtue also meant hard-earned skill and merits, particularly among ambitious civil servants and entrepreneurs. In eighteenth-century moral discourse, utility and public benefit became increasingly influential criteria for 'the greatest good', contrasted against idleness and the free reign of passions. Thus, in Sweden, virtue became the emergent ideal that provided the rational means for controlling and channelling the energy of passions into thrift and industry.[60]

Gudmund Jöran Adlerbeth – The steadfast man

It is against this backdrop of increasing criticism of duels and changing meanings of honour and virtue that Baron Gudmund Jöran Adlerbeth's reaction to allegations of cuckoldry should be considered. During the course of his marriage, a rival, who was 14 years his junior and a soldier awarded for bravery, was rumoured to have seduced Adlerbeth's wife. The rumour turned out to be true, but instead of confronting the man Adlerbeth assumed the fictive role of cheating husband in order to facilitate a swift divorce. This allowed his ex-wife to marry her lover immediately, although it failed to silence innuendos about cuckoldry. While Gyllenstierna had been haunted by humiliation, Adlerbeth tried to cope by shifting the meanings of 'courage' and 'bravery'. In his writings he distinguished between courage 'that merely consists of an inbred antipathy to risk' and another, far more admirable type of courage 'based on a sense of duty, which spies danger but disarms it with sober deliberation and outfaces it'. Only the latter is a practical virtue, since it could be exercised in 'negotiation' and 'conference' (meaning Adlerbeth's civil affairs) as well as on the field of battle. The source of his humiliation was similar to Gyllenstierna's, but instead of seeking recourse through the sword and litigation, Adlerbeth chose the pen and oratory to argue in favour of a kind of courage that was not dependent on the constant need to do battle – or to take revenge. These contrasting reactions were not merely the result of personal disposition but were representative of a more fundamental historical transition in the emotional regime and concepts of male prestige, led by the Church and king.

Men continued to duel in the late eighteenth century, however, and the most talked-about duel of the entire century in fact took place only a few years before Adlerbeth's divorce. Count Adolph Ribbing fenced with Baron Hans Henric von Essen over one of the country's wealthiest and purportedly most beautiful young ladies, Charlotta Eleonora De Geer. In contrast to Charles XI, for whom the suppression of duelling was a hallmark of royal autocracy, Gustav III (1772–1792) was rather permissive when it suited him, and the duellists were never tried, despite the fact that von Essen had been seriously wounded.[61] Like other noblemen, Adlerbeth was thus well acquainted with the rhetoric of duelling, but among his friends and acquaintances (mostly intellectuals, poets and high officials), the world of duellists was distant. One of his associates, Count Johan Gabriel Oxenstierna, recorded in his diary that he had once narrowly escaped being challenged to a duel by a certain captain and then had promised himself to avoid thereafter confronting such 'conceited individuals' at any price. This aversion to duelling was expressed more programmatically in a scriptum in French on 'the true sense of honour', which Oxenstierna had been assigned to define as a student. A person, he wrote, who is driven by a false sense of honour and 'proffers his decisive argument on the point of the rapier' is wracked by envy and anxiety and sees everything through a lens of anger, while a true sense of honour supports its possessor with 'a calm, steady mind in times of adversity and misfortune'.[62] Similarly, Count Gustaf Fredrik Gyllenborg (1731–1808), another of Adlerbeth's close friends, wrote in his memoirs about 'a most ridiculous incident' that occurred during the royal coup d'etat of 1772. An aristocrat of the highest rank was so besotted with royalist enthusiasm that he rode through the streets looking for possible antiroyalists to challenge with his rapier. Gyllenborg distastefully remarks that the revolution was not made by such 'madcaps' and pathetic 'don Quixotes'.[63] Instead, he celebrates in his poetry the kind of courage 'born from the strength of the soul'.[64] A steady mind and an inner strength are the qualities that capture the attitudes expressed by Adlerbeth and the circles in which he moved, which also valued the ideals of sociability in a cult of passionate friendship.

While Gyllenstierna appeared as a frustrated duellist a century earlier, Adlerbeth could find pride in being a steadfast man. Strains of stoicism were evident in some of Adlerbeth's formulations about 'retaining one's strength unaltered in moments of fast changes', about the need 'to think in the same way in prosperity and adversity' and 'to follow one's conscience and conviction without regard to inclination or revenge'.[65] Adlerbeth did not confine himself to the strength of indifference and endurance however;' he actively sought to adapt traditionally male qualities like courage to his own professional practice. Oxenstierna may in fact have come closer to a stoic attitude in such self-ironic comments as, 'arguments are the only battles I could win since nature had given me the tongue as my only weapon and a pair of light feet'. A poet colleague who had been challenged to a duel was described in similar terms: 'poets are usually not very courageous, I'm expecting to hear how he has been beaten and composed an apology put into rhyme'.[66] Oxenstierna was notably one of the first to introduce Rousseau's philosophy in early modern Sweden, and he read the critical passages on duelling in *Julie*, which were later to be published in Swedish.[67]

Adlerbeth's attitudes were indicative of a shift of focus in moral discourse during the eighteenth century, away from God's commandments and heroic virtue to a keener emphasis on utility and public service pursued with diligence and thrift as the greatest good. Steadfastness was in this context used synonymously with honesty and integrity and in contrast to the free reign of passions, associated with a lack of virtue. Thus, the Royal Swedish Academy of Letters launched an essay contest in 1777 on the theme of 'A steadfast man or a fable with the moral: honesty is the best policy'.[68] The theme was already illustrated in the play *The Swedish Spark* (first performed in 1737), in which Baron Steadfast is confronted by Count Brisk, recently back home from France. The epithet Brisk refers to the inconstancy and shallowness of a spark who has submitted himself to the latest fashions and conventions à la mode.[69] The notorious vanity of this more sociable spark was extended further by satirists into an inordinate need to please (held to be a typical female quality), which made him a weathervane for his own whims and the whims and affections of others, the very personification of an 'unsteady mind'.[70] Steadfastness in civil life as well as civic virtues like thrift and diligence were in this way given a more manly, and thus prestigious character through the contrastive effect of a highly feminized counterimage of mischievousness. Adlerbeth went a step further in his efforts to connect civility and self-restraint to manly courage.[71] While virtue's masculinization offered new ways of displaying manliness, authentic honour was redefined as an inner quality, distinct from the state-administered system of honourable rewards and sentences of infamy. 'True honour', the author of a 1766 antiduelling tract declared, 'does not originate in the vain judgment of others, but in the heart of each and every man, and cannot be lost because of another man's insulting words or regained by combat, but solely by living virtuously'.[72] 'True honour' was becoming virtue. Thus, in terms of social prestige and violence, Adlerbeth and Gyllenstierna lived in distinct conceptual and emotional worlds. Bound by a horizontal and aristocratic concept of honour, Gyllenstierna had to be suspicious and perpetually on his guard against insulting provocations from his peers, while Adlerbeth could find support in socializing with friends across horizontal borders in newly established societies that promoted and rewarded civic virtues.

From honour to virtue

The shifting logics of masculinity and duelling reflect a long-term development, which could be described as a change from an emotional regime encouraging self-assertiveness and touchiness as signs of a true sense of honour and manliness to a regime premiering sociability and strivings for the benefit of society as expressions of virtue. In the older regime, taking immediate action either in 'spontaneous' acts of violence or a challenge to fight was a living norm; in its place a steadfast and virtuous mind came to be seen as the means for directing the energy of passions into useful activities. The positive evaluation of emotional spontaneity was at the same time transferred to displays of sympathy and compassion as true signs of masculine friendship and civic virtue.[73] At last, the link between male prestige and interpersonal violence was seriously questioned.

Although the fatal logic of an exclusive and horizontal honour lingered in aristocratic military circles, the 'most talked about' duel of the eighteenth century represented in fact the final act in an historical drama about the culturally prescribed necessity of risking one's life for an insulting word. The last formal duel in Sweden with a fatal outcome was fought in 1816. After that, ritual duelling seems to have quietly disappeared.[74] In contrast to shifts in codes of honour in contemporary Europe, as Robert Nye discusses, the Swedish development was distinct. While challenges to fight were practised among farmers and ordinary soldiers during the seventeenth century, the new middle classes emerging in the eighteenth and early nineteenth centuries seem not to have appropriated the duel as a way of confirming or defending their recently acquired status. In contrast to France as well as to the German world, the emerging bourgeoisie never appropriated the duel in nineteenth-century Sweden, in which the practice was marginalized across classes.[75] In this regard the Swedish experience comes closest to Britain where duels vanished after 1840.[76] The discursive and conceptual changes sketched in this chapter give a hint of where to look for deeper and more complex explanations in the shifting relationship between masculine emotions, honour and violence.

Notes

1   Dag Lindström, 'Homicide in Scandinavia: Long-Term Trends and Their Interpretations', in *Violence in Europe: Historical and Contemporary Perspectives*, ed. Sophie Body-Gendrot and Pieter Spierenburg (New York: Springer, 2008), 43–64.

2   Jonas Liliequist, 'Violence, Honour and Manliness in Early Modern Northern Sweden', in *Crime and Control in Europe from the Past to the Present*, ed. M. Lappalainen and P. Hirvonen (Helsinki: Publications of the History of Criminality Research Project, 1999), 174–207.

3   For a critical review of this thesis, see Barbara H. Rosenwein, 'Controlling Paradigms', in *Anger's Past: The Social Uses of an Emotion in the Middle Ages*, ed. Barbara H. Rosenwein (Ithaca, NY and London: Cornell University Press, 1998), 233–47.

4   *Grettir's Saga* Chapter XV eBook collection (EBSCO host), 15.

5   Minutes of the Privy Council, oktober 1636, *Handlingar rörande Sveriges historia*, ed. Seved Bergh (Stockholm: 1891), del VI., 622.

6   Fabian Persson, 'Bättre livlös än ärelös: Symbolik och sociala funktioner i stormaktstidens dueller', *Scandia*, 65, 1 (1999): 2–23; Christopher Collstedt, *Duellanten och rättvisan: Duellbrott och synen på manlighet i stormaktsväldets slutskede* (Lund: Sekel Bokförlag, 2007), 88–97.

7   Liliequist, 'Violence', 196.

8   Frank Henderson Stewart, *Honor* (Chicago: University of Chicago Press, 1994), 54–63.

9   Trial record (Second Lieutenant Stierncrantz) Military Court 22 July 1713, Generalauditören 12 July 1714 no. 11, Swedish National Archive (RA).

10   Quoted in Liliequist, 'Violence', 189.

11   F. G. Bailey, *The Tactical Uses of Passion: An Essay on Power, Reason, and Reality* (Ithaca, NY and London: Cornell University Press, 1983), 58–100.

12   For example, Trial Record (Lindmeijer) Town council of Stockholm 28/5 1688, AIIA:23, Stockholm City Archive, SSA; Trial Record (Lieutenant Humble) Military Court 31/8 1711, Generalauditören 12/12 1711, *RA*.

13   This is specifically mentioned as a defamatory provocation in the Royal Ordinance of 1682.

14   For a brief summary of his theoretical perspective, see William M. Reddy, 'Sentimentalism and Its Erasure: The Role of Emotions in the Era of the French Revolution', *Journal of Modern History*, 72, 1 (2000): 113–19.

15   Daniel Tilas, *Curriculum vitæ I–II, 1712–1757 samt fragment av dagbok september–oktober 1767*, ed. Holger Wickman (Stockholm: Kungl. Samfundet för utgifvande af handskrifter rörande Skandinaviens historia, 1966), 138–40.

16   Collstedt, *Duellanten*, 174–178.

17   Parliamentary Records of the Noble Estate/*Sveriges Ridderskaps och Adels Riksdagsprotokoll (RAP)*, IV, 1 (1645–1649) (Stockholm: 1871), Bil. D31 January 1649: 14, 244.

18 Parliamentary Records of the Noble Estate/*Sveriges Ridderskaps och Adels Riksdagsprotokoll (RAP)*, IV, 1 (1645–1649), Bil. F17 February 1649: 14, 263.

19 Jonas Liliequist and Martin Almbjär, 'Early Modern Court Records and Supplications in Sweden (c. 1400–1809)', *Frühneuzeit-Info*, 7 (2012): 9.

20 Royal Ordinance 23/12 1662, in *Kongl. Stadgar…* ed. J. Schmedeman (Stockholm: 1706), 325.

21 *RAP* (1664), 244, 431,442.

22 Minutes of the Privy Council 24 oktober 1671, Lindschöld volume 58, f. 384, RA (emphasis author's own).

23 There is a short biography and summary of the course of events in Stina Hansson, 'Inledning', in *Lars Johansson (Lucidor): Samlade dikter*, ed. S. Hansson (Stockholm: Svenska Vitterhetssamfundet, 1997), 7–12.

24 Sven Grauers, *Ätten Wachtmeister genom seklerna* (Johannishus: Andra Delen, 1946), 14–16.

25 Court records published in Fredrik Sandwall, 'Nya akter i rättegången om Gilliare Kwaal', *Samlaren*, 9 (1926), 33–108.

26 Gunnar Bolin, 'Lucidor som student i Greifswald och Leipzig', *Samlaren*, 20 (1939): 1–38.

27 Court records published in Birger Schöldström, *Lars Johansson Lucidor: en litterär studie* (Stockholm: Author, 1872).

28 Sven Delblanc, 'Hercules magnanimus: Ett bidrag till tolkningen av Stiernhielms Hercules', *Samlaren*, 82 (1961): 5–72; Leif Runefelt, *Hushållningens dygder: Affektlära, hushållningslära och ekonomiskt tänkande under svensk stormaktstid* (Stockholm: Almqvist och Wiksell International, 2001), 91–118; Bengt Lewan, *Med dygden som vapen: Kring begreppet dygd i svensk 1700-talsdebatt* (Stockholm: Symposion, 1985), 21–34.

29 Kurt Johannesson, 'Om furstars och aristokraters dygder: Reflexioner kring Johannes Schefferus Memorabilia', in *1600-talets ansikte*, ed. Sten Åke Nilsson and Margareta Ramsay (*Krapperup*: Symposier på Krapperups borg 3, 1997), 311.

30 Peter Englund, *Det hotade huset: Adliga föreställningar om samhället under stormaktstiden* (Stockholm: Atlantis, 1989), 157–72.

31 Royal Ordinance 22/8, 1682 in Schmedeman, 764–71.

32 Bo H. Lindberg, *Praemia et poenae: Etik och straffrätt i Sverige i tidig ny tid* (Uppsala: Uppsala Universitet, 1992), 401–03.

33 Simon Isogaeus, *Carla Segerskiöld* (Stockholm: Carl Hedeman, 1714),781, 784.

34 Rudolph Clingel, *En Liten Tractat*, second question, second point unpaginated.

35 Minutes of the Royal Council (1669), Lilljeflycht, volume 52, 1/7 f. 191h, RA.

36 Isogaeus, *Carla Segerskiöld*, 607–08.

37 Clingel, second question, second point unpaginated.

38 Gunnar Mascoll Silfverstolpe, 'Rumsinredningarna i konsthistorisk belysning', in *Stockholms slotts historia II: Det Tessinska slottet*, ed. J. Böttiger (Stockholm: Norstedt & Söner, 1940), 263.

39 Kristoffer Neville, 'Gothicism and Early Modern Historical Ethnography', *Journal of the History of Ideas*, 70, 2 (2009): 213–34.

40 Axel Friberg, *Den svenska Herkules: Studier i Stiernhielms diktning* (Stockhlom: Wahlström & Widstrand 1945), 175–81.

41 Johannes Messenius, 'Signill: Thet är en lustigh och sanfärdigh tragoedia (1612)', in *Johannes Messenius samlade dramer*, ed. H. Schück del 1 (Uppsala: Svenska Litteratursällskapet, 1886), 41–44.

42 Petrus Rudbeckius, *Insignis Adolescentia. En Ny Wijsa, Om Starcke* (Stockholm: M. Petro J. Rudbeckio, 1624), verses 15–20, 23, 26, 27–29 unpaginated.

43 *1500-och 1600-talets visböcker*, tredje bandet, 'Samuel Älfs visbok' ed. A. Noreen och A. Grape (Uppsala, 1916–25), nr 23 [51b], verse 10 and verse 5 respectively.

44 Johannes Botvidi, *Tree predikningar håldne Uthi Häärfärden ååt Lijfland* (Stockholm: Christoffer Reusner, 1627), 45.

45 Archbishop Rudbeckius sermon 6 November 1633, quoted in Lars Gustafsson, *Virtus Politica: Politisk etik och nationellt svärmeri i den tidigare stormaktstidens litteratur* (Uppsala: Lychnos bibliotek, 1956), 95.

46 Silfverstolpe, Rumsinredningarna i konsthistorisk belysning, 266.

47 Sven Delblanc, *Ära och minne: Studier kring ett motivkomplex i 1700-talets litteratur* (Stockholm: Bonnier, 1965), 114–15; Collstedt, *Duellanten*, 94–95; Göran Inger, *Vanfrejd: från infamia till förlust av medborgerligt förtroende* (Uppsala: Inger, 2001).

48 Eric Lindschöld, 'Den Stoora Genius: Ballet til Hans Konungl. Mayst. Konung Carl den Elfftes Födelse Dag den Fämptonde dansad på Stockholms Slåt anno 1669', in *Samlade vitterhetsarbeten IV*, ed. P. Hanselli (Uppsala: Hanselli, 1866), III inträdet, 110–11.

49 Sven Gudmund Strömwall, *Historiska och politiska anmärkningar* (Stockholm: F. Phil. Paulssen, 1736), 62–63.

50 Isogaeus, *Carla Segerskiöld*, 781.

51 Isogaeus, *Carla Segerskiöld*, 805.

52 *Sedolärande Mercurius* 10 (1730).

53 Carl Hallman, *Donnerpamp, comedie uti en act, blandad med sång, samt intermede* (Stockholm: Carl Stolpe, 1782).

54 For example, Carl Fredric Holm, *Medel at förekomma dueller* diss. (Åbo: 1776), 6.

55 Olof Kexél, 'Bergslags-Fröken eller Rivalerne: Comedie i Tre Akter. Uppförd på Kongl. Dramatiska Theatern första gången den 5 Maj 1789', in *Olof Kexéls skrifter*, ed. P. A. Sondén, del 1 (Stockholm: Förlagsföreningen, 1837).

56 'Duells-Placat den 28 Januari 1738', in *Utdrag Utur alle ifrån 1729 års slut utkomne Publique Handlingar, Placater, Förordningar, Resolutioner och Publicationer*, ed. R. G. Modée (Stockholm: Andra delen, 1746), 1340–344.

57 Archibald Campelld, *Underwisning För en Ung Herre, skrefwen utaf hans Fader* (Stockholm: Burchardi, 1700), 92–93.

58 *Täncke-Skrift: Innehållande åtskilliga Christeliga Dygde= och Lefnads=Läror*
    (Västerås: Pet. Devall, kongl.: consist. och gymn. boktr., 1744).

59 Sylvestri Du Four, *Sede-Bok eller Kort Begrep, At underwisa ungt folk til en
    ärbar och försichtig wandel* (Stockholm: Henrich Keyser, kongl. bokt., 1683),
    section II, unpaginated.

60 Leif Runefelt, *Dygden som välståndets grund: Dygd, nytta och egennytta i
    frihetstidens ekonomiska tänkande* (Stockholm: Stockholms universitet, 2005),
    19–45.

61 *Hedvig Elisabeth Charlottas Dagbok, II, 1783–1788*, ed. Carl Carlsson
    Bonde (Stockholm: Nordstedts, 1903), 211–17; *Grefve Fredrik Axel von
    Fersens historiska skrifter, Sjunde delen*, ed. R. M. Klinckowström (Stockholm:
    Norstedts, 1871), 10–13.

62 Johan Gabriel Oxenstierna, *Ljuva ungdomstid: Dagbok för åren 1766–1768*,
    ed. and trans. Ingrid Estabout (Uppsala: Bokgillet, 1965), Diary originally
    written in French, translated into Swedish, 157–59.

63 Gustaf Fredrik Gyllenborg, 'Ur, "Mitt lefverne"', in *Svenska Parnassen: Ett
    urval ur Sveriges klassiska litteratur*, ed. D. E. Meyer (Stockholm: Fahlcrantz &
    Co., 1889), 150–51.

64 Gustaf Fredrik Gyllenborg, 'Ode till själens styrka', in *Svenska Parnassen: Ett
    urval ur Sveriges klassiska litteratur*, 150.

65 Quoted in Leif Landen *Gudmund Jöran Adlerbeth: En biografi* (Stockholm:
    Kungl. Vitterhets historie och antikvitets akad., 2000), 239.

66 Oxenstierna, *Ljuva ungdomstid: Dagbok för åren 1766–1768*, (1965), 84;
    Dagboks-anteckningar: åren 1769–1771 af Johan Gabriel Oxenstierna, ed.
    G. Stjernström (Uppsala: Svenska litteratursällskapet, 1881), 59.

67 *Bref angående dueller, af J.J. Rousseau, öfversättning* (Stockholm:
    C.F. Marquard, 1799).

68 Inge Jonsson, *Vitterhetsakademien 1753–2003* (Stockholm: Kungl. Vitterhets
    historie och antikvitets akad., 2003), 27.

69 *Swenska Sprätthöken: Komedi av Carl Gyllenborg*, ed. Lennart Breitholz &
    Einar Törnqvist (Uppsala: Gebers, 1959).

70 Jonas Liliequist, 'Från niding till sprätt', in *Manligt och Omanligt i ett
    Historiskt Perspektiv*, ed. A. M. Berggren (Uppsala: FRN, 1999), 85–88.

71 Similar reformulations of manliness and courage could in fact be found among
    civil servants already in the late seventeenth century. Cf. Åsa Karlsson 'En man
    I statens tjänst: Den politiska elitens manlighetsideal under det karolinska
    enväldet 1680–1718' in Berggren, 122–25.

72 Carl Fredric Holm, *Medel at förekomma dueller* diss. (Åbo: Johan Christopher
    Frenckell, 1776), 6–7.

73 Jonas Liliequist, 'The Political Rhetoric of Tears in Early Modern Sweden', in
    A History of Emotions, 1200–1800, ed. Jonas Liliequist (London: Pickering &
    Chatto, 2012), 181–205.

74 Christopher Collstedt, 'Duellpolitik och duellestetik', in *Våld: Representation
    och verklighet*, ed. E. Österberg and M. Lindstedt Cronberg (Lund: Nordic
    Academic Press, 2006), 89.

75 David Tjeder, *The Power of Character: Middle-Class Masculinities, 1800–1900* (Stockholm: Författares bokmaskin, 2003), 162–163; Robert A. Nye, *Masculinity and Male Codes of Honour in Modern France* (New York: Oxford University Press, 1993); Ute Frevert, *Men of Honour: A Social and Cultural History of the Duel* (Cambridge: Polity Press, 1995).

76 Stephen Banks, *A Polite Exchange of Bullets: The Duel and the English Gentleman, 1750–1850* (Woodbridge: Boydell & Brewer, 2010).

4

'For the Shame of the World, and Fear of Her Mother's Anger': Emotion and child murder in England and Scotland in the long eighteenth century

Dana Rabin

Historians of crime and justice and women's historians have devoted considerable attention to the subject of child murder, particularly the killing of newborns and infants.[1] Recent scholarship on the history of emotion can, however, shed new light on existing evidence of the crime's history. By drawing on judicial case notes and medical opinion, as well as the last dying speeches pamphlet writers ascribed to women convicted of murdering their children, we can analyse the significance accorded to the emotive comportment of the condemned in their final days and moments.[2] Such speeches, allegedly delivered at the gallows, were published and edited by anonymous authors who wrote for a public eager to read about the feelings and thoughts that led women to kill. With two exceptions, the cases examined here involved unmarried women in England and Scotland who were accused of newborn child murder between the late seventeenth- and early nineteenth- centuries. While these texts did not typically invoke the language of honour to justify or explain their crimes, they do devote attention to the anger of parents towards their daughters, as well as the anger of married women towards their wayward husbands. The prominence granted to anger in these accounts suggests the significance ascribed to the honourable reputations of parents of unmarried daughters, as well as the ways in which child murder could express a married woman's defence of her own honour in the face of her husband's infidelity.

Although these women experienced sex, pregnancy and child birth privately, even secretly, their speeches were addressed to the larger emotional community – local and national – and as such related to the rhetorical and emotional performances anticipated of all convicted criminals.[3] What is the record of affect in these sources? In the last dying speeches of these doomed women we can see the significance of space and place: the site of the crime, the courtroom and the gallows all made a significant appearance in last dying speeches, and they elicited distinct emotional responses, both from the women accused and from the judges who ruled on their cases.[4]

The emotion revealed in these cases calls for concerted analysis through the close reading of extant sources. By moving beyond trial transcripts, characterized by their flat and detached tone, this chapter deepens our understanding of emotion in the eighteenth century by focusing on pamphlets written after the trial, in which women's anonymous editors or ghostwriters accounted for a brutal crime and the emotions surrounding it. Post-execution tracts provide a means to trace the ways in which writers and readers struggled to understand and reconcile themselves to violence and its consequences. The greatest elaboration from the defendants themselves at trial came in their descriptions of their states of mind, and interest in their accounts grew over the course of the eighteenth century.[5] Judicial case notes and medical opinion about the crime provide further evidence about coexisting systems of feelings.[6] These sources are by no means comprehensive, and the last words uttered by the women on the scaffold cannot be verified; nevertheless, existing evidence indicates patterns in the representation of women's emotional performances in such cases.[7] This textual trail documents systems of emotional exchange and the ways in which these shared systems of emotion worked to constitute imagined communities.[8] As we will see, these sources articulated conflicting expectations and clashing emotional exchanges, and they failed as often as they succeeded to bind readers. Over the long eighteenth century, however, the emergent culture of sensibility altered what was considered an appropriate emotional response in these intense situations, as assumptions of women's presumed agency and responsibility for their violence declined.

The shifting legal context and meanings of child murder

In seventeenth- and eighteenth-century England single women deemed responsible for killing their own newborns were tried under the 1624 'Act to prevent the destroying and murthering of bastard children', which presumed that any mother of an illegitimate child who concealed its death was guilty of murder unless she could establish by the oath of at least one witness that the child had been stillborn.[9] The statute claimed to address the problem of 'lewd women' and asserted that they committed these crimes 'to avoid their shame' and 'to escape punishment'. The statute and its enforcement suggest that in the seventeenth century infanticide by an unmarried woman was considered a reasoned, premeditated (though immoral and criminal) act undertaken to preserve her reputation and her economic well-being. Although the statute was repealed in 1803, recent research has shown that infanticide convictions dropped sharply by the early eighteenth century.[10] Scholars have suggested that the jury's sympathy with the plight of the unwed mothers accused of the crime and the discomfort of legal authorities with the harsh statute of 1624 and its presumption of guilt accounted for this phenomenon.[11] The attitude of legal authorities towards women who committed infanticide was determined primarily by the marital status of the accused. A married woman accused of killing her child was not charged under the Act of 1624 because she was thought to lack the intent to conceal the birth; instead married women were charged with murder, and they were often acquitted when they claimed to have suffered temporary insanity.[12] Unmarried women seldom used the insanity defence when charged with infanticide because a plea of insanity would entail some (even implicit) admission of guilt and, if unsuccessful, would lead to immediate conviction and possible execution. Instead, these women drew on the 'loopholes' in the statute of 1624: single women accused of infanticide testified that the baby was born dead, that the baby died immediately after birth because they were delivered alone, that they had not concealed the pregnancy or that they had prepared for the delivery and the birth of the child. In the 'preparation defence', women cited the provisions they had made for the child during pregnancy as evidence of their intentions to nurture the baby after its birth. Their stories were usually confirmed by a woman in the community who told the court that she knew of the pregnancy and that the mother had made some arrangements for the lying in, and that she had prepared necessary provisions for the child such as items of clothing. At trial the defendants in these cases related their evidence with very little affect and no personal details. The testimony was entirely uniform, formulaic, repetitive and generally successful, resulting in the mother's acquittal.[13]

By 1715 convictions under the infanticide statute became rare. The preparation defence had become the legal mechanism by which the courts negotiated the gap between the statute and popular understanding of the crime. Of the women tried for infanticide at the Old Bailey during the eighteenth century, 85 per cent were acquitted and there were no convictions for infanticide after 1774. Juries and judges may have felt an implicit sympathy for the accused who were mostly young working women with few means to support a child.[14] They may have disliked the presumption of guilt written into the statute of 1624, as William Blackstone (1723–1780) did when he wrote that the law 'savours pretty strongly of severity'.[15] Nevertheless, the legal fiction by which the crime was negotiated, the preparation defence, affirmed the statute of 1624 and the legal system that produced it.[16]

Emotional communities, memory and place

Bessy Turnbul, tried in Scotland under the 'Anent Child Murder Act' (1690), was executed 'for Murdering her own Child' on 6 April 1709 in Edinburgh, as a broadside stated. On the same day an adjoining broadside announced that Margaret Inglis was hanged for the same crime.[17] These two accounts, published together, were tellingly paired by the author, and the explicit contrast exposes traces of the history of emotion. According to the broadside, Bessy had not been discovered during her pregnancy and had instead 'voluntarily confessed the fact while none accused her or look'd upon [her] as Guilty'. She said that she murdered the child 'and threw it into a holl (sic), and afterwards went to England'. The account attributed her confession to 'the pricking of her Conscience'. The text allows us to examine the meaning of this phrase, which reveals the intersection of memory and emotion surrounding the crime. Bessy said that after she absconded to England, 'still wherever she went, the innocent murdered Bab (sic) appeared before her', which she reported had 'troubled her so much that she came back again to the place where she committed the Murder'. Crucial to the account is the convergence of place and emotion. When Bessy came home, she went to the minister, confessed and 'carried him to the place where she had buried the Infant'. Once apprehended, Bessy seems to have experienced a change of heart: she used the preparation defence claiming that she had delivered 'without help of Women, tho severals were at hand, and a medwife (sic) also hard by. And says the Child was Dead Born'. The narrative ends with an assessment of Bessy's performance of those emotions expected of a condemned criminal at the moment of execution: grief, guilt and repentance. The author pronounced that in comparison to 'her Comrad', Margaret Inglis, Bessy 'seem'd much more Affected…, but not so much as could be wished'.[18]

Various meanings about emotion might be discerned from these two short texts. Bessy and Margaret belonged to an emotional community of other single women whose information about sex, pregnancy and childbirth was limited as fitting to their status, since unmarried women were not supposed to be sexually active. Laura Gowing has argued that their knowledge of childbirth would also have been extremely restricted, as those who attended births generally were married women who already had children.[19] Their silence and detachment would be considered appropriate because they lacked a public way to speak about their failed sexual relationships, perhaps coerced by dishonourable masters or their sons or based on a promise of marriage that did not work out, and because they were burdened by the shame of an illegitimate pregnancy. In fact, their preoccupation during these prohibited experiences would have been to hide and conceal them.[20]

The detached demeanour of Margaret Inglis (Bessy's comrade) troubles the pamphlet's author in his account of her execution. According to the writer, she 'did not seem to have any suitable concern about Death till within a few days before her Execution'. Her family worked tirelessly trying to secure a pardon for her, and only when her sister informed her that there was little hope that the efforts would succeed did Margaret begin 'to be a little more concerned about her condition, but not to the degree that were to be wished'. In recounting her lack of an appropriate public emotional response, the pamphlet observes that despite overwhelming evidence (a dead child found in her house and her physical condition matching that of a woman who had just delivered a baby), 'she never appeared to be duly affected and still denied that she violently took away the Child's Life'. The pamphlet circles around again to Margaret's continued lack of repentance or performance of emotion: 'even after all hopes of a Reprieve she was ever still continued little affected with her condition'.[21] Although Bessy is not mentioned in the broadside about Margaret, the implicit comparison is unfavourable: Margaret disappointed her ghostwriter and those listening to her last words because she failed to exhibit a sufficient level of contrition and remorse on the scaffold.

The content and tone of these texts, their gaps and contradictions and their particular preoccupations indicate that they spoke to several audiences at once, trying to satisfy various social, cultural, political and emotional expectations, not always successfully or completely. This may explain the frustration of their authors when the women did not perform as expected. At the scaffold, condemned criminals, usually flanked by members of the clergy, generally sought forgiveness from their neighbours and from God, accepting execution as a just punishment for a sinful life. Often the prisoner asked onlookers to join him or her in prayer, performing repentance and seeking religious reconciliation. For the purposes of the state, the legal authorities and even those in attendance in the crowd, the last dying speech was supposed to render a performance of guilt and contrition that would conform to the anticipated ritual of execution and affirm the legal system, its findings and its punishments.[22] A good execution was necessary to vindicate the conviction and uphold the truth-finding capacity of the legal system as a whole. But the scaffold speech was a contingent setting and the stakes were high as was the incidence of transgression in which the punished refused to follow the prescripted format.[23] As she awaited her punishment, Margaret Inglis continued to deny her guilt, and 'she did not seem to have any suitable impression of her condition or future state, and gave but a very indifferent account of the grounds of her faith'. Rather than confessing her guilt at the scaffold, asking the crowd's forgiveness and remonstrating against gateway sins such as swearing, drunkenness and Sabbath breaking, Margaret's recalcitrant attitude persisted: 'she did not give full Satisfaction to the Ministers who attend her; neither with Respect to the grounds of her Hope, nor in a Confession of the Crime for which she Suffered'.[24] Instead of reciting the usual cautionary tale from the repentant criminal, the pamphlet's author had to warn his readers himself to live a good and faithful life.

In contrast to Margaret Inglis, Agnes Craig's emotions were described in more detail, accommodating the expectations of a condemned prisoner awaiting execution. The broadside on her case revealed that she confessed to fornication in 1717 with William Hiddelston, the father of the newborn child, whom she said was born dead. The account of her trial and execution referred to a wide range of emotions that included desperation, shame, sorrow and repentance. Agnes said she was 'very Desperate' when her mother discovered her second pregnancy outside of marriage and beat her for it. After she gave birth to her stillborn child, alone and outside on a snowy night, Agnes recounted that she 'took her Napkin from about her Neck and wrapt it therein, and laid it betweixt two Stones, in her Mother's Yeard Dike'. When asked why she did that, Agnes answered that 'she did it for the shame of the World, and fear of her Mother's Anger'. Duly convicted, she concluded her speech 'Professing' that she was 'truly Sorrowful and Penitent for her sins'.[25]

Unlike the trope of the single woman, away from her family and facing pregnancy out of wedlock alone, this pamphlet prominently features the parents of both Agnes and William and their emotional responses to these events. Agnes' mother 'was so enraged at her' when she learned of the pregnancy, while William's father spoke at him 'in a great passion' when he discovered the pregnancy and that William had fed Agnes what she thought were plums and locked her in the mill. She later found out that they were bullfist, a toxic fungus that grew in the yard. It is unclear whether William hoped that the fungus would act as an abortifacient, but it did cause Agnes immediately to become 'sick and disordered'.[26] Her confession called upon herself 'the Wrath of God', which Agnes believed she deserved for concealing her pregnancy and delivery and 'all her other sins'. This description of the parents' involvement conveys the anguish of the families, similar to the parents and sister of Margaret Inglis, who feared the fatal consequences of their children's transgressions. The rage of both sets of parents contributed to and shaped the shame and despair that Agnes expressed in her confession. Her expansive expression of grief, sorrow and repentance indicates the stakes for her mother's reputation in the community and the family's right to command respect, and it may also have served as a daughter's apology.

Another apology comes from a pamphlet concerning 30-year-old Janet Hutchie, executed in Edinburgh's Grass-market on 30 August 1721. Her *Last Speech and Dying Words*, unusually lengthy at two pages, weaves several different emotions through the narration of her life. In addition to repentance she expresses great shame, not only for the murder of the infant but more so for having wrongfully accused one Peter Vallance of fathering it. To these she adds regrets about promising to marry William Stewart, another man, and breaking that engagement, in addition to lying and drunkenness. Her language reached a great pitch as she described herself as 'more Brutish then a Brute' and accused herself, 'a Rational Creature' in God's image, 'indowed (sic) with a reasonable Soul to Act, as if I had no Soul at all'.[27]

In the introduction to Margaret Millar's scaffold speech in February 1726, the author of the pamphlet explained that even those crimes undetected by human investigation will be exposed by the 'the all-seeing Eye of the Almighty'. Once revealed, the offender's public punishment served to provide 'Terror and Example to others'. Here we see clearly the scaffold as a scene of emotional exchange; the performance of guilt, grief and repentance by the convicted criminal was to elicit fear and terror as well as pity and sorrow among the witnesses in attendance. Margaret Millar's ghostwritten scaffold speech addressed this expectation explicitly, situating these accounts as a genre: 'Dear People, since I am by the Just Sentence of the Law, condemned to suffer this Day a shameful and cursed Death, for that unnatural and cruel Fact, it will be expected by you all, to hear something from me.' The narrative begins with a biographical sketch recounting her birth in Dysart, her upbringing among a series of relatives, and her work as a collier. She had a child with her master's son, who was fostered until he or she died at the age of three from smallpox. Margaret's work then took her to Coldencleugh, a move of which she said, 'I most solemnly regret this Day.' Margaret attributed her 'Hurry of Despair' to constant hard work and continued poverty, which 'prompted her to greater Vice, as most unhappily hath now fallen out'. She explained that she engaged in a relationship with George Lauder, coal-grieve (mine overseer or manager), and became pregnant. 'Finding no subsistence from him' when she was about to deliver, she killed the child. She counselled her listeners by her example: 'Vice hath brought me to this unhappy and untimely End.'[28]

A visit to the scene of the crime or a memory could interrupt the detached and seemingly emotionless account and produce a surge of affect, grief and horror. As discussed above, when Bessy Turnbul returned home to Scotland, she went to the minister, confessed and 'carried him to the place where she had buried the Infant'. Unlike the single women who appeared in court for newborn child murder, an unnamed widow from Stephney is the perpetrator in *Murder Will Out* (1675). This pamphlet tells of the loss of her husband when her child was one and a half years old. The widow was devoted to her child and worked hard to support the two of them. The child suffered 'a lingering distemper' and 'its continual crying a nights made its Mother's life very uncomfortable'.[29] Although at first she 'bore up under it as well as could be expected for a weak vessel', the author explained that the cost and work involved in rearing this child soon took a toll, and 'she began to murmur at the hard providence...that had brought her into so sad a condition'.[30] As was common in other crime narratives written in the late seventeenth century, the narrator attributed the woman's evil thoughts about the child and her contemplation of his death to Satan's visitations. The woman speaks of her 'sad condition' while Satan reminds her, 'you are unhappy onely in this child of yours'. He is blamed for tempting her to remove the child from her life in the hopes of remarrying, and she 'resolves that she will not lead such an uncomfortable life any longer'.[31] Presumably because the child was sickly, the crime went undetected and the neighbours considered the child's death, caused by putting the child under a tub, the result of 'a Fit'. The widow remarried, had a son and lived with her husband for 30 years before she exposed her own crime. Affect and memory played an important role in eliciting her confession. The woman became ill with a serious cold and a fever that seemed to all around her to be mortal, 'Upon which she was exceedingly Disquieted at the Remembrance of her former bloody crime, and could not rest till she had revealed it in manner as before'.[32] The tone of the pamphlet is matter of fact, with little sensationalistic rhetoric. The author explained simply that 'as Chollar proceeds from the passions', murder was instigated by the Devil. This formulation distances the perpetrator from the crime. The detachment may have allowed readers and the local community to reconcile themselves to the crime and the murderer who lived among them for decades.

The anguish, regret and shame that typified the confessions of the single women convicted of newborn murder and the widow's account from Stephney stand in contrast to the anger, vengeance and rage that animate Francis Parker in an *Account* from 1705. Francis was married to a mariner, the father of her child. The marriage, however, did not work out as planned. Mr. Parker sailed for Leghorne and 'the ship returning without him [Mrs. Parker] had news that he had Married one of the natives of that country'. Upon confirming this rumour with a visit to London, Francis Parker 'was resolved to Revenge her self of this for it's (*sic*) Father's folly; and so resolved to put it out of the World'.[33] She returned home to Chatham in Kent on 5 July 1705, and immediately fetched her child, one and a half years old, from the neighbour. As the *Account* continued, 'no sooner did she enter the Room, but she lock'd her Door to her, and afterward lookt a Case-Knife and cut it's (*sic*) Throat'. The author ascribed feelings of revenge and rage to Francis and articulated them: at the moment of the murder the offender was alleged to have pronounced that 'since it's (*sic*) Father had left her, she would destroy the seed, and not be plagued with anymore of his Blood'. By concluding that Francis 'committed this Barbarous Fact, without any Remorse or Dread of either the Laws of God or Man'[34] the *Account* records an expression of the anger of a married woman wronged by a husband who has left her. It represents the murder as a planned but rageful response to a husband's abandonment. The pamphlet does not condone, excuse or justify Parker's crime, but it nevertheless acknowledges her emotional explanation for her violent act, balanced by her appropriate behaviour after her condemnation. Once convicted and imprisoned to await execution, 'she behaved herself very well', and at her execution she asked several ministers to pray with her and asked that the onlookers join her in prayer. She asked for 'Divine Assistance: help me, O Father, and give me a Heart of Repentance'.[35]

A poem attributed to Parker, titled 'Her Legacy to the World', appends the pamphlet. In verse she warned other 'tender Mothers' and made reference to several emotions. Citing 'discontent' caused by her wayward husband, she explained that she was 'in Passion' when she killed her child. Although she repeated that she died 'in shame' and 'in scorn' with no pity from anyone, she mentioned her 'Friends … who for me grieve', attributing sadness to them.[36] This poem and the wide range of feelings it expresses allow us to see the text's capacity to speak to the different emotional communities addressed. The despair and passion that drove Parker to murder seem to be directed at men, specifically married men, but they also address women and wives. The shame and scorn are those of a condemned and regretful criminal. The sadness of friends reminds us of Parker's neighbours who watched her child while she was away. Although short and unelaborated, this poem renders a picture of Parker nested in layered and complex networks of affective relationships.[37]

(Male) opinion: Judicial and medical

Ideas about the expression of emotion in the eighteenth century, especially the emotive lives of elite men, were significantly shaped by the emergence of the language and culture of sensibility. By the mid-eighteenth century 'sensibility', which had referred to physical sensitivities, came to mean an emotional and moral faculty: it denoted a special and admirable susceptibility to one's own feelings and the feelings of others. As Adela Pinch has remarked, this period was marked by a 'fascination with trying to account for where feelings come from and what they are'.[38] Sentiment and sensibility and the relationship between emotion and morality preoccupied the literature of sensibility from the 1740s to the 1770s.[39] Although novels are the best-known expression of the culture of sensibility, philosophical essays, newspapers, sermons and crime pamphlets also shared these concerns. According to Pinch, 'the era of sensibility defined relations between middle class British men and women and their social others: Indians, slaves, the poor, and the mad'.[40] These relations were modelled in the literature of sensibility built upon the assumption that life and literature were directly linked. In their capacity to teach, both fictional and true-crime texts 'showed people how to behave, how to express themselves in friendship and how to respond decently to life's experiences'.[41]

Eighteenth-century judges and medical experts confronted infanticide in the context of this emergent culture, and their expertise and feelings, as well as their interpretations of emotion, figure prominently in their trial notes and opinions. As chief justice of the King's Bench from 1754 to 1756, Sir Dudley Ryder (1691–1756) presided at criminal trials at the Old Bailey, London's central criminal court; he also served as an assize judge on the Home Circuit during the summers of 1754 and 1755.[42] On Friday 9 August 1754 at Chelmsford in Essex, Ryder heard the case of Frances Cheek, accused of murdering her six-month-old child. A neighbour found Cheek 'kneeling over the body of [her] child, cut plainly with a chicken hook lying by bloody'. When asked why she did it, Cheek 'said nothing but that she should be hanged and knew nothing of the matter'. A clergyman who saw her after the crime testified that 'she was then distracted'. In his notes on the case Ryder concluded that 'she was two days after clearly not out of her senses, nor now at her trial nor during the intermediate time, nor any evidence given of her having been disordered before, but one witness said she was a hasty passionate woman'.[43] When he charged the jury, Ryder told them 'they must consider whether she did the fact, and if so whether she was out of her senses when she did the fact, immaterial whether she was so afterwards when she reflected what she had done'.[44]

A disagreement between the judge and the jury ensued. The jury 'first said they were satisfied she killed the child but doubted her sanity', which would suggest an acquittal. Despite his own admission that Cheek 'looked wild and disturbed' at her trial, Ryder 'explained again to them the nature of the case rather against the prisoner' and sent them back to deliberate further. Ryder seemed concerned to distinguish between Cheek's distraught emotional performance at the trial and her emotional state when she killed the child. An hour and a half later, a lengthy deliberation in the eighteenth century, the jury brought in a conviction. Ryder noted that he 'told them I was very well satisfied' and pronounced a death sentence to be followed by dissection – the ultimate punishment.[45] In view of the declining conviction rate for infanticide by the second decade of the eighteenth century, this 1754 conviction stands out as unusual.

The separation of justice and sensibility did not, however, lead Ryder to repress his emotions or portray himself as an unfeeling man, insensitive to the emotional testimony he heard. Quite the contrary: when he handed down Cheek's death sentence, Ryder reported that 'I made a very proper speech *extempore* and pronounced it with dignity.' In his diary, he described his feelings as he pronounced the sentence: 'I was so affected that the tears were gushing out several times against my will.'[46] Self-conscious about the public nature of his emotional outpouring, Ryder noted gratefully that 'it was discerned by all the company – which was large – and a lady gave me her handkerchief dipped in lavender water to help me'.[47]

Was Ryder oblivious to the irony of his claim to have cried against his will as he sentenced to death a woman, whom some believed had acted against her *own* will? His use of the phrase 'against my will' implied his failure to distance his emotions from 'his very proper speech'. Yet his feelings did not prevent him from performing his judicial duty with honour. By leaving his show of emotion until the pronouncement of the death sentence, Ryder achieved what he deemed an appropriate balance of emotion and justice. When he rejected acquittal and directed the jury to convict Frances Cheek, he asserted his authority over the trial. He enforced justice by insisting on a conviction, and he displayed sensibility when he pronounced the death sentence, accompanied by a speech that attempted to reclaim his own authority and that of middle-class masculinity. Addressing jurors as fellow men of sensibility he reconstituted the trial as the setting for the traditional masculine values of reason, self-control and stoicism. Ryder's tears at the sentencing may have signalled some limited exchange of emotion, perhaps even compassion, as appropriate only at the post-trial phase of the criminal legal process. Was the judge performing for the jury, the prosecutor, the defendant, those seated in the gallery or a combination of audiences? The multidirectionality of affective performance leaves its object ambiguous.[48]

In a similar incident the judge in Ann Arnold's case from 1813 advised the jury that in view of the circumstances and the prisoner's confession, there was 'little ground to doubt the truth of the charge'. The jury brought in a guilty verdict after consulting for 'a few minutes'. The judge then addressed the prisoner 'in the most affecting manner', saying it was 'painful to reflect that a person of your years should be condemned to die, but when we consider the extent of your crime, it is necessary'.[49] He castigated Arnold for mismanaging her life and not caring for her child: 'one should have thought that after having once recovered from the shame of your illicit connection, you would have been careful as to your future conduct, and endeavoured, with maternal affection, to cherish that child'.[50] After that he pronounced a sentence of death by hanging followed by dissection and anatomization. The pamphlet's concluding lines echo Dudley Ryder's diary: 'his Lordship was so much affected in passing sentence that he could not refrain from tears'. In contrast, 'the prisoner appeared but little affected with her awful state'.[51] Both of these cases reveal the gendered affective impact of the courtroom and the power dynamics in the room.[52] The male judges concerned to perform their heightened emotions inhabit a position of power that enables them to do so while still upholding notions of an objective justice that considers only 'the nature of the case rather against the prisoner'. The female defendant, clearly subordinated and lacking the right of expression, masked her emotions and left the impression that she was 'but little affected with her awful state'. Her apparent emotional detachment is unsurprising, considering the relational composition of disposition in the eighteenth century: in a courtroom with no one from her emotional community, no emotional exchange took place.[53]

The language of sensibility gestures towards ideas about honour as they related to the reputation of both men and women grappling with the consequences of this brutal crime. In the evidence we have seen from judges, they wished to preserve the honour of the courtroom with a balance of justice and sentiment. While men who committed infanticide are not the focus of the discussion here, there are many instances in the record of men who killed their illegitimate children or their pregnant lovers. These men used their last words in an attempt to excuse their actions in order to restore their honour and reassert their dominance in the social and familiar order.[54] Francis Parker indicated that the murder of her small son was meant to expunge the contamination of her husband, so that 'she would destroy the seed, and not be plagued with anymore of his Blood'.[55] The pamphlet suggests that, like a stain, the trace of her husband's blood impugned her honour and that violence was the means to erase it.

The heightened interest in emotions is reflected in the medical literature, which articulated a remarkable shift in the attitudes towards single women accused of infanticide. By the end of the eighteenth century, the assumption of guilt and of criminal intent were called into question, and the crime itself became evidence of a heightened emotional state that required little or no supporting testimony of mental alienation. William Hunter's lecture read to the members of the Medical Society on 14 July 1783 reflected this change of opinion. Dr. Hunter (1718–1783) was a renowned physician, anatomist, surgeon and man-midwife. In his lecture titled, 'On the uncertainty of the signs of murder in the case of bastard children', Hunter warned his colleagues against 'early prejudice' in cases that looked like infanticide and reminded them that the act could not be considered a murder unless it was

> executed with some degree of cool judgement, and wicked intention. When committed under a phrenzy from despair, can it be more offensive in the sight of God, than under a phrenzy from a fever, or in lunacy?[56]

Hunter pointed to the diagnosis of temporary insanity when he reminded his audience that

> in making up a just estimate of any human action, much will depend on the state of the agent's mind at the time; and therefore the laws of all countries make ample allowance for insanity. The insane are not held to be responsible for their actions.[57]

Hunter suggested instead that single women 'with an unconquerable sense of shame', who found themselves pregnant out of wedlock, might be 'overwhelmed with terror and despair' until their 'distress of body and mind deprives them of all judgement and rational conduct'.[58] He speculated that these women were driven by a 'violently agitated' mind experiencing 'a conflict of passions and terror', and that in this emotional state 'an irrational conduct may appear very natural'.[59] The shame of such a pregnancy drove one of his patients to suicide when she was 'struck with panic and lost her judgement and senses'.[60] Hunter explained the deaths of seemingly healthy babies born to women who delivered alone, 'distracted in… mind, and exhausted in… body, [and who] will not have strength or recollection enough to fly instantly to the relief of the child'.[61]

Hunter's speech signalled a change in the attitude of the medical community with regard to the effects of pregnancy out of wedlock on the mother's emotions and her behaviour. He argued that the very motives cited in the statute of 1624, shame and fear, produced emotional distress leading to 'phrenzy'. For Hunter, the villain was not the infanticidal mother, whom he thought 'weak, credulous, and deluded', but rather the dishonourable father of the child who, like Frances Parker's husband, 'is really criminal', because he has abandoned his paternal duty and his responsibilities as a husband and a provider.[62] Turning the emotional table on legal authorities, physicians and the friends and family of the single woman, Hunter concluded that

> every humane heart will forget the indiscretion or crime, and bleed for the sufferings which a woman must have gone through; who but for having listened to the perfidious protestations and vows of our sex, might have been an affectionate and faithful wife, a virtuous and honoured mother, through a long and happy life.[63]

The errant men deserve only disdain because they have robbed the women of their honour by denying them their place in society as faithful wives and virtuous mothers. These men personify dishonour because they have failed to fulfil their roles as husbands and providers. Hunter's interpretation of the crime of infanticide and its causes serves as a strong example of the humanitarian narrative defined and deconstructed by Thomas Laqueur.[64] Stripped of all agency granted to them, however harshly, by the statute of 1624, Hunter presented the women as the passive victims of their male seducers while the physicians took on the role of their obstetrical and psychological saviours.

Conclusion

Barbara Rosenwein has encouraged us to see emotions as 'narratives of negotiation' that can inform us about what people valued in the past.[65] The pamphlets, legal documents and medical opinion of the long eighteenth century leave traces of these negotiations. The women at the centre of this story, the mothers, wed and unwed, accused and convicted of murdering their children, deployed the scaffold speech in complicated ways that served to uphold and affirm ideas about sin and redemption as well as the judicial system and its findings and also to express their shame, contrition, sorrow and repentance. The words attributed to them convey apologies, expressions of faith, anger, resentment, sadness, grief, repentance, justification, excuse and regret. Whether they wrote them or not, these sources represent an attempt by an individual and her communities to grapple with a violent rupture and reconcile themselves to the implications of a criminal transgression. The emotions expressed served as thresholds that 'separate[d] and connect[ed]'.[66] They distanced the criminal from the crime and simultaneously drew her closer to her emotional communities. They also served as a signal of the crime itself, providing assurance that such crime would inevitably be discovered – even if it was undetected for 30 years.

In trial transcripts of infanticide cases defendants typically appeared as isolated and solitary figures who rarely spoke, unless to utter a submissive and formulaic defence, and they stood accused, often correctly, of trying to hide and conceal from their families and households. In contrast the pamphlets allow us to see the affective lives of these women within their multiple worlds of household, families and villages. The sudden outpouring of emotion from a seemingly detached speaker – whether an accused woman or a judge – confirms that the affective and unemotional should not be defined as opposites, particularly in an historical context in which sensibility was valued and honoured. Similarly this evidence 'unsettles the dichotomous distinctions' between the private affective response as authentic and the public as instrumental.[67] These interactions are multilayered and reveal the contradictory strands of these women's lives and their attempts to resolve them in their final moments. The high stakes of such performances for both the individual and those interested in her fate are evidenced when we consider how much work these last words had to do. The emotional expectations, responses and performances that surround these extreme cases may allow us to reconstruct the emotional histories of more ordinary people in less extraordinary situations.

Notes

1   The term infanticide is, as Mark Jackson has argued, vague and anachronistic. Almost all of the cases discussed here involved the death of a newborn infant. Mark Jackson, *New-Born Child Murder: Women, Illegitimacy and the Courts in Eighteenth-Century England* (Manchester: Manchester University Press, 1996), 5–6. For a literary and cultural analysis, see Josephine McDonagh, *Child Murder and British Culture, 1720–1900* (Cambridge: Cambridge University Press, 2003).

2   For a cultural and social analysis of execution in early modern England, see Andrea McKenzie, *Tyburn's Martyrs: Execution in England, 1675–1775* (London: Hambledon Continuum, 2007); for the United States, see Karen Halttunen, *Murder Most Foul: The Killer and the American Gothic Imagination* (Cambridge, MA: Harvard University Press, 1998). For more on broadsides, see *Ballads and Broadsides in Britain, 1500–1800*, ed. Patricia Fumerton, Anita Guerrini and Kris McAbee (Burlington, VT: Ashgate, 2010).

3   My analysis of emotional communities draws heavily on Barbara Rosenwein's work, especially 'Worrying about Emotions in History', *American Historical Review*, 107 (2002): 821–45 and 'Problems and Methods in the History of Emotions', *Passions in Context: Journal of the History and Philosophy of the Emotions*, 1, 1 (2010), unpaginated, available online at http://www.passionsincontext.de/index.php?id=557, accessed 17 June 2013.

4   On spatially defined emotional styles, see Benno Gammerl, 'Emotional Styles – Concepts and Challenges', *Rethinking History: the Journal of Theory and Practice*, 16 (2012): 161–75 and Doreen Massey, *For Space* (London: Sage, 2005) and 'Places and Their Pasts', *History Workshop Journal*, 39 (1995): 182–92.

5   Dana Rabin, 'Bodies of Evidence, States of Mind: Infanticide, Emotion, and Sensibility in Eighteenth-Century England', in *Infanticide: Historical Perspectives, 1550–2000*, ed. Mark Jackson (London: Ashgate, 2002), 73–92, and Rabin, *Identity, Crime, and Legal Responsibility in Eighteenth-Century England* (New York: Palgrave, 2004), Chap. 4. The work on sensibility is tremendously rich and provocative. Some of the most helpful insights for this study emerged from Nancy Armstrong, *Desire and Domestic Fiction: A Political History of the Novel* (Oxford: Oxford University Press, 1987); G. J. Barker-Benfield, *The Culture of Sensibility: Sex and Society in Eighteenth-Century Britain* (Chicago: University of Chicago Press, 1992); Barbara Benedict, *Framing Feeling: Sentiment and Style in English Prose Fiction, 1745–1800* (New York: AMS Press, 1994); R. F. Brissenden, *Virtue in Distress: Studies in the Novel of Sentiment from Richardson to Sade* (New York: McMillan, 1974); Alan T. McKenzie, *Certain, Lively Episodes: The Articulation of Passion in Eighteenth-Century Prose* (Athens, GA: University of Georgia Press, 1990); John Mullan, *Sentiment and Sociability: The Language of Feeling in the Eighteenth Century* (Oxford: Oxford University Press, 1988); Adela Pinch, *Strange Fits of Passion: Epistemologies of Emotion, Hume to Austen* (Palo Alto: Stanford University Press, 1996); Janet Todd, *Sensibility: An Introduction* (London: Methuen, 1986); and Ann Jessie Van Sant, *Eighteenth-Century Sensibility and the Novel: The Senses in Social Context* (Cambridge: Cambridge University Press, 1993).

6   Rosenwein, 'Worrying about Emotions', 842.

7   Barbara H. Rosenwein et al., 'AHR Conversation: The Historical Study of Emotions', *American Historical Review*, 117 (December 2012), 1503.

8   Rosenwein et al., 'AHR Conversation', 1504. For an analysis of women's scaffold speeches, see Frances E. Dolan, '"Gentlemen, I have one thing more to say": Women on Scaffolds in England, 1563–1680', *Modern Philology*, 92 (1994): 157–78.

9   21 Jac. 1, c. 27. The statute is also known as the Concealment of Birth of Bastards Act.

10 43 Geo. III., c. 58, *Offences against the Person Act* is known as Lord Ellenborough's Act. The drop in convictions for infanticide is described in J. M. Beattie, *Crime and the Courts in England, 1660–1800* (Princeton: Princeton University Press, 1986), 113–24; Peter Hoffer and N. E. H. Hull, *Murdering Mothers: Infanticide in England and New England, 1558–1803* (New York: New York University Press, 1981), 65–91; Jackson, *New-Born Child Murder*, 133–34; and R. W. Malcolmson, 'Infanticide in the Eighteenth Century', in *Crime in England 1550–1800*, ed. J. S. Cockburn (London: Methuen, 1977), 196–98. Jackson points out that the drop in trial jury convictions accompanied a rise in grand jury dismissals of accused women and findings of natural death or still birth by coroner's juries.

11 Beattie, *Crime in the Courts*, 120–24, Jackson, *New-Born Child Murder*, 133–50.

12 Matthew Hale (1609–1676) treated the crime of infanticide as a special case within the category of insanity. *History of the Pleas of the Crown*, ed. Sollom Emlyn, 2 Vols. (London: E. and R. Nutt and R. Gosling, 1736), Vol.1, 36.

13 Beattie, *Crime in the Courts*, 120–24 and Malcolmson, 'Infanticide', 197–98.

14 Jackson, *New-Born Child Murder*, 113–28. Jackson's analysis of the humanitarian narratives also considers the opposition to these accounts that emerged even at the end of the eighteenth century.

15 William Blackstone, *Commentaries on the Laws of England: Vol. 4 Of Public Wrongs* (Chicago: University of Chicago Press, 1979), Vol. 4, 198. Beattie, *Crime and the Courts*, 124. Mark Jackson gives a detailed explication of the statute and changing laws of evidence and standards of proof in *New-Born Child Murder*, 145–51.

16 Although the preparation defence was the most common, some women also claimed the child was stillborn or that the child had died during or immediately after birth. These other defences did not exclude a preparation defence.

17 The Act was based to a large extent on the English statute. A broadside is a one-page pamphlet, sometimes with an illustration. It was sometimes printed on a larger sheet of paper used for public notices or advertisements.

18 *The confession and last words of Bessy Turnbul, who was execute [sic] at Edinburgh, 6th April 1709; for murdering her own child* (Edinburgh: John Reid, 1709), 1.

19 Early modern understandings of pregnancy, the body and childbirth are described as circulating in a sphere of female networks and knowledge. *Women as Mothers in Pre-Industrial England: Essays in Memory of Dorothy McLaren*, ed. Valerie Fildes (London: Routledge, 1990). Laura Gowing describes how knowledge about the birthing process was controlled by married women and suggests the impact this had on single pregnant women in 'Secret Births and Infanticide in Seventeenth-Century England', *Past and Present*, 156 (1997): 87–115 and in 'Ordering the Body: Illegitimacy and Female Authority in Seventeenth-Century England', in *Negotiating Power in Early Modern Society*, ed. Michael Braddick and John Walter (Cambridge: Cambridge University Press, 2001), 43–62. In 'Pregnancy, Childbirth, and the Female Body in Early Modern Germany', *Past and Present*, 150 (1996): 84–110, Ulinka Rublack suggests that married men were often included and involved in their wives' pregnancies and labour.

20 For more on illegitimacy, see Richard Adair, *Courtship, Illegitimacy and Marriage in Early Modern England* (Manchester: Manchester University Press, 1996).

21 *The last words and confession of Margaret Inglis, who was executed at Edinburgh the 6th of April 1709* (Edinburgh: John Reid, 1709).

22 J. A. Sharpe, '"Last Dying Speeches": Religion, Ideology and Public Execution in Seventeenth-Century England', *Past and Present*, 107 (1985): 144–67.

23 For more on the contingency of the scaffold speech, see Thomas Laqueur, 'Crowds, Carnival and the State in English Executions, 1604–1868', in *The First Modern Society: Essays in English History in Honour of*

Lawrence Stone, ed. A. L. Beier, David Cannadine, and James Rosenheim (Cambridge: Cambridge University Press, 1989), 305–55 and Peter Linebaugh, 'The Tyburn Riot against the Surgeons', in *Albion's Fatal Tree: Crime and Society in Eighteenth Century England*, ed. Douglas Hay, Peter Linebaugh, John G. Rule, E. P. Thompson, and Cal Winslow (London: Allen Lane, 1975), 65–117.

24   *The last words ... Margaret Inglis.*

25   *The Confession of Agnes Craig, daughter to the deceased John Craig and Agnes Grierson, who lives at the bridge-end of Minnijve in the paroch of Glencairn when the said Agnes Craig was execute in Drumfries, on Wednesday being the 5th of June, anno 1717. For the murdering of hct [sic] own child* (Edinburgh, s.n., 1717), 1.

26   Bullfist, a fungus (*Lycoperdon sp.*) was believed to be poisonous (Oxford English Dictionary online editions). *The Confession of Agnes Craig ...*, 1.

27   *The last speech and dying words of Janet Hutchie, who was executed in the Grass-market of Edinburgh, upon the 30th of August 1721, for the murder of her own child* (Edinburgh: Printed by Robert Brown in the middle of Forrester's-Wynd, 1721), 2.

28   *The last speech and dying words of Margaret Millar, coal-bearer at Colden-cleugh who was executed 10 February 1726 at the Gibbet of Dalkeith, for murdering her own child* (Edinburgh, s.n., 1726).

29   *Murther will out; or A true and faithful relation of a horrible murther* (London: Printed for C. Passinger, 1675), 2.

30   *Murther will out; or A true and faithful relation of a horrible murther*, 2–3.

31   *Murther will out; or A true and faithful relation of a horrible murther*, 3.

32   *Murther will out; or A true and faithful relation of a horrible murther*, 6.

33   *A full and true account of the tryal and condemnation, and execution of Francis Parker (a sea-mans wife) at Maidstone in Kent, on Tuesday the 24th of July, 1705 ... Together with an account how she murdered her child, ...* (London: printed by D. Brown, 1705), 3.

34   *A full and true account of the tryal and condemnation, and execution of Francis Parker*, 4–5.

35   *A full and true account of the tryal and condemnation, and execution of Francis Parker*, 6.

36   *A full and true account of the tryal and condemnation, and execution of Francis Parker*, 8.

37   Rosenwein et al., 'Historical Study of Emotions', 1519.

38   Pinch, *Strange Fits of Passion*, 2.

39   Todd, *Sensibility*, 9.

40   Pinch, *Strange Fits of Passion*, 11.

41   Todd, *Sensibility*, 2.

42   Ryder presided at the Old Bailey sessions held in October 1754, April 1755, October 1755, and April 1756. His use of shorthand enabled him to record many of the trial's details. John Langbein has written extensively about

Ryder's Notebook and his Assize Diary. For more on this source, its reliability and its uses for legal historians, see his 'Shaping the Eighteenth-Century Trial: A View from the Ryder Sources', *University of Chicago Law Review*, 50 (1983): 1–136.

43   Notes made by Dudley Ryder on cases at the Home Circuit assizes, 1754–55. 'Legal notebook of Sir Dudley Ryder, 1754/55', Document 19(f), Volume 1129 of the Harrowby Manuscripts, Sandon Hall (typescript), 4.

44   Ryder, 'Legal notebook'.

45   Ryder, 'Legal notebook'.

46   Ryder, 'Legal notebook', 5. For an excellent analysis of another 'weeping judge' in a slightly later period, see Thomas Dixon, 'The Tears of Mr Justice Willes', *Journal of Victorian Culture*, 17, 2 (March 2012): 1–23.

47   Notes made by Dudley Ryder on cases at the Home Circuit assizes, 1754–55, 4.

48   Dixon makes this point in a cautionary note against the interpretation of tears as merely indicative of 'sentiment'. 'The Tears', 3.

49   *The Trial at Large of Ann Arnold, for The Wilful Murder of Her Infant Child, under Five Years of Age, by Drowning Him in a Pond at Spexhall, in The County of Suffolk* (Bury St. Edmunds: Printed by Gedge and Barker and sold by T. Middleditch, 1813), 15.

50   *Trial at Large of Ann Arnold*, 15.

51   *Trial at Large of Ann Arnold*, 15.

52   Rosenwein et al., 'Historical Study of Emotions', 1496 and Gammerl, 'Emotional Styles', 164–66.

53   Rosenwein et al., 'Historical Study of Emotions', 1504.

54   For the case of Robert Foulkes, a married man who murdered his illegitimate baby after delivering it, see David Turner, '"Nothing is so Secret but Shall be Revealed": The Scandalous Life of Robert Foulkes', in *English Masculinities, 1660–1800*, ed. Tim Hitchcock and Michèlle Cohen (London: Longman, 1999), 169–92.

55   *A full and true account of… Francis Parker*, 4.

56   William Hunter, 'On the Uncertainty of the Signs of Murder, in the Case of Bastard Children', *Medical Observations and Inquiries*, 6 (1784): 271.

57   Hunter, 'On the Uncertainty of the Signs of Murder, in the Case of Bastard Children', 268.

58   Hunter, 'On the Uncertainty of the Signs of Murder, in the Case of Bastard Children', 272–73.

59   Hunter, 'On the Uncertainty of the Signs of Murder, in the Case of Bastard Children', 278.

60   Hunter, 'On the Uncertainty of the Signs of Murder, in the Case of Bastard Children', 279.

61   Hunter, 'On the Uncertainty of the Signs of Murder, in the Case of Bastard Children', 288–89.

62   Hunter, 'On the Uncertainty of the Signs of Murder, in the Case of Bastard Children', 269.

63 Hunter, 'On the Uncertainty of the Signs of Murder, in the Case of Bastard Children', 270.

64 Thomas Laqueur, 'Bodies, Details, and the Humanitarian Narrative', in *The New Cultural History*, ed. Lynn Hunt (Berkeley: University of California Press, 1989), 176–204.

65 Rosenwein, 'Passions in Context', 11, 20.

66 Gammerl, 'Emotional Styles', 162.

67 Gammerl, 'Emotional Styles', 169, 164.

5

'Unbridled Passions', honour and status in late eighteenth-century Cape Town

Nigel Worden

No-one will want to deny that it is the most grievous offence that can be done to an upright and right-minded person when one's honour and reputation is damaged by people who cannot master their own unbridled passions since, in accordance with calm and rational understanding and natural reasoning, there is nothing more precious or valuable after life itself than the maintenance of honour and reputation.

Council of Justice Judgement (1782)[1]

The defence of honour as a key element in violent physical conflict over matters of reputation is well documented in the history of Europe and its colonies. The familiar picture is of a victim of insulting words or deeds that have challenged his reputation (for it was usually a male) who responds with violent action against the perpetrator. Extensively studied as a cause of armed conflict in the ritual of the European duel, honour was also a common element in less formalized outbreaks of public violence.[2] There is growing evidence that honour defined as a 'right to respect' was not confined to social elites; indeed, reputation among one's equals and the right to defend one's honour and to receive respect from others were central to the social ordering of many early modern societies, encompassing both genders and all ranks, including servants and slaves.[3] Honour and respect were enforced through rituals, language and gesture in everyday practice; furthermore, the law, both criminal and civil, recognized the right to remedy for infringements of honour and respect.

Studies in the history of violence commonly draw a direct line of causal connection from infringement of honour to anger and on to violence. Understanding of the cultural context of brawling in early modern Europe, for example, has been deepened by awareness of the participants' felt need to contest slights to reputation, especially among single young men of lower rank.[4] Relatively few of these insights, however, have been tested in contexts where European concepts and practices had to adapt to new situations in which distinct ideas and practices prevailed. This chapter examines some of the various ways in which both Europeans and Asians expressed emotion in relation to reputation and honour in eighteenth-century Cape Town, a rough and ready colonial port town with a remarkably diverse population. Here, one might expect to find a population particularly prone to use violence to defend honour. Indeed, this pattern is present, but alongside it is striking evidence of frequent resort to the civil court system for the resolution of conflicts that might otherwise have ended in violence.

Several demographic, economic and political features explain the nature of conflicts over honour and reputation in eighteenth-century Cape Town, which was under the control of the Dutch East India Company (VOC) with its headquarters in Batavia (now Jakarta). First, a large number of its inhabitants were young and single men who asserted themselves in relation to other males in public surroundings, often by brawling. Second, the capacity to command respect played a key role in a VOC-controlled settlement, where status legally defined access to political and social privileges. For example, only burghers – those VOC employees who had been granted permission to establish themselves as independent colonists and their descendants – had the right to marry, own property and hold lucrative Company supply contracts, while the existence of slavery and convict labour made free legal status an important mark of distinction, as it was in nineteenth-century Buenos Aires (as Martha Santos discusses in her chapter).[5] Asserting and defending one's position in relation to others was particularly important in a highly transient and fluid community where the continual arrival of strangers and newcomers from Europe, Asia and elsewhere in Africa meant that nothing could be taken for granted. Reputation was critical, and people felt obliged to defend their honour if it were challenged.[6] Women as well as men from all classes of society – high-ranking officials, military and naval officers, free burghers and artisans, soldiers, sailors, freed slaves and convicts – were enmeshed in this obligation.

Analysis of these conflicts has hitherto relied on the extensive and well-preserved criminal court records of the Cape Council of Justice. This evidence indicates that the VOC authorities brought charges of homicide, violent assault or disturbance of the public peace against brawlers, most of whom were soldiers, sailors, low-ranking Company employees, slaves and convicts. At least some of these encounters were characteristic of what Pieter Spierenburg has described as 'popular duels', meaning one-to-one fights which followed specific codes of practice, albeit ones demonstrated through actions rather than by written rules.[7] However, there are also extensive records of hundreds of civil cases brought before the Council by individuals whose honour had been impugned and who sought redress in ways which did not involve physical retaliation. Most of such plaintiffs were burghers who considered violence to be an unworthy response for men of their status. As the opening quotation to this chapter indicates, Cape judges and social elites connected the 'maintenance of honour and reputation' to control over 'unbridled passion'.[8]

Analysing evidence drawn from civil honour cases thus sheds new light on the history of emotion, a field of study which in recent decades has received much attention by historians of early modern Europe and North America but which has thus far been almost entirely neglected in the historiography of the early Cape Colony.[9] One result of such work has been the identification of the eighteenth century as a period of 'great transformation' in north-western Europe and colonial North America, as individual anger became more explicitly condemned, although in differing ways for men and women and with differing degrees of acceptance across social classes.[10] In relation to honour, such work argues that as violence became a monopoly of the state, public defence of individual honour rested increasingly in judicial settlement rather than physical retaliation.[11] Evidence from civil proceedings over honour disputes in Cape Town suggests that the state did not control this process. Rather, local social values, which emphasized the importance of avoiding emotional outbursts, rendered the regulation of passion a civil, as well as a criminal, matter.

All the inhabitants of Cape Town, whether free or slave, or of European, African or Asian origin, came under the aegis of a single legal structure established by the VOC. This framework was based on Roman-Dutch law and adapted to colonial circumstances under statutes passed in Batavia and locally at the Cape.[12] Cases entailing public brawling and overt violence, usually involving sailors and slaves, were subject to criminal prosecution by the Company and any claims of provocation were routinely repudiated as a defence.[13] Yet individuals who considered their honour and reputation to be damaged by the actions of others (usually burghers, military officers and those of higher social rank) brought civil actions against their assailants. In such cases the Company Council of Justice sought reconciliation or imposed a fine and demanded that apology and recognition of the honour of the victim be publicly asserted by the culprit. The ways in which individuals in Cape Town perceived their honour, and expressed their feelings in reaction to attacks made on it, thus differed markedly according to their status, gender and place of origin, although the Company's legal system recognized only some of these differences as valid. Brawling and duelling enabled an offended individual to restore his honour by inflicting violence on the offender, and the criminal law system subjected both parties to similar punishment for breaching the peace. In this sense, criminal law formally rejected the public defence of honour. Nevertheless, the civil law system in Cape Town provided a means by which both parties could recover honour by abjuring violence. The distinctive feature of this civil system was that it upheld the notion that personal honour was a matter of entitlement to respectful treatment, while it also offered a nonviolent channel through which honour might be restored.

Uncurbed passion

Cape Town was a military defence post as well as the market for the rapidly expanding agrarian colony of its colonial hinterland and a key port for provisions and repairs for the hundreds of European trading vessels en route between the Atlantic and Indian Oceans. It had a small resident population (some 7,000 individuals in the 1770s), made up of people of extremely diverse origins and status including: Dutch, German and Scandinavian officials, artisans, soldiers, free burghers and convicts; and South and Southeast Asian, Malagasy and Southeast African slaves, freed slaves, convicts and exiles. To this mix was added the characteristically transient population of a busy port – soldiers and sailors from Europe and Asia, along with travellers and officials en route between Europe and Asia. Cape Town was thus a complex, socially fragmented and multiethnic society, each social and ethnic category having its own understanding of status and slights and its own concepts of honour.[14]

A key element of the Cape Town civil cases involving attacks on reputation and honour was the concept of *drift*, a Dutch word which in the late eighteenth century referred not only to the swift track of a ship in water but also to the passions of 'anger, zeal, ardour, desire, love, eagerness'.[15] *Drift* was an undesirable quality, an excess of emotion which accentuated the calumnies committed by persons who, in the words of the opening quotation to this chapter, could not 'master their own passions'. In contrast, the 'upright and right-minded' victims of such outbursts, who displayed 'calm and rational understanding and natural reasoning', were regarded with respect. *Drift* was often cited in the civil records as the cause of attacks on the honour of burghers. Plaintiffs stressed that the perpetrators had lost control of their passions and that their impulsive and wilful behaviour was irrational and thus without due cause. In arguing this way, they diverted attention from any rational account as to why they should have been insulted: rather than claiming their innocence, plaintiffs stressed their entitlement to the respect that persons with uncontrolled temper had denied them.

Thus the burgher Willem Stricker recounted how he had been sitting outside his front door one warm October evening in 1780 when, 'suddenly and without any previous exchange of words', his neighbour, the burgher Hanje Janse Swartsenburg, began to scold him as a 'rogue, scoundrel and a man who strips others and then clothes them again'. No explanation was given for these curious words, and the neighbours and friends who were with Stricker tried to persuade Swartsenburg to be quiet. He refused to listen to them, though, and he went to his house and returned with a thick stick in his hands. Stricker sensibly retreated indoors while the others tried to 'calm Swartsenburg down'. When he refused to 'curb his passion' and started throwing stones at Stricker's door his neighbours found it necessary to go indoors and 'shut everything up'.[16]

There are strong echoes in this behaviour of a ritual known as 'house-scorning', a practice that was particularly prevalent among lower-class men in sixteenth- and early seventeenth-century Germany, where one man would insult another in front of his house and throw stones at it until he appeared to answer the challenge. Many Cape Town burghers were of German origin. However, as Jan Plamper has reminded us, the transfer of an emotional culture across time and space does not necessarily preserve its meaning in a different context.[17] In Germany such actions were seen as peasant customs sanctioned by the village community and their effectiveness lay in the power of local men to challenge those who were suspected of breaking community norms and values.[18] In late eighteenth-century Cape Town, however, such behaviour by a fellow burgher was an unacceptable display of anger. Stricker told the Council that he was bringing a case against Swartsenburg of 'severe insult, threat and violence' because he feared that he would go further in his 'rage' (woede). He had spoken to him about his behaviour before, but had more recently in a 'premeditated way kept silent and in this way sought to avoid further consequences'. However, this recent episode made him realize 'how little the defendant was able to master his aroused anger and bad passions'. Realizing that reason could not prevail over such uncontrolled rage, and insulted by the public verbal insult and physical shaming of his home, Stricker sought redress from the Council. He demanded that Swartsenburg apologize and declare him publicly to be an honourable man, 'in front of open doors at the sounding of the clock bells'. He also suggested that Swartsenburg pay the sizeable fine of 1,000 Cape guilders to the poor fund in acknowledgement of his guilt.[19] Such actions would restore the reputation of a man of Stricker's standing, which ignoring the insult or responding to it with anger would have failed to accomplish. A public judgement along these lines might have humiliated Swartsenburg, but it also gave him the opportunity to restore his own standing as a balanced man, able to accept past misbehaviour and with the means to make material amends.

There are several notable features of this case. At no point did Swartsenburg defend himself by explaining why he had attacked Stricker and there is no hint in the records of the cause of this friction between neighbours. Two weeks later the two men reappeared before the Council saying that they had resolved their differences and thanked it for the pains it had taken in helping them to do so. Swartsenburg received a warning to behave more circumspectly in future, but he paid no fine.[20] There are various possible explanations for Stricker's acceptance of this settlement, including relief at the taming of an irascible neighbour, a genuine desire to forgive and forget for the sake of a more peaceful neighbourhood and a satisfaction that his appeal to the authorities had yielded reconciliation. But it is unlikely that he would have agreed to reconcile with Swartsenburg unless he had felt that the assaults on his honour had been annulled. To insult someone publicly in front of his house and in the presence of friends and neighbours inflicted greater damage to their reputations than to their houses. If Stricker had taken no action in response, this inaction would have permanently shamed him. But instead of reacting with violence himself, he took the matter to the Council to effect a peaceful resolution. His complaint to the Council constantly emphasized the contrast between his own reasonableness and 'premeditated' self-control and the inability of Swartsenburg to 'master' his 'passion' (*drift)* and 'fury' (*woede*). Witnesses who gave testimony to the Council each made a special point of stressing how they had tried to subdue Swartsenburg without success.[21] Furious anger, the inability to master one's own passions, exacerbated the situation and placed burgher Swartsenburg, rather than Stricker, in a shameful position. Insult through angry words or action was amplified when carried out in a public place and in the presence of witnesses. It was particularly outrageous when the place and people concerned were of high status. Reconciliation restored honour for them both, albeit in different ways. The state in this instance did not claim a monopoly of violence, but rather stood in reserve to encourage members of society to desist from it on their own account.

Whereas the argument of Stricker and Swartsenburg late one evening in front of their neighbours and friends was resolved by mutual agreement, another case which came to the Council in the same month was less easily resolved. Burgher Jeremias Auret was in the council chamber of the Council of Justice one Thursday morning in September 1780 where a large number of prominent burghers and senior VOC officials had gathered. One of them, burgher Hendrik Hermanus Bos, began to tell him a long story about how the landdrost of Swellendam had acted badly in a case involving runaway slaves. Auret soon grew tired of this, told him that he knew nothing about the matter, that he would have acted in the same way if he had been the landdrost and that he now needed to get on with his business. Bos then shouted out in the hearing of everyone, 'Then God damn it, you are just as louse-infested as the landdrost is'.[22] Auret responded with 'Be quiet, be quiet', words which were intended to calm Bos down, but he subsequently complained to the Council that 'no-one can dispute that calumnies and invectives, especially when uttered with incitement and in passion in the presence of many people at a place where right-minded people can witness it, fall bitterly on an honourable living soul, since honour is the most valuable thing after a man's life itself'.[23] Consequently, he demanded an apology and the restoration of his good name.

In his defence, Bos admitted to the Council that he had indeed described Auret as louse-infested but that he had not lost his temper and had spoken 'gently/softly' (*saagtjes*). By contrast, he claimed, Auret responded to him with 'passion' (*drift*), both in cutting short his complaint about the Swellendam landdrost and by telling him to be quiet.[24] The Council determined that Bos was guilty and that he must restore Auret's good name by a public apology and payment of a fine, a judgement which would have involved public humiliation and some diminution of status for him. Bos, however, gave notice that he would take the case to appeal in the Dutch East India Company's courts in Batavia.[25] Auret's loss of face by the insulting words of Bos in the presence of senior and respected burghers and officials in the very meeting hall of the Council of Justice was not in question. What was at issue was which of the two men had spoken in uncontrolled 'passion' and anger.

For angry insults should not be parried with violence, least of all by men of status. In the fluid social milieu of Cape Town, those of high status had a strong interest in establishing and adhering to standards of peaceable living. As the claimant in another case in 1783 stated, 'forceful and uncontrolled passions should be answered with an appeasing approach', in order to promote 'regular living and [the] good order of society'.[26]

Who do you think you are?

While uncontrolled anger was generally considered unacceptable for a man of status, there were, nonetheless, circumstances in which it could be justified. By distancing themselves from a form of anger which they considered indicative of the loss of self-control and critical reasoning, some Cape Town men also articulated a specific form of righteous 'anger as outrage' that was 'controlled and carefully aimed'. These claims were made by men of European origin and of higher rank and status, drawing on concepts of vertical honour which they transferred to a colonial context. Accordingly, they were both class- and gender-specific, though always interpreted in the context of the special configuration of race and ethnicity in the complex community of the Cape.[27]

One such justification for anger was provocation when social status was called into question, especially in instances when the respective ranks of the plaintiff and defendant were uncertain. Thus in 1777 Jacobus de Meijer, captain of the Company ship *Popkensburg*, defended himself on the charge of 'insulting' a senior lieutenant, one Jacobus Herder, whom he called a 'damned fellow' and challenged to a fight in front of his companions. The cause of the dispute was that several days out on the voyage from Asia to the Cape, Herder had complained at being served fish and pineapple instead of meat and vegetables, and insinuated that De Meijer had pocketed the money that the higher-ranking passengers had paid for their food. De Meijer was particularly incensed that Herder was challenging his authority and status: 'You are just a passenger here, who do you think you are? I consider you as just the same as my ship's boy.'[28] Another witness reported that De Meijer had angrily asked Herder if he thought that the ship's captain was the cook. Herder brought the case to the Council on their arrival in Cape Town, demanding that De Meijer apologize for such insulting words. De Meijer's response was that he may well have spoken in anger and that he was prepared to give Herder satisfaction and recognize him to be a man of 'honour and probity' as the Council directed, but that he had done so because his authority on board ship had been challenged by a passenger, in front of the other passengers and officers and within hearing of the ordinary crewmen.[29]

A similar contestation of status took place a few years later when Georg Karel Wentz was in charge of a burgher night watch patrol. On the evening of 25 January 1783, he grew frustrated at the noise they were making and their refusal to obey his orders to be quieter and to walk more slowly. Wentz pulled one of them aside and thrusting his fist under his nose said, 'You African armpit farm flies, red-nosed louse-ridden rascals, you've never had a hair on your chin, I'd rather do service with savages and *Caffers* than with burghers such as you'. The patrol members were highly offended by these words since they did not know 'what creature there is on this earth who has less honour than a *Caffer*'. They therefore brought a case of damage to their honour against Wentz.[30] Wentz admitted that he had spoken in anger but justified his behaviour by stating that he felt his authority as the duty sergeant on the watch was being undermined by young burgher men who refused to obey his orders. In so doing he demeaned the immature local farm yokels as worth less than the lowest of the low. The term *caffer* was not only a generic word of Arabic origin to refer to 'heathens' but in Dutch Cape Town it was specifically used for slaves who worked for the Company as 'executioner's assistants and a type of police force'. The insult was thus more than a racial one since it associated the young burghers with a particularly dishonourable and despised job.[31] Once again anger and the threat of a punched nose was the result of a challenge to authority and status, but the matter was settled by mediation once Wentz had justified to the Council the reasons for his angry words and physical threats.[32]

Alternative codes of honour: The failed duel

Although men of high status in late eighteenth-century Cape Town tended to turn to the authorities for judicial redress of insult to their honour rather than resorting to physical retaliation and violence, there is evidence that alternative codes of violent resolution among social elites also existed. In one case from 1782 these differences came clearly to the fore. In 1782 Pieter Meiring, the VOC's Commissioner for Civil and Matrimonial Matters, brought a civil action against Carel Matthijs Willem De Lille, a military captain stationed at the Cape Town Castle garrison. Both were men of rank and therefore the case may be seen in one sense as an example of 'horizontal' honour-related conflict between men of similar social status.[33] However, such conflicts also highlight the tensions that existed between resolving such matters by self-regulation and violence or by turning to the judicial authorities for redress.

The Commissioner's and captain's dispute arose one November evening during a fire which threatened several houses in the town. Both men were helping to extinguish, and in the presence of everyone De Lille shouted to Meiring 'in a passionate and hot-headed voice', demanding that he help him put out the flames of the house of one of his friends. 'If you won't set to', he shouted, 'you're a goddamn louse, a bad fellow, a scoundrel'. This episode was akin to the aforementioned cases involving public insult. As Meiring later told the Council they were 'shameful, heart-grieving and, for an honourable and good-natured man, intolerable words'. Meiring responded by telling De Lille that this was neither the time nor the place to be arguing but De Lille then hit him with his fist. When Pieter Cloete, one of Meiring's associates, intervened, De Lille threatened him with a dagger vowing, 'I'll stab you through and through'.[34] Cloete was raring for a fight and responded, 'shall we allow ourselves to be insulted here in the presence of all these onlookers, he has scolded you as well as me in ways that are most ugly'. Meiring persuaded Cloete to return home and for the moment an awareness of risk won over impulsive anger, as Meiring and Cloete realized that they were outnumbered by several soldiers standing by who were 'comrades' of De Lille.[35] The matter, however, did not rest there. The following morning De Lille insisted on following a more definitive means of violent resolution. He appeared at Cloete's house to announce 'we had issues last night, if you want satisfaction now come with me and I will give you satisfaction', adding that he would wait for him in the Company gardens, a clear invitation to settle matters in a duel.

Although duelling was most often associated with higher-ranking elites, especially among the military, it was not approved by the authorities. Most duels therefore took place out of public sight and so did not usually appear in the court records.[36] Meiring, however, was present and attempted to dissuade De Lille from being, as he put it, 'his own judge', an indication that he believed that honour-based disputes such as this should be resolved by the judicial authorities and not by self-regulation. Yet, he also showed his awareness of the conventions of the duel by adding that a proper match would be impossible since Cloete 'had no second' and that it would be best to delay the whole matter until that afternoon. De Lille retaliated in frustration and lunged at Cloete with his sword. Meiring then sprang between them and separated them, at which De Lille stormed out of the house.[37]

Instead of responding with like violence, Meiring laid a civil complaint against De Lille and the matter came before the Council of Justice. The opposing parties were reconciled once De Lille publicly expressed regret for his actions and words. He admitted that he had acted 'in haste' and he acknowledged Meiring to be 'an upright and honourable' (*braaf en eerlijk*) man.[38] Meiring's responses throughout this episode indicate that it was possible for members of the Cape Town elite to settle honour-based disputes judicially, rather than with violence. However, as both De Lille and Cloete's responses show, the possibility was not always taken up: codes of righteous anger and violent resolution still existed among men of rank, doubtless exacerbated by the presence of the military garrison. An emotional and legal regime that rejected passionate anger and sought settlement of honour disputes though judicial processes coexisted in late eighteenth-century Cape Town with patterns of honour-based violence that are familiar from other contexts.[39]

A matter for men?

The cases so far described came to the civil courts as actions brought by men of some status who believed that their honour should be restored by legal redress. Women appeared much more rarely as participants in such episodes. This may be because their social status was not as dependent on their public behaviour as was the case for men, although, as in other European and Asian societies discussed in this collection, they were particularly vulnerable to shaming on the grounds of inappropriate private and especially sexual conduct.[40]

An exceptional civil case that involved a female plaintiff indicates that women could also seek to protect their honour through the courts. In 1775 Elizabeth Esterhuijsen, unusually a married woman who was separated from her burgher husband, brought a case of injury to reputation against burgher Hendrik Stoute. Stoute was hiring a room in her house but gave notice that he wanted to leave. When he demanded part of his rent back she replied that he must leave his room clean and in the state in which he had received it, to which Stoute retorted in anger in the presence of other residents of the house: 'I've no need of this strumpet who has been rejected by the community!' He further insinuated that her daughter had sold herself for 300 rixdollars.[41] Esterhuijsen brought a case of civil injury against Stoute on the grounds that although she and her daughter 'were poor people, they were truly honourable folk'.[42]

Stoute claimed at the hearing that Esterhuijsen had not wanted to refund him his overpaid rent, and had called him a 'a 'louse-ridden blighter' (*luijse blixem*), so he 'had thus in anger scolded her back'.[43] It is significant that his 'scolding' took the form of a sexual accusation against both Esterhuijsen and her daughter, a form of insult which does not appear in the Cape Town records when applied to men. Moreover, Stoute stressed that Esterhuijsen was 'put aside by the community', a terrible indictment which may have been uttered in anger but which may indeed have been the case, reflecting the vulnerability of burghers to loss of reputation in an insecure colonial settler community.[44] Whether this accusation was related to the suspicion that Esterhuijsen and her daughter were involved in prostitution or whether it reflected the plight of a separated woman who was neither unmarried nor a widow is uncertain. The fact that Esterhuijsen was 'poor' also made her vulnerable to such accusations. But as a woman anxious to defend her reputation – and doubtless also because she needed this to maintain her living by renting rooms in her house – she brought the case to the authorities. The Council determined that both parties were guilty of dishonouring the other, and that they should each declare the other to be 'honourable persons'. Its sympathy for Esterhuijsen, however, was shown by the fact that it ordered Stoute to pay the costs.[45]

A contrasting case of anger and slander in public by a woman took place in 1784, when Rosetta van Bengal, a former slave who had married the burgher Harmen Aarts, insulted the wife and daughter of burgher Joseph Elsen. The two women were sitting outside their house when Rosetta assailed them with crudities that even the hard-bitten Council of Justice apologized for recording as, 'You old skunk, you animal I'll (pardon the phrase) kick your cunt so that you won't go any more.' Elsen reported that Rosetta appeared to be drunk, but two days later she again accosted his daughter as she was going to church with the words, 'that she'd better pray honestly'. Since she shouted this out in public, 'honour must have blushed', as Elsen later stated. When his daughter was walking back after the service, the taunts continued as Rosetta 'in a mocking manner asked again, "Leentje, Leentje, have you prayed, have you also prayed for me?"'.[46] A neighbour who witnessed all of this further reported that Rosetta added, 'you damned animal, who are you opening your cunt for, are you opening it for the dyer or the hangman?'[47] Elsen protested to the Council at such extreme public shaming of his wife and daughter, but Rosetta defended herself by saying she had been scolded and attacked by Elsen's wife, who had pulled her hair and hit her, and although she admitted acting hastily, Rosetta claimed she had acted in self-defence. The Council concluded that there had indeed been wrongs on both sides, and ordered that all parties, including Rosetta, should be declared as honourable persons and the costs be divided between them.[48] The severity of such explicit sexual insults, and especially the heinous association with the 'hangman', combined with the mocking of a woman on her way back from church, drove Elsen to make an official complaint.[49] The more notable aspect of the episode is that harsh words from a former slave woman with a foul mouth were treated on the same legal basis as insults between high-ranking men.

The honour of slaves

Rosetta van Bengal's name indicates that she was of South Asian origin, most likely a freed slave. In the records of civil courts, slaves and 'free blacks' (as emancipated slaves were called by the VOC) rarely appeared, a notable contrast to their regular appearance before the Council of Justice in criminal cases.[50] Slaves were viewed by the authorities and by those set above them as being without honour and so unable to bring any legal claim that it had been attacked. Yet while the honour of slaves might not have been recognized from their social superiors in colonial society, this lack of standing did not mean that they lacked a sense of honour themselves or failed to demand it from others. Slaves possessed a clear sense of selfhood asserted in a range of cultural and social forms as the rich historiography of Cape slavery has demonstrated.[51] Moreover, as Reid has shown for Southeast Asia, a region from which many Cape slaves originated, certain Asian legal codes recognized the rights of slaves, 'including the right to defend their dignity if abused'.[52] Several cases of public violence in Cape Town involving slaves were similar in form and function to those of free men in the town, clearly indicating that slaves had an equally developed sense of honour and that they responded to challenges to it with similar demonstrations of passion.[53]

One such manifestation by Cape Town slaves took a particularly violent, public and self-destructive form. This was running amok, characteristic of some regions of India and Southeast Asia and brought to the Cape by its Asian slave and convict migrants. Amok was an urban phenomenon involving seemingly random violence that was carried out by, and usually directed at, men in the public streets.[54] Sometimes dismissed as irrational mental illness, amok has been categorized as a specifically cultural form of response to depression, involving trance and belief in spirit possession.[55] Analysts of Makassarese and Bugis societies, from which many Southeast Asian slaves at the Cape originated, have also associated it with an acute awareness of rank and the intensity of *siri'*, meaning both 'self-worth' and 'shame'.[56] Suicidal violence was an acute response to shame, for 'it was better to die in defence of one's *siri'* ... than to live without it'.[57] Jungwon Kim and Alison Bailey explore this issue in their chapters in this volume.

As several scholars have shown, there are very few clear cases of amok in the Cape Town records, but public acts of violence by slaves were evidently triggered by affronts to *siri'* induced by disrespectful or inappropriate treatment. In 1739, for instance, Alexander van Macassar was affronted when he was sent to the kitchen and not allowed to serve at table, and in 1757 Baatjoe van Mandhaar was unwilling to work because nobody had remembered that it was his birthday.[58] Nor was this a response by slaves alone. Kerry Ward attributes the running amok of the Batavian convict and *caffer* Soera Brotto in 1786 to his loss of face and status after he was refused repatriation.[59] All of these affronts provoked anger which took the form of violent public attacks on other men, free and slave, in the vicinity.

Such forms of slave and convict anger in Cape Town followed patterns and codes of practice which were Asian rather than European in origin. As such they followed distinctive cultural expectations, but these were not ones that were recognized as mitigating by the VOC authorities, unlike the righteous anger of offended officials and burghers.[60] As with lower-ranking public brawlers, those who expressed anger in such demonstrative ways were treated as criminals to be duly punished by the full weight of the authorities.[61]

Conclusion

Angry outbursts frequently accompanied attacks on honour and reputation in late eighteenth-century Cape Town. As in seventeenth-century Sweden and nineteenth-century Brazil, anger could lead to violent confrontations in the form of duels or brawls. Such incidents were dealt with in the criminal courts and may thus be considered part of the global process by which the state has gathered to itself an ever more encompassing monopoly of the right to punish violently. Parallel to this familiar system, however, was a system of civil law in which the public expression of anger – unambiguously seen as a likely prelude to physical violence – was excoriated in both offender and victim. Although the possibility of righteous anger existed, most angry outbursts were considered to be unwarranted, and the possibility that circumstances might have justified an angry outburst was often not even raised in the court proceedings. These cases usually involved men of relatively high rank in the town, such as VOC officials, officers and free burghers, but freed slaves could also be involved. Although there were circumstances under which inhabitants of Cape Town turned to ritualized forms of violence to resolve such attacks on honour, such as house scorning and duelling, most men of higher status sought to avoid such behaviour. Still, aggrieved men of rank could successfully justify anger when their status was challenged by those not entitled to do so. Passionate anger was for the most part seen as inappropriate public behaviour, while restraint and emotional control were highly valued in this volatile, diverse colonial port.

Recourse to the law of defamation and appeal to the courts for restitution of status were characteristic tactics of the new commercial and middle classes of early nineteenth-century Cape Town, when the colony came under the control of Britain's mercantile empire.[62] This chapter shows that legal action and emotional restraint in response to challenges to honour were already encouraged and rewarded among the burghers of Cape Town in the later eighteenth century. The experience of Cape Town challenges the perception that the criminalization of duelling and brawling was the principal means by which civilizing processes reduced the incidence of violence in public life in the eighteenth and nineteenth centuries. The criminalization of violence generally implied that insults were no longer to be taken so seriously that they justified a violent response,[63] but the civil law system in Cape Town functioned to affirm the importance of honour, while offering an alternative to violent defence against attacks on it.

Notes

1   Western Cape Archives Repository (CA), Council of Justice (CJ), 1124, Eijsch
    [Claim] of Hendrick de Waal Corneliszoon, 1 August 1782, f. 288–9.

2   See, for instance, S. Gayo, '"Honor Moderno": The Significance of Honor in
    Fin-de-Siècle Argentina', *Hispanic American Historical Review*, 84, 3 (2004):
    475–98.

3   For example, L. Johnson and S. Lipsett-Rivera, 'Introduction', in *The Faces of
    Honor: Sex, Shame and Violence in Colonial Latin America*, ed. L. Johnson
    and S. Lipsett-Rivera (Albuquerque: University of New Mexico Press, 1998),
    11–12. A key study of honour and violence among the slaves and freed slaves
    of the nineteenth-century Cape Colony is R. Watson, *Slave Emancipation and
    Racial Attitudes in Nineteenth-Century South Africa, 1834–1842* (Cambridge:
    Cambridge University Press, 2012). For the application of ideas of honour
    to African material, see especially J. Iliffe, *Honour in African History*
    (Cambridge: Cambridge University Press, 2005).

4   For example, Robert Muchembled, *A History of Violence* (Cambridge:
    Polity, 2012); Pieter Spierenburg, *A History of Murder* (Cambridge:
    Polity, 2008); Anton Blok, *Honour and Violence* (Cambridge: Polity, 2001);
    Pieter Spierenburg, ed. *Men and Violence: Gender, Honor, and Rituals in
    Modern Europe and America* (Columbus: Ohio State University Press,
    1998); and Julius R. Ruff, *Violence in Early Modern Europe, 1500–1800*
    (Cambridge: Cambridge University Press, 2001). A recent study focusing on
    the Netherlands is Benjamin B. Roberts, *Sex and Drugs before Rock 'n' Roll:
    Youth Culture and Masculinity during Holland's Golden Age* (Amsterdam:
    Amsterdam University Press, 2012), especially Chapter 4.

5   For the fullest explication of this, see Robert Ross, *Status and Respectability in
    the Cape Colony, 1750–1870: A Tragedy of Manners* (Cambridge: Cambridge
    University Press, 1999), Chapter 2. On burgher status and aspirations to it, see
    Gerald Groenewald, 'Kinship, Entrepreneurship and Social Capital: Alcohol
    Pachters and the Making of a Free-Burgher Society in Cape Town, 1652–1795'
    (Ph.D diss., University of Cape Town, 2009); Teun Baartman, 'Fighting for the
    Spoils: Cape Burgherschap and Faction Disputes in Cape Town in the 1770s'
    (Ph.D diss., University of Cape Town, 2011); and Nigel Worden, 'Artisan
    Conflicts in a Colonial Context: The Cape Town Blacksmith Strike of 1752',
    Labor History, 46 (2005): 155–84.

6   On the forging of social identities in this context, see Nigel Worden, ed., *Cape
    Town between East and West: Social Identities in a Dutch Colonial Town*
    (Hilversum: Verloren and Johannesburg: Jacana, 2012).

7   Spierenburg, *A History of Murder*, 81. For material on such episodes in
    Cape Town, see Nigel Worden, 'Public Brawling, Masculinity and Honour',
    in Worden, ed., *Cape Town between East and West*, 194–211, and Nigel
    Worden, 'Demanding Satisfaction: Violence, Masculinity and Honour in Late
    Eighteenth-Century Cape Town', *Kronos*, 35 (2009): 32–47.

8   I am grateful to the editors of this volume for their invaluable assistance in
    shaping this argument. This research is part of a wider project entitled *Empires*

of Honour: Violence and Virtue in Colonial Societies, 1750–1850, funded by the Australian Research Council and directed by Penny Russell, University of Sydney. A database index of civil cases dealing with issues of honour and reputation for the period 1770–1808, on which this chapter is based, was compiled for the project by Teun Baartman in 2011–2012.

9 Peter N. Stearns, 'History of Emotions', in *Handbook of Emotions: Issues of Change and Impact*, 3rd edn., ed. Michael Lewis, Jeannette M. Haviland-Jones and Lisa Feldman Barrett (New York and London: Guilford Press, 2008), 17–31; Jan Plamper, 'The History of Emotions: An Interview with William Reddy, Barbara Rosenwein and Peter Stearns', *History and Theory*, 49 (2010): 237–65; Nicole N. Eustace et al., 'The Historical Study of Emotions', *American Historical Review*, 117, 5, (2012): 1486–531. For the Cape, a pioneering work is D. Van Zyl, '"Gij kent genoeg mijn gevoelig hart": Cape Dutch Emotion around the Turn of the Eighteenth Century' (M.A. diss., Leiden University, 2009).

10 For example, Carol Z. Stearns and Peter N. Stearns, *Anger: The Struggle for Emotional Control in America's History* (Chicago: University of Chicago Press, 1986); Nicole N. Eustace, *Passion Is the Gale: Emotion, Power and the Coming of the American Revolution* (Chapel Hill: University of North Carolina Press, 2008), especially 151–99; and Dorothee Sturkenboom, 'Historicising the Gender of Emotions: Changing Perceptions in Dutch Enlightenment Thought', *Journal of Social History*, 34, 1 (2000): 55–75.

11 See, for example, Robert Shoemaker, 'Male Honour and the Decline of Public Violence in Eighteenth-Century London', *Social History*, 26, 2 (2001): 190–208.

12 For discussion of the ways in which indigenous and the diverse immigrant inhabitants of the Cape were incorporated into a single legal system under VOC control, see R. Ross, 'The Rule of Law at the Cape in the Eighteenth Century', *Journal of Imperial and Commonwealth History*, 9 (1980): 5–16.

13 For examples of such cases related to sailors, see Nigel Worden, 'Strangers Ashore: Sailor Identity and Social Conflict in Mid-18th Century Cape Town', *Kronos*, 33 (2007): 72–83.

14 Nigel Worden, Elizabeth van Heyningen and Vivian Bickford-Smith, *Cape Town: The Making of a City* (Cape Town: David Philip and Hilversum: Verloren, 1998), Chapter 2.

15 John Holtrop, *Neerduitsch en Engelsch Woordenboek* Vol. 2 (Dordrecht: Blusse en Van Braam, 1823–4), 219.

16 CA, CJ 1119, Eijsch of Willem Stricker, 9 November 1780, f. 307–9.

17 Eustace et al., 'AHR Conversations', 1527.

18 Such practices also took place in early modern Rome, although the precedent for Cape inhabitants was more likely to come from rural Germany from where many VOC employees originated. Spierenburg, *A History of Murder*, 69 citing Ruth E. Mohrmann, *Volksleben in Wilster im 16. und 17. Jahrhundert* (Neumünster: Wachholtz, 1977), 271–7.

19 CA, CJ 1119, Eijsch of Willem Stricker, 9 November 1780, f. 311–12.

20 CA, CJ 874, Civiele Regtsrolle, 23 November 1780, f. 484–5.

21 CA, CJ 1119, Testimony of burgher Wilhelm Wernick, 16 October 1780, f. 313–4.

22 CA, CJ 1121, Eijsch of Jeremias Auret, 26 October 1780, f. 434–6.

23 CA, CJ 1121, Eijsch of Jeremias Auret, 26 October 1780, f. 429–30.

24 CA, CJ 874, Civiele Regtsrollen, 26 October 1780, f. 389–90.

25 CA, CJ 875, Civiele Regtsrollen, 25 January, 1 February and 15 February 1781, f. 43–6 and 69.

26 CA, CJ 1135, Eijsch of Christoph Lijste, 15 January 1784, f. 4–6.

27 This distinction is made in William I. Torry, 'Social Change, Crime and the Defense of Provocation', *Crime, Law and Social Change*, 36 (2001): 310. The quotation specifying class and gender comes from the analysis of late colonial North America in Eustace, *Passion Is the Gale*, 187.

28 CA, CJ 1110, Statement of *opperstuurman* Paulus Best, 25 January 1777, f. 15.

29 CA, CJ 871, Civiele Regtsrollen, 31 January 1777, f. 19–21.

30 CA, CJ 1125, Eijsch of Jacobus Smoudt, Johannes Mostert Louiszoon, Hendrik Kruger, Abraham Arendsz Loon, Jacobus Cornelis de Kat, Gielion Frederick Kock, Johannes Olckers and Hendrik Goedhart, 27 February 1783, f. 140.

31 Robert C. H. Shell, *Children of Bondage: A Social History of the Slave Society at the Cape of Good Hope, 1652–1838* (Hanover, CT: Wesleyan University Press, 1994), 189.

32 CA, CJ 1125, Report of the Mediators, 27 March 1783, f. 136–7.

33 On the differences between 'horizontal' honour involving the right of respect from an equal as opposed to 'vertical' honour involving respect due from those of differing rank, see especially Frank H. Stewart, *Honor* (Chicago: University of Chicago Press, 1994), 54–63.

34 CA, CJ 1125, Eijsch of Pieter Meiring, 5 December 1782, f. 34–5.

35 CA, CJ 1125, Statement of Pieter Cloete, 15 November 1783, f. 43v.

36 Ignaz Matthey, *Het Duel in de Nederlandse Geschiedenis* (Zutphen: Walburg, 2012), Spierenburg, *A History of Murder*, 77; A. J. Van Weel, 'De Wetgeving tegen het Duelleren in de Republiek der Verenigde Nederlanden', *Nederlands Archievenblad*, 81 (1977): 282–96. For a rare example of (a somewhat botched) duel between ship captains in Cape Town, see Worden, 'Public Brawling', 200–01.

37 CA, CJ 1125, Statement of Pieter Cloete, 15 November 1783, f. 43–44.

38 CA, CJ 1125, Report of the Mediator, Documents in Civil Cases, 16 January 1783, f. 53–54.

39 On the association of violence with differing emotional and legal regimes and the ambiguities of duelling in this regard, see especially Ute Frevert, *Emotions in History – Lost and Found* (Budapest: Central European University Press, 2011), 53–70. The classic study of the emergence of alternative 'bourgeois' regimes of male codes of honour is Robert A. Nye, *Masculinity and Male Codes of Honor in Modern France* (Berkeley: University of California Press, 1993).

40   This observation appears in most foundational and subsequent studies of honour's gendered character. See, for instance, Julian Pitt-Rivers, 'Honor and Social Status', in *Honour and Shame: the Values of Mediterranean Society*, ed. Jean G. Peristiany (London: Wiedenfeld and Nicholson, 1965), 43–6.

41   CA, CJ 1106, Testimony of *matroos* (sailor) Jan Hendrick Smit, 13 November 1775, f. 247–8.

42   CA, CJ 869, Civiele Regtsrollen, 21 December 1775, f. 214–15.

43   CA, CJ 869, Civiele Regtsrollen, 21 December 1775, f. 214–15. The insult is a variation of the common term of abuse, *luishond* meaning a 'scoundrel'.

44   On the importance of reputation in securing financial, social and political position in the Cape Town burgher population, see Gerald Groenewald, 'Entrepreneurs and the Making of a Free Burgher Society', 45–64 and Baartman, 'Protest and Dutch Burgher Identity', 65–83 both in *Cape Town between East and West: Social Identities in a Dutch Colonial Town*, ed. N. Worden (Johannesburg: Jacana and Hilversum: Verloren, 2012).

45   CA, CJ 869, Civiele Regtsrollen, 21 December 1775, f. 214–15.

46   CA, CJ 1132, Eijsch of Joseph Elsing (*sic*), 8 April 1784, f. 110–112.

47   CA, CJ 1132, Testimony of Hermanus van der Schijf, 5 April 1784, f. 117.

48   This seeking of mutual restoration of honour was a strong emphasis of the resolutions of the Cape Council of Justice, perhaps more so than in Europe. For discussion of this, see Teun Baartman, '"The Most Precious Possession": Honour, Reputation and the Council of Justice', unpublished paper, Violence and Honour in Settler Societies Conference (University of Cape Town, December 2012).

49   On the dishonour of association with the hangman, see Kathy Stuart, *Defiled Trades and Social Outcasts: Honour and Ritual Pollution in Early Modern Germany* (Cambridge: Cambridge University Press, 1999), 69–93.

50   For discussion and transcriptions of slave evidence in the criminal records, see Nigel Worden and Gerald Groenewald, ed., *Trials of Slavery: Selected Documents Concerning Slaves from the Criminal Records of the Council of Justice at the Cape of Good Hope, 1705–1794*, Second Series, No. 36 (Cape Town: Van Riebeeck Society, 2005).

51   This has been a key theme of the extensive historiography of slavery in the past few decades. For such work on the Cape, see especially Robert Ross, *Cape of Torments: Slavery and Resistance in South Africa* (London: Routledge, 1983) and Shell, *Children of Bondage*.

52   Anthony Reid, '*Merdeka*: The Concept of Freedom in Indonesia', in *Asian Freedoms: The Idea of Freedom in East and Southeast Asia*, ed. D. Kelly and A. Reid (Cambridge: Cambridge University Press, 1998), 144.

53   For work on this in the VOC period, see especially Kate Ekama, 'Honour among Slaves at the Eighteenth-Century Cape' (B.A. Hons diss., University of Cape Town, 2010) and Worden, 'Public Brawling', 207–10. For slave and freed slave honour in the nineteenth-century Cape, see Richard L. Watson, *Slave Emancipation and Racial Attitudes in Nineteenth-Century South Africa, 1834–1842*, Chapter 10.

54 John C. Spores, *Running Amok: An Historical Inquiry* (Athens, OH: Ohio University Center for International Studies, Southeast Asia Series,1988), 61–8; Ekama, 'Honour among Slaves', 36–45.

55 Spores, *Running Amok*, 104–10.

56 Leonard Y. Andaya, *The Heritage of Arung Palakka: A History of South Sulawesi (Celebes) in the Seventeenth Century* (The Hague: Martinus Nijhoff, 1981), 6; Christian Pelras, *The Bugis* (Oxford: Blackwell,1996), 206–7; and William Cummings, *Making Blood White: Historical Transformations in Early Modern Makassar* (Honolulu: University of Hawai'i Press, 2002), 164–5.

57 Andaya, *Arung Palakka*, 70.

58 For details of these cases, see Worden and Groenewald, *Trials of Slavery*, 169–75, 220–31 and 337–44.

59 Kerry Ward, *Networks of Empire: Forced Migration in the Dutch East India Company* (New York: Cambridge University Press, 2008), 266–7. See also Edna Bradlow, 'Mental Illness or a Form of Resistance? The Case of Soera Brotto', *Kleio*, 23 (1991): 4–16.

60 Torry, 'Social Change', 311–13.

61 For criminal sentencing and punishment and the ways in which these varied according to the status of the accused, see especially K. Bergemann, 'Crime and Punishment in the Cape Colony in the 1730s' (M.A. diss., University of Cape Town, 2012).

62 Kirsten McKenzie, 'Of Convicts and Capitalists: Honour and Colonial Commerce in Cape Town and Sydney', *Australian Historical Studies*, 118 (2002): 199–222; Kirsten McKenzie, *Scandal in the Colonies: Sydney and Cape Town, 1820–1840* (Melbourne: Melbourne University Press, 2004).

63 Honour-related violence continued to be condoned when it had to do with defending the honour of others. As Frevert points out, noble rage in defence of the weak remained acceptable for men, even when the violent defence of their own honour had been criminalized. See Frevert, *Emotions in History*, 97.

6

Death on a river: Honour and violence in an Australian penal colony, 1826–1827

Penny Russell

In the autumn of 1826, four convict workers plotted together to commit a murder. They were cedar-cutters, members of a timber gang who laboured in country north of Port Stephens, a lonely outpost of settlement in the penal colony of New South Wales. Around midday, witnesses would later allege, one man lured a ten-year-old Aboriginal boy to their hut with the promise of food. Two others then took the boy in a boat to a lonely stretch of river. They bound him tightly with wet bark and left him in the water to die.

The murder of a child may seem an unlikely place to seek evidence of the significance of honour in a colonial world. Yet the crime and its repercussions were entangled with threads of honour, both explicit and implicit. The case was soaked with emotion, from the violent context of its initial enactment to the discursive sites in which it was subsequently embedded while individuals and communities sought its just resolution. At each site, competing cultural understandings emerged of right and wrong, compassion and self-interest, justice and revenge. Analysing readings of the murder by colonial officials, the victim's indigenous community and the convicts themselves, this chapter examines honour's complex implication in violence, from a tense and isolated community on the Myall River to the penal capital of Sydney and the colonial public sphere.

Violence in these communities was varied and spectacular. The force of the law was displayed in New South Wales in the 1820s in frequent flogging of convicts and public hangings; its limitations could be seen in killings of Aboriginal Australians that often escaped official attention. Frontier violence was officially condemned, but in a decade of rapid pastoral expansion characterized by ruthless dispossession many colonists were becoming inured to its horror. Sanctions were limited and hard to enforce. Hitherto only one white man – and that too a convict escapee – had been hanged, in December 1820, for the murder of an Aboriginal person.[1] During the later months of 1826 the governor, Ralph Darling, did strive to prosecute an officer of the mounted police for the brutal murder of a captive Aboriginal man, but his efforts were thwarted first by the collusion of landholding magistrates in the area and later by the sympathies of a military jury.[2] Lieutenant Nathaniel Lowe's acquittal in May 1827 was greeted with enthusiastic applause from his assembled friends and supporters.[3] Colonists who deplored the wanton violence of the frontier, including mass murders that were often rumoured but until the infamous Myall Creek massacre in 1838 never successfully prosecuted, had to defer retribution to that 'tribunal where the Judge will exact the full and eternal penalty of his oft violated law'.[4]

In this environment the cold-blooded murder of a young Aboriginal child might have gone unnoticed by any but his own people. But three white men were sufficiently sure of the circumstances, and sufficiently indifferent to the fate of the culprits, to bring the case to official attention. By so doing they seemed to offer colonial authorities an opportunity to enact exemplary justice at little cost. The four cedar-cutters were all convicts, at various stages between bondage and freedom; they had no powerful friends or defenders, and no one bothered to question their culpability. The crime itself, moreover, seemed to defy explanation or justification. The case took some months to proceed to trial, but the verdict was swift and sure. All four were found guilty and, to emphasize the governor's 'just Reprobation' of such 'wanton and unprovoked Acts of Atrocity', condemned to death.[5] Yet through a series of twists, only one of the four was hanged, and that was for a different crime.

Insofar as they have taken notice of the incident, historians have seen it as embodying the paradoxes of British sovereignty. While Aboriginal people were, in theory, British subjects, the protection offered them by the law was, as Alan Atkinson has put it, 'meagre and inconsistent'.[6] Thus the men were condemned to death because they were relatively powerless and manifestly guilty, but reprieved because the authorities ultimately judged even these white lives to be of more value than Aboriginal lives. This is true as far as it goes, but there is more to be said. The trial itself was straightforward, productive of little but damning, if circumstantial, evidence of the cedar-cutters' guilt. In the extra-legal dimensions of the case, however, we find a more complicated story.[7] The formal administration of justice was everywhere entangled with the perplexities of a colonizing society.

In this broader social context we glimpse the varied 'community-based or spatially defined emotional styles' of penal New South Wales.[8] These can be discerned, as Benno Gammerl suggests, by tracing the ways in which the 'experience, fostering, and display of emotions' were connected to 'embodied practices', as well as to culturally sanctioned aesthetic expressions.[9] Eugenia

Lean underlines that historians must also attend to 'actual historical space and spatial linkages' when examining emotions, since they 'move and traverse over space, small-scale and large, and in messy, unexpected ways'.[10] In this spirit, I examine the spatial and cultural contexts in which emotional styles were formed and performed in a British penal colony, and focus on the ways in which honour operated as a motive and justification for violence.

The variety of discursive material generated by the case provides rich material for this endeavour. The language of honour framed the reactions of moralists and lawmakers, who praised the integrity and moral courage of those who brought the case to justice. In the deliberations of the courts and Executive Council, the private correspondence of the Chief Justice, the reactions of the press and comments on the case in the published memoir of Robert Dawson, the Port Stephens magistrate whose involvement made the trial possible, we find one understanding of honour. But Dawson's account, in particular, also offers insight into an honour culture that might easily be overlooked – that of the Worimi people, Tommy's community, who were swift to resent and avenge his death. And deep in the official records lies buried a glimmer of the moral reasoning and emotional style of the cedar-cutters themselves, a group on whose behalf no one spoke, and who seemed incapable (with one belated exception) of speaking for themselves.

In penal New South Wales, racial and social inequalities were stark and divisive. As in colonial Cape Town, discussed by Nigel Worden, disparate communities negotiated a fraught and often destructive coexistence with minimal protection from the state. Cedar-cutters as a group were particularly despised. Their labour was hard, their living rough and their conditions of life precarious: they lacked either protection or respect.[11] In turn, they were notorious for their ruthless violence towards Aboriginal people, in whose lands they toiled and whose humanity they manifestly failed to respect. Yet emotions may be found even in contexts where no codes of conduct or feeling were formally articulated or expressly recognized, including among such isolated or systematically subordinated groups as these. In the inarticulate emotional community of the cedar-cutters, elements of honorific violence can be identified.

Even in its 'most brutal and enigmatic forms', Anton Blok argues, violence is 'often honorific – especially under conditions of political insecurity when people "have to make themselves respected" in order to survive'.[12] His insight has particular relevance for this era of colonial governance in New South Wales, during which the authority of the state, its 'monopoly of violence', was by no means assured. Seeking the operation of an 'enigmatic', inarticulate concept of honour may help render past acts of violence more intelligible, despite the lack of an articulated or culturally sanctioned 'honour culture' among colonists. At the same time, the pervasiveness of violence dramatized what was at stake in the diversity of emotional styles that pertained among individuals and groups brought together through invasion and colonization.

Teasing out the multiple threads of Tommy's murder and its aftermath exposes the emotional, even visceral, freighting of moral principle in an uncertain world – the role of repugnance and disgust, the craving for dignity and respect, the importance of self-love and self-preservation. Reading the cultural narratives that were woven around this 'brutal and enigmatic' act of violence takes us a little closer to that intersection of embodied emotion and cultural expression where the concepts of integrity, humanity and honour reside. Different emotional communities, forged in diverse material circumstances, are revealed through the stories men told, and failed to tell, to justify their acts of violence.

The Myall River: Frontiers of violence

Fortune did not smile on Joseph Pennington, though he pursued her across the world. Arriving with his family in New South Wales as a free settler in October 1822, he was granted 1,500 acres of land on the Hunter River. Fifteen convict servants were also assigned to him; these he found a mixed blessing at best. Within the year he tried, without success, to give two of them back – one whose blasphemous language thwarted his efforts to maintain 'good order and regularity', and another whose disobedience to orders would, he feared, cause 'insubordination and confusion' among the rest.[13]

Perhaps because the management of men and land was not his forte, Pennington's farm did not prosper. By the early months of 1826 he had established his wife and daughter in Newcastle, given up his land to his neighbour, the wealthy emancipist Simeon Lord, and accepted employment from Lord as superintendent of a cedar-cutting gang on the upper reaches of the Myall River, north of Port Stephens.[14] In 1816 Governor Lachlan Macquarie had issued the first timber-cutting licence for this area, and since then gangs of men had been hard at work, felling the mighty trees, fashioning them into rafts and floating them downriver to Port Stephens, to be shipped to Sydney. A decade of intensive labour had destroyed almost all the accessible cedar; now only a few gangs lingered, Lord's among them, to clear away the last of the felled trees.

For thousands of years, this region had been the home of the Worimi people. In an environment where natural resources could be scarce, their social organization maintained a delicate balance. The population was thinly spread: small bands or loose agglomerations of families lived together within carefully observed territorial boundaries, coming together in large assemblies only for the purposes of ceremony or battle. Breaches or transgressions – of territory or protocol – generally brought swift retribution. Hostilities were fierce, but rarely fatal. Disputes between different bands were settled in formal battles that followed a strict and mutually understood format, in accordance with established codes. Internal differences or misdemeanours likewise met with formal punishment, the most common requiring a man to defend himself against spears flung at him by those he had offended. Since the formalities of retribution were understood by all, they facilitated an uneasy peace and respect for each others' interests, needs and territory. Shared codes of conduct created common cultural understanding and commonly experienced emotional registers.[15] Sympathetic white observers could readily interpret these patterns of behaviour within a frame of masculine honour. Robert Dawson, for example, understood that it was a 'point of honour' and manly pride among Worimi men not to shrink from hostile encounters or punishment.[16] The colonial press, however, was more inclined to dismiss the logic of retribution as the 'wild impulse of an untutored savage to revenge a real, or fancied wrong by the law of retaliation'.[17]

The arrival of cedar-cutters in the region dramatically destabilized a balance that had evolved over millennia. The cedar-cutters worked in small gangs consisting mainly of convicts and ex-convicts. Structurally, they were in a vulnerable position. Their contract work was back-breaking and poorly paid, and their employers took little responsibility for their safety. They were few in number and, for the most part, unarmed, in an unfamiliar environment inhabited by people they were quick to regard as treacherous enemies. Many of them had only recently been torn from their familiar rural or urban surroundings in Britain. Oblivious to and uncaring of the laws they were offending, and in any case lacking the power of choice, they soon became both agents and targets of violence.

The timber station on the Myall River, riven by multiple lines of authority and hierarchy, represented a distinct but by no means unified 'emotional community'.[18] It comprised just three huts – one occupied by Pennington alone, a storehouse nearby and a third on the far side of a small creek, which housed five labourers.[19] The physical boundary of the creek marked a social gulf between Pennington and the convict workers, but their daily propinquity irked him nonetheless. He found them impossible to manage, and each day he helplessly recorded instances of their idleness and insubordination. The men worked with deliberate slowness; they could turn a search for stray cattle into an excuse to avoid heavy logging work for a day at a time; Pennington regarded them as 'Sculkers'. For one, the 'double faced Stanley', he cherished a particular antipathy, and hoped to be 'rid' of him as soon as possible. The others he did not trouble to name individually. It was their corporate entity, their habit of association, that made them formidable. Being a new arrival to the region, he despised the men but was intimidated by them. Daily he deducted wages or withheld rations as punishment, but with little effect. His feeble authority was not helped when an injury to his leg confined him to his hut.[20]

In the crowded hut across the creek, the emotional and social cross-currents may have been more complicated than Pennington recognized. Thomas Stanley, at 37, was older than the rest and had been in the colony for longest: he held a conditional pardon and was probably the leader of the timber gang. John Ridgway, around 30 years old, had been assigned to Simeon Lord on first arriving in the colony in 1819. Now holding a ticket of leave, he had returned to his service in 1825.[21] Samuel Chipp and Edward Colthurst had been just 19 when transported for life for theft, in 1822 and 1824 respectively; both were assigned to Lord on arrival. Sandy-haired Colthurst, a bare five feet tall, was probably the slightest as well as the youngest and the most recent arrival among the men; his lowly status was reflected in his role as hutkeeper. These four had now worked together for about a year: within the last week or so they had been joined by another assigned servant, Daniel Woodhill, who had been in the colony for some years but only recently transferred to Lord's service. Though he necessarily shared the space of the others he, like Pennington, was an outsider. He became a critical witness to events.[22]

There are few hints of what the great rupture of transportation must have meant to these men, each so young when he left his home and family behind forever. For some, indeed, displacement may have begun earlier still. Convicts have been conventionally understood as a vagrant and rootless class, but recent interpretations have begun to explore the importance of domestic and emotional ties.[23] We can only speculate on the nature of such ties for these four men. Ridgway, 24 years old when convicted, bore tattoos on his forearms that perhaps recalled a wife or sweetheart left in England.[24] Colthurst had spent almost a year, first on a prison hulk and then on a transport ship, in the company of half a dozen men who had been convicted alongside him at the Chester Assizes. Only on arrival at Sydney was he separated from these now familiar associates and thrust, alone among strangers, into an environment filled with new terrors.[25] The ties convicts formed with each other were regularly thus disrupted, partly through the arbitrary dispensations of the convict system, partly as a matter of deliberate policy to discourage dangerous associations among a large and disaffected group. New associations were repeatedly formed, if only as a strategy for survival, but they were often fragile alliances.

The four seasoned workers on the Myall seemed united in their evident contempt for their new superintendent and in their edgy hostility towards the Worimi people. Pennington's fear and contempt were reserved for the men in his charge. The contrast in emotional style was especially apparent in their attitude to the child Tommy, who frequented the huts for several weeks before he met his death. Pennington, believing he had 'domesticated' the boy, regarded him with easy and indulgent kindness and allowed him to sleep in his hut. As one Sydney newspaper later commented, 'The poor little fellow had even rendered himself much regarded by his master, and was esteemed for his faithfulness and diligence in those various kind offices which he affectionately performed.'[26] For the labourers, as their actions showed, Tommy was not a child to be indulged, but a representative of the enemy they feared and loathed.

'Black Native Tommy disappeared this afternoon', Pennington recorded in his day-book on 8 May 1826.[27] At around midday, he and the boy had been resting in his hut when the sawyers returned from an unsuccessful search for cattle. Soon afterwards Colthurst, the young hutkeeper, came in, woke Tommy and invited him over to the men's hut for a meal. The invitation was a ruse: Daniel Woodhill would later testify that Chipp and Stanley took the boy away in a small boat, claiming they were taking him to see the cedar raft they were building down the river. Before they left, Stanley gathered a quantity of wet kurrajong bark, a strong and flexible fibre used by Aboriginal people and newcomers alike in place of rope. Colthurst and Ridgway then set off on foot in the same direction, saying that they were going kangaroo hunting, but refusing to let Woodhill go with them. All four men returned an hour later. There was no sign of Tommy, nor did they attempt to explain his absence.[28]

Three days later, 'a Black Man apparently the Chief of the Boys tribe' – perhaps his father – came to the station, on the pretext of bringing the men a kangaroo. He 'inquired particularly several times where was his piccaninny'. Stanley replied that he must have gone in search of the 'Bunyip' (a mythical monster, supposedly feared by all Aboriginal people). The callous remark intensified the anxiety and suspicion manifested by Tommy's father, who appeared 'dissatisfied…and unhappy about the boy'. He repeated his questions, but to no avail. Daniel Woodhill also seemed to notice the cruelty underlying Stanley's flippant remark: later he would testify that this exchange first led him to think that Stanley 'had made away with the boy'.[29]

Joseph Pennington was already certain that dark deeds had been afoot. Sending his employer a litany of complaints about Stanley, he added murder to the list. 'This fellow I strongly suspect (*but I have no proof*)', he wrote, 'enticed, by Duplicity, a poor little Black boy out of my Hut,… and with the assistance of others, dastardly Cowardly assassins like himself, took him in the Boat and forcibly drowned him'. He had not seen Tommy since – 'such are the Scoundrels I have about me'. His anger over the suspected action was intensified by the men's inappropriate emotional response. He had overheard their 'merriment' over the exploit, he wrote, and their warnings to each other 'not to say anything about it to me'.[30] Pennington did not ask whether all were equally amused by the exploit, or equally responsible. Pondering the relative ages, physique and experience of the cedar-cutters, we might wonder how much choice young Colthurst, especially, had over the part he played – and whether the mirth Pennington overheard was in some cases a trifle forced. It is impossible now to determine what role fear may have played in the men's apparent unity of action – but Stanley seems like a man few would have cared to cross.

Nor did Pennington pause to wonder why, with so much open space surrounding them, the 'warnings' were uttered within his hearing. He was careful not to reveal his suspicions, later telling the court that he had been 'afraid to make any enquiries, from an apprehension that some plot would be laid for him if he did so'.[31] In 'so remote and sequestered a situation',[32] he felt himself to be 'in the power of these men'.[33] If their imperfect concealment of the crime and their ostentatious merriment over it were, in fact, designed to exaggerate his helplessness and their strength, they succeeded in the short term. Pennington made no comment on Tommy's disappearance, either at the time or ten days later, when a floating object on the river proved to be a bloated, disintegrating corpse, 'much disfigured from being eaten... by the crows', which had drifted upstream on the rising tide. Pennington simply gave directions for the small body to be brought ashore and buried.[34]

If Pennington's own testimony is to be believed, fear kept him silent before the murder as well as after. As the men passed his hut at noon on 8 May, he later claimed, he overheard one say to the others, 'let us drown the little b-g-r'.[35] This detail does not appear in the records he made at the time, so he may have invented the remark, allowing his desire to see the men convicted to override his commitment to truth. But the implication of his words is that he overheard the men plotting to drown Tommy, yet did nothing to defend or even warn the child when Colthurst immediately afterwards came to fetch him. No one ever hinted that this failure made him an accessory to the crime. Robert Dawson applauded Pennington's 'natural good feelings and strong sense of justice' in the case;[36] the Attorney General, Saxe Bannister, likewise praised his 'integrity and right feeling'.[37] Even the most upright colonial observer did not expect that a white man should put his safety at risk for the sake of an Aboriginal child.

To the extent that honour is a 'moral imperative', based on the desire for respect among one's peers, its potential to conflict with the alternative imperative of obedience to authority and command is ever present.[38] This was likely the case among the cedar-cutters, who carved their own path in the forest with minimal respect for the orders of their superintendent. Indeed, they asserted the primacy of their peer group by ostentatiously withholding from Pennington what Alexander Welsh terms 'recognition respect' – the degree of consideration that one person or group accords another when deliberating over possible actions.[39]

The desire for respect or esteem, based on a sense of relative merit, may also be internalized as an individual understanding of rectitude and integrity, carrying with it a moral right to social status. For Joseph Pennington, conscience and the desire for social authority were always intertwined. Living in an isolated community on the edge of colonial society, his ideas of integrity, justice and order were under continual threat – not only from men whose moral codes were very different but from the peculiar demands of frontier life. Like many colonists, his hopes of bringing civilization to an untamed world were battered by the lawless savagery he encountered and which threatened to overwhelm him.[40]

Pennington's moral sensibility was sustained by his sense of belonging to a wider community whose moral standards he upheld, and whose coercive powers he could, in extremis, invoke. In this frontier environment, however, that law-abiding, middle-class, upstanding Briton and right-thinking Christian community had only a tenuous presence. Pennington's dislike for the rough men who were only nominally under his authority flowed from his recognition that the structures of authority and morality he had once taken for granted had failed him. His dislike preceded Tommy's disappearance and was intensified, not created, by his disgust at the murder he suspected. The murder seemed to underline his powerlessness – but it also licensed him to seek help from central authorities to do what he had longed to do, and neatly 'rid himself' of Stanley. At the first opportunity, he sought out the magistrate at Port Stephens, made his deposition and thankfully resigned the matter into his hands.

Port Stephens: Honour, retribution and justice

Like Pennington, magistrate Robert Dawson belonged to a new generation of colonizers, free emigrants who trusted that their commitment to agriculture, civilization, religion and justice would transform the raw violence of the penal colony into a well-regulated and harmonious society. As chief agent for the Australian Agricultural Company (AAC), in charge of its million-acre land grant and several hundred workers, bond and free, he had better opportunities than most to make the experiment. A respectable yeoman farmer from Essex, he had arrived at Port Stephens in the early months of 1826 and there established a rudimentary village settlement, which he intended should be characterized by harmonious black–white relations.[41]

Dawson believed in 'honourable colonisation' – that is, he assumed that an amicable exchange of civilization for land might be negotiated between Aboriginal Australians and a humanely disposed colonizer.[42] His sense of conscious rectitude was revealed in his respectful acknowledgement of the humanity of Aboriginal people. He argued passionately that a 'germ of good within' raised them above mere 'barbarous ferocity'.[43] Developing this idea in the account he later published of his time in Port Stephens, he was careful to point out the cultural logic that underpinned their apparently random acts of violence. His carefully cultivated rapport with the local communities allowed him some insight into their moral reasoning, though at times the gulf of understanding was too great and he could only be told that 'all black pellow do so'.[44] Acts of retaliation against white people, however, were to him not inexplicable, but culturally specific expressions of grief, anger and retribution.

While thus sympathetically drawing out the human responses of Aboriginal people, Dawson represented the sawyers who had preceded him to the district as fundamentally inhumane. These 'white savages' had no redeeming features. Before going to Port Stephens, he was warned 'against the savage and treacherous conduct of the tribes' in this part of the colony. He found the warnings unnecessary, and indeed misconceived: meeting many widows and orphans of Aboriginal men who had been shot for the most 'trifling causes', he thought it not surprising that the locals should now avoid the marauders and 'seek revenge, either openly or otherwise, for such injuries'. The Worimi were 'naturally a harmless people, and desirous to seek rather than to shun the society of white persons, as soon as they saw a disposition to treat them with humanity'. The cedar-cutters, by contrast, were 'not remarkable either for humanity or honesty', and treated the Aboriginal people 'as if they had been dogs'.[45] Sickened by the things he witnessed and worse things he heard about, Dawson had no desire to seek an explanation for these actions in natural human feelings. The barbarism of Aboriginal people was a product of culture and ignorance, he believed; the barbarism of the whites betrayed their voluntary, unforgivable descent into ungoverned and brutish passion.

Most of the white violence Dawson heard about could not be punished under law. Colonial courts did not allow Aboriginal testimony; nor could a man be incriminated by his own avowal of a deed. So when some Worimi people accused a white sawyer, in Dawson's presence, of killing ten of their friends and relations, the 'wretch did not deny it, but said he would kill them whenever he could. It was well for him', Dawson added, 'that he had no white man to depose to the facts, or I would have had him off to jail at once'.[46]

The appearance of Joseph Pennington gave Dawson an opportunity he had longed for, to bring some of these 'wretches' to justice. This time there were two white witnesses: not Pennington alone but also the convict servant, Woodhill, were willing to testify to all they had seen and suspected. Dawson immediately issued a warrant for the arrest of all four of the alleged murderers. By the time his police reached the station on the Myall River, Chipp and Stanley had fled. But Ridgway and Colthurst, who perhaps had not realized they too might be charged with murder, were arrested and brought to Carrington.

Dawson's retributive desire to bring white murderers to justice had an additional motive: to assert the arrival of a new moral culture at Port Stephens that would interrupt and quiet the cycle of retaliatory violence. Convinced that the Worimi people had a keen sense of justice, he hoped that if they could trust him to punish aggressors, they would moderate their own impulse to revenge. He was gratified that local Aboriginal people, whose resentment had been stirred by Tommy's death, attentively observed his examination of Ridgway and Colthurst. They displayed great satisfaction at seeing the men thus 'in charge of the soldiers and constables', and plied Dawson with 'many pertinent questions'.[47] Pursuing the case with vigour, he at once asserted his own authority, gave voice and some force to his sympathy for the plight of the local Aboriginal people and endeavoured to guard the white convicts and settlers under his administration from the danger of retaliatory attack. Thus a rule of law, mediated by his own central authority, might eventually prevail.[48]

Dawson next travelled up the Myall with Pennington, intending to question another witness. There he found that Tommy's nearest relatives, at least, had not been content to leave the dispensation of justice to white law. The man he had hoped to interview lay exhausted, terrified and close to death in his hut, 'hewn almost to pieces by an axe'. He told Dawson that he had been attacked 'in revenge for the murder of the boy', and thus suffered 'for the crimes of others'. Dawson's sympathy was limited, for he learned at the same time that sawyers in this district 'had slaughtered the natives indiscriminately, and left their carcasses to be devoured, as they actually were, by their dogs! Who could then wonder at the revenge the natives seek?'[49] McDonna had not committed the crime for which he paid, but to Dawson, as to the Worimi people, he represented a body of men with blood on their hands. Thus, though he did not explicitly condone the retaliatory violence of the Aboriginal people, Dawson again described it as comprehensible in human terms, as an angry response to the prior and indiscriminate violence of the cedar-cutters themselves.[50]

Only justice could forestall such well-founded resentment. When Dawson returned to Port Stephens, it was to find that one of his constables had accidentally shot an Aboriginal man, and that AAC sawyers now dreaded that they too would become the targets of vengeance. Dawson declined to issue them with firearms, trusting that his 'influence over the natives' would be sufficient to 'preserve the peace which had hitherto so happily been maintained between us'. Though soon convinced that this shooting was indeed an accident, he made a great display of sending the constable under military escort to Sydney for trial. He had 'sent two white fellows off to be hanged for killing little Tommy', he reminded his Aboriginal friends; now he promised to have his constable hanged too. He was pleased to find that his promises of justice had apparently staved off the threat of retaliation, and congratulated himself that the Aboriginal community's confidence in him had served to 'moderate those feelings of revenge which might otherwise have been indulged on this tragical occasion'.[51]

The humane or 'honourable' colonization that Dawson imagined was always a myth. By attributing the violence of colonization to the disposition of a lower social order, he evaded a less palatable reality: that it was inherent in the act of dispossession, in which landholders like himself were fully implicated.[52] The brutality of the cedar-cutters, sickening though it might be, would in the long term prove less destructive, physically and culturally, than Dawson's humane and enlarged understanding, his commitment to peace and justice and his million-acre land grant.[53] Dawson, bringer of civilization and justice, planned to impose a new social order at Port Stephens. His benevolent despotism was the first step in a campaign of total displacement, in which Worimi lands would be made over to colonial agriculture, and the lifeways that gave meaning to their honour culture would be gradually obliterated. The larger story of dispossession he represented ensured that the cycle of retaliatory violence could never be closed in a court of law.

Sydney: Narratives of violence and humanity

On 12 September 1826, John Ridgway, Samuel Chipp, Edward Colthurst and Thomas Stanley were tried before the Supreme Court in Sydney. Chipp had been arrested and committed for trial in June; Stanley, still on the run, was declared to be 'equally prosecuted' with the rest.[54] Dawson and Pennington were summoned to Sydney as witnesses.

In her perceptive discussion of culture and punishment in nineteenth-century British Columbia, Tina Loo suggests that the success of a cultural defence hinged on the 'quality of the story told in court' – its narrative coherence, internal consistency and plausibility in relation to those stories through which judges and juries ordered and understood the world. Narratives on behalf of those who were complete 'cultural outsiders' could be more effective than those that evoked a cultural defence for white working-class masculinity, which was more likely to be seen as debased and degraded than fundamentally 'different'.[55] Loo's insight applies to the cedar-cutters' case, both within and beyond the courtroom. Whereas some attempt was made to narrate instances of Aboriginal retaliatory violence in culturally intelligible terms, there was no discernible effort to weave an intelligible story around the cedar-cutters' actions. Attorney General Saxe Bannister, who acted as prosecutor, thought it 'as foul a murder as is possible to be conceived', and that a 'more unmitigated case was never presented to a court of justice'.[56] Chief Justice Francis Forbes felt the same: 'a more cruel, unprovoked, and atrocious murder I never tried'.[57]

The men offered no defence, and none was offered on their behalf. Telling no stories, they nevertheless stood condemned equally by their silences and their words. When Dawson had examined Ridgway and Colthurst at Port Stephens, they denied everything, insisting that none of them had seen the boy about the place that day. Summing up at the trial, Forbes reminded the jury that these denials were directly contradicted by 'the positive testimony given by the witnesses, some of whom were of their own party'. Their stubborn silence was moreover belied by the incriminating effect of the reports, offered freely and often verbatim by witnesses, of their speech on the day of Tommy's disappearance and after. Colthurst had invited Tommy to the hut. Chipp had suggested taking the boy down the river. Stanley had gathered a quantity of kurrajong bark and asked Chipp if it would 'do'. Chipp had agreed that it would, if there was 'enough of it'. When Chipp and Stanley put Tommy in their boat, Ridgway had warned them not to let the 'little bugger' get away. 'We will take damned good care of that', Stanley assured him. As the boat departed Woodhill heard the frightened boy protesting and demanding the promised meal, only to be told, with a growl, that he would get his 'pipe' tomorrow. Pennington had heard all the men warning each other to say 'nothing about it' to him. Later Stanley had – 'inadvertently', as the *Gazette* later opined – identified the bloated and disfigured corpse as Tommy, and then tried to cover the slip by surmising that he must have fallen accidentally into the river.[58]

All 'were engaged in one common transaction', Forbes instructed the jury; therefore 'what one said or did, was to be taken as evidence against the whole'. Thus condemned out of their own mouths, the cedar-cutters offered no alternative account of their actions. The judge declared that the evidence, although circumstantial, had impressed 'strongly upon his mind, throughout the whole of the case, that the boy had been made away with'. The jury agreed, and after a short consultation returned a guilty verdict. Forbes proceeded at once to sentence the prisoners. The court, he told them, had 'in vain looked for any thing like a motive which could have induced them to perpetrate the crime'. Finding none, and hoping that their example would 'show others that they could not destroy the natives with impunity', he ordered their execution the following week.[59]

If the executions had taken place as planned, the story would have ended there, with few voices raised in protest. By hanging four men whom nobody cared about, the government could have reinforced its message that the indiscriminate killing of Aboriginal people would not be tolerated, and for everyone else it would have been business as usual. Instead, through a series of twists and delays, sympathy gathered for the plight of the condemned men. The nature of their crime receded from view as the convicts' story was caught up in different narratives of recurrent social concern. Debates about the emotional underpinnings and honourable justification of state and personal violence continued, but amid those debates the pain of the original victim and his community was swiftly forgotten.

Throughout the trial and sentencing, Forbes had insisted that all four men were equally guilty. Immediately afterwards, however, he referred the case to the Executive Council, which recommended that Ridgway and Colthurst, whom they judged to be 'less criminal', should be reprieved.[60] Dawson disapproved, telling the Sydney *Monitor* that these notoriously bad characters 'deserved no pity, looking to their other misdeeds', but the paper concluded that it was 'well to err on the side of mercy'.[61] In any case, some considered their new fate – life imprisonment with hard labour on Norfolk Island – to be worse than death. Governor Darling had recently revived Norfolk Island as a place of secondary punishment, and the *Monitor* in particular was appalled by the spectre. Removed from civilization, female companionship and any prospect of freedom, it was presumed that prisoners would descend into an inescapable abyss of misery and vice.[62]

In December 1826 the brig *Wellington* set off for Norfolk Island with 66 convicts aboard, Ridgway and Colthurst among them. Two days from their destination, about half the convicts broke free and seized the brig, hoping to escape to South America. Recaptured when they stopped to take on water in New Zealand, they were returned to Sydney and placed on trial. In February 1827, 23 'pirates' were condemned to death. Among them was young Edward Colthurst, although several witnesses testified that he had taken little part in the uprising.[63]

The pirates' 'natural' desire for liberty, combined with the magnanimity they showed to their overthrown gaolers, had attracted widespread public sympathy.[64] Daunted by the prospect of hanging so many men before an indignant crowd, the Executive Council chose to extend mercy to the majority. In the end they selected five men to hang, mainly on the basis of the 'vicious course of their previous lives'.[65] These were men who had previously been reprieved from death sentences – they were held to have abused the clemency thus offered them and to have forfeited their lives more than once. The compromise satisfied most Sydney editors, who agreed that justice had been tempered by mercy. The *Monitor* alone demurred. This act of piracy was no crime at all, the paper argued, but a manly bid for freedom. It was wrong that men should hang for such an act, and equally unjustifiable that they should hang for a crime for which they had previously been pardoned. The executions thus showed the government to be both tyrannical and capricious.

Edward Colthurst was one of the unlucky five. 'I die innocent!' he cried from the scaffold on 12 March 1827, awaiting the fatal drop. Although the *Monitor* believed he was referring to Tommy's murder, most observers understood him to mean only that he was innocent of piracy.[66] And by this time, the piracy was all that mattered: amid the upsurge of popular feeling it evoked, Colthurst died before a sympathetic, not a hostile crowd.

The night before he died, Colthurst told Anglican clergyman William Cowper that he was not involved in Tommy's murder. He confirmed that Chipp and Stanley had killed the child, but he insisted he had not been present, and offered a justification, of sorts, for their actions. Though his story made no direct mention of 'honour', it nevertheless hinted at the exercise of 'honorific violence'. Tommy, he said, had previously persuaded two of the men to go with him to a place across the river, where (in Cowper's words) they found 'a number of Blacks were waiting and devising the[ir] destruction or injury': the boy had 'led them into danger before they were aware of the plot against them'. They managed to escape, but were bent on revenge. Relaying this story to the Colonial Secretary, Cowper added that Stanley likewise had told him 'that it is no uncommon thing for the Blacks to use their own people' in this way as decoys.[67]

Colthurst's story is a reminder that while the cedar-cutters were certainly aggressors, they had also become targets in a cycle of violence of which Tommy's death was more a consequence than a cause. Whether their earlier aggressions were unprovoked or a response to perceived or actual danger, their effect had been to make the danger real indeed. Tommy's murder paradoxically reveals the depth of their fear, the lengths to which they felt they must go to keep the upper hand in a relatively even contest. It seems to have been a strategy aimed at reprisal and survival, a ruthless and deliberate claim to recognition. This is further hinted in Stanley's reported remark, after Tommy's body was hauled from the water, that he 'did not think the blacks would come again about the place to be used as guides, on account of the boy being put aside'.[68] In their unprotected state the cedar-cutters certainly acted on the assumption that a reputation for ruthlessness was their only safeguard. The 'honour' they sought was not moral esteem, but 'recognition respect': the Worimi people would never esteem them, but must learn to fear them.

When Colthurst died, the 'principals' in the murder, Chipp and Stanley, were still alive. It had been decided that, to emphasize the government's message that atrocities against Aboriginal people would not be tolerated, these two should be hanged in Port Stephens, close to the site of their misdeeds.[69] 'To spare such men would, indeed, be a waste of mercy', wrote the *Sydney Gazette*. 'Oh, that the living – the living – may lay such things to heart, and profit by the awful spectacle that will take place.'[70] But as Stanley was still on the run when the sentence of death was passed, Chipp's execution was delayed until his associate also could be tried and sentenced. Stanley was taken up in October, but for want of a principal witness his trial was postponed until early March.[71] Then the sentence of both men was again respited to allow them to be conveyed to Port Stephens.[72]

When Robert Dawson received official notice to prepare for the 'fatal ceremony', the news produced 'painful excitement' in his tiny community. Coffins were made ready and a platform and drop erected between two high trees; the arrival of the 'unhappy criminals' was awaited with 'anxious expectation'. Dawson was dismayed to have responsibility thus returned to him. To hold the executions locally, he feared, would exacerbate, not allay, racial tensions. His anxiety deepened when some Aboriginal men visiting the region wounded an AAC shepherd with a spear. Dawson feared the 'unfavourable effect' of this incident upon his convict servants, at a moment when men of their class were about to suffer for what he now described as a 'similar offence'. To show the convicts that he desired to protect *all* parties, he at once set off on a spectacular but abortive expedition to secure the offenders. Before he left, he wrote to beg the governor to 'suspend the intended executions until the result of my pursuit should be known'.[73] Darling complied.[74]

The decision to hang the men in Port Stephens was intended to lend spectacular emphasis to the power of central authority. Instead, it re-embedded the case in the complicated local politics of authority, justice and race relations where it had originated. Little of this was apparent to watchers in Sydney, who saw only a succession of frivolous delays. Even by December, Chipp had been regarded as an 'unfortunate being' as he languished in gaol with a death sentence over his head; by early April the *Australian* could 'hardly believe, that after so long a delay, it can seriously be designed to put these men out of existence';[75] and by mid-April the paper freely expressed the hope that the 'unfortunate wretches' would not be hanged.[76] By this time Darling had decided, and even Forbes agreed, that justice could no longer be served by the executions.[77] On the morning of 27 April, the two men solemnly followed their coffins to a brig bound for Port Stephens – only to be removed in the afternoon to a prison hulk, whence they would be forwarded to Norfolk Island to spend the rest of their lives in chains.

The fiasco appalled Saxe Bannister, who had left the colony before Stanley's trial. Dawson's published account of the Worimi people had convinced Bannister that they had a 'keen sense of justice', and that if assured that justice was being done, they would 'repress their dispositions to do it in their own way'. Alas, without the 'slightest justification', the administration of the law had been 'taken out of the proper channel'. Dawson was noted for 'his kind consideration of the natives.... Yet in such a case of really frightful atrocity, the humane magistrate sets up a plea of expediency, and the governor yields to it, and pardons murderers in a way that in England would at once cause universal remonstrance'.[78] Bannister roundly condemned Darling's acquiescence in Dawson's logic.

In the stormy debate over the execution of Stanley and Chipp, Colthurst's meagre defence was never publicly aired. The decision to reprieve the men stemmed partly from Dawson's judgement of local politics and 'expediency' and partly from humanitarian views about the length of time for which men could be held in limbo under sentence of death. When sympathy swung towards the murderers, it was for the plight of their vulnerable bodies, not recognition of the circumstances that had prompted the crime.[79] One Sydney paper, indeed, invoked the lack of motive as cause to doubt their guilt. The pro-government *Gazette* retorted that the 'bad passions of men instigated by malice, hatred, or envy, will not seek long for a motive to prompt them to the commission of the greatest enormities'.[80]

These swings between sympathy, expediency and arguments about humanity in the later stages of the case were aired in an emotional community far removed from that in which the murder was plotted and carried out. The emotional and ethical underpinnings of violence were susceptible to discordant interpretations as their narration shifted from a tiny community at the fringe of settlement to the more articulate discourses of courts and press in the city. Honour was felt, experienced and expressed by human individuals located within particularities of time, place and circumstance.

In the frankly brutal society of a penal colony that was also a frontier settlement, stark moral choices were faced, and justified, by individuals and by communities large and small, vocal and inarticulate. These choices were not abstract musings on principle but – as Joseph Pennington was acutely aware – could have immediate, practical implications for personal safety. The lines of respect owed to peers, to rivals and to self ran jaggedly between considerations of what was right and what would maintain a balance of power judged essential for survival. An overarching story of dispossession thus framed multiple complex interactions, grounded in time and place, in which raw emotions and raw violence were composed into imperfect narratives of honour.

Notes

1   *R v Kirby and Thompson*, 14 December 1820, Decisions of the Superior
    Courts of NSW (NSWSupC), ed. Bruce Kercher, published by the Australasian
    Legal Information Institute, http://www.austlii.edu.au/au/cases/nsw//
    NSWSupC/1820/11.html, accessed 8 May 2013.

2   *R v Lowe*, 18 May 1827, NSWSupC, http://www.austlii.edu.au/au/cases/nsw//
    NSWSupC/1827/32.html, accessed 8 May 2013. Among many discussions of
    this notable case, see Kelly K. Chaves, '"A Solemn Judicial Farce, the Mere
    Mockery of a Trial": The Acquittal of Lieutenant Lowe, 1827', *Aboriginal
    History*, 31 (2007): 122–40; Lisa Ford, *Settler Sovereignty: Jurisdiction
    and Indigenous People in America and Australia 1788–1836* (Cambridge,
    Mass: Harvard University Press, 2010), 120–28; Lauren Benton, *Law and
    Colonial Cultures: Legal Regimes in World History, 1400–1900* (Cambridge:
    Cambridge University Press, 2002), 187–91.

3   *Australian* (Sydney), 23 May 1827.

4   *Sydney Gazette* (hereafter *Gazette*) 30 September 1826.

5   *Gazette*, 27 September 1826.

6   Alan Atkinson, *The Europeans in Australia, Vol. 2* (Melbourne: Oxford
    University Press, 2004), 164. See also R. H. W. Reece, *Aborigines and
    Colonists: Aborigines and Colonial Society in New South Wales in the 1830s
    and 1840s* (Sydney: Sydney University Press, 1974), 114–16; Brian H. Fletcher,
    Ralph Darling: A Governor Maligned (Melbourne: Oxford University Press,
    1984), 188.

7   See *Qualities of Mercy: Justice, Punishment and Discretion*, ed. Carolyn
    Strange (Vancouver: UBC Press, 1996) for model explorations of
    postconviction justice.

8   Benno Gammerl, 'Emotional Styles – Concepts and Challenges', *Rethinking
    History: The Journal of Theory and Practice*, 16, 2 (2012): 161.

9   Gammerl, 'Emotional Styles', 163.

10 Eugenia Lean, '*AHR* Conversation: The Historical Study of Emotions',
    American Historical Review, 117, 5 (2012): 1518.

11 For a defence of the cedar-cutters' reputations, see Norma Townsend,
    'A Strange, Wild Set? Cedar-cutters on the Macleay, Nambucca and Bellinger
    Rivers, 1838 to 1848', *Labour History*, 55 (1988): 9–21.

12 Anton Blok, *Honour and Violence* (Cambridge: Polity, 2001), 9.

13 Joseph Pennington to E.C. Close, NSW Colonial Secretary Papers, Letters
    received, NRS 897, 4/1809: 98–103S, AONSW.

14 Emancipists were convicts whose sentences had ended, by expiry or free
    pardon.

15 This sketch is based on descriptions in Robert Dawson, *The Present State
    of Australia; A Description of the Country, its Advantages and Prospects*
    (London: Smith, Elder & Co, 1830), eg 64–65; 287–89. See L. R. Hiatt
    Arguments About Aborigines: Australia and the Evolution of Social

Anthropology (Cambridge: Cambridge University Press, 1996), 83–84; Mark Finnane, '"Payback", Customary Law and Criminal Law in Colonised Australia', *International Journal of the Sociology of Law*, 29 (2001): 297–302, G. W. Trompf, *Payback: The Logic of Retribution in Melanesian Religions* (Cambridge: Cambridge University Press, 1994).

16   Dawson, *Australia*, 64–65.

17   *Gazette*, 20 April 1827.

18   See Barbara H. Rosenwein, 'Worrying about Emotions in History', *American Historical Review*, 107, 3 (2002): 821–45.

19   *Gazette*, 23 September 1826.

20   Joseph Pennington to Simeon Lord, 23 May 1826, NSW Executive Council Minute Books, 1119, no 2, AONSW.

21   Tickets of leave enabled convicts to work for wages; conditional pardons provided the rights of a free citizen within the colony, but they did not allow former convicts to return to England.

22   Information compiled from Convict Transportation Registers Database, http://www.slq.qld.gov.au/resources/family-history/info-guides/convicts. NSW Convict Indents, 1788–1842, NRS 12188 AONSW: accessed via ancestry.com, 8 May 2013.

23   Kirsty Reid, *Gender, Crime and Empire: Convicts, Settlers and the State in Early Colonial Australia* (Manchester: Manchester University Press, 2007); Paul Donnelly, '"When This You See Remember Me": Convict Love Tokens and Related Keepsakes', *Australasian Victorian Studies Journal*, 3, 1 (1997): 22–37.

24   NSW Certificates of Freedom, 41/123 26 January 1841, NRS 12210, Item 4/4364, Roll 1008, AONSW: accessed via ancestry.com, 8 May 2013.

25   England and Wales Criminal Registers; UK Prison Hulk Registers and Letterbooks; Australian Convict Transportation Registers: accessed via ancestry.com, 8 May 2013.

26   *Gazette*, 30 September 1826.

27   Pennington to Lord, 23 May 1826.

28   *R v Ridgway, Chipp, Colthurst and Stanly*, 20 September 1826, NSWSupC, http://www.austlii.edu.au/au/cases/nsw/NSWSupC/1826/62.html; *R v Stanley*, 3 March 1827, NSWSupC, http://www.austlii.edu.au/au/cases/nsw//NSWSupC/1827/12.html.

29   Appendix to Executive Council: Minutes 4/1438, AONSW.

30   Extract from Mr Pennington's letter to Lord, dated 11 May 1826. Appendix to Executive Council: Minutes 4/1438, AONSW.

31   *R v Ridgway et al.*

32   Dawson, *Australia*, 43.

33   *R v Stanley*.

34   *R v Ridgway et al.*

35   *R v Ridgway et al.*

36   Dawson, *Australia*, 233.

37   Saxe Bannister, *Humane Policy; or Justice to the Aborigines of New Settlements* (London: Thomas and George Underwood, 1830), ccxl.

38   Alexander Welsh, *What Is Honor? A Question of Moral Imperatives* (New Haven: Yale University Press, 2008).

39   Welsh, *What Is Honor?*, 3.

40   See Penny Russell, *Savage or Civilised? Manners in Colonial Australia* (Sydney: University of New South Wales Press, 2010), esp. 27–34.

41   Dawson, *Australia*; see also E. Flowers, 'Dawson, Robert (1782–1866)', *Australian Dictionary of Biography*, Vol. 1 (Melbourne: Melbourne University Press 1966), 298–300; Damaris Bairstow, 'With the Best Will in the World: Some Records of Early White Contact with the Gampignal on the Australian Agricultural Company's Estate at Port Stephens', *Aboriginal History*, 17, 1 (1993): 6–8; Mark Hannah, 'Aboriginal Workers in the Australian Agricultural Company 1824–1857', *Labour History* 82, (2002): 17–33; Russell, *Savage or Civilised?*, 53–79.

42   For critical accounts of this erroneous belief, see John Docker, *The Origins of Violence: Religion, History and Genocide* (Sydney: University of New South Wales Press, 2008), esp. 161–87; and Richard Waswo, *The Founding Legend of Western Civilization: From Virgil to Vietnam* (Hanover, CT: Wesleyan University Press, 1997), esp. 236–52.

43   Dawson, *Australia*, xiii.

44   Dawson, *Australia*, 288, 321. Dawson used 'pellow' (meaning fellow) to depict Aboriginal speech.

45   Dawson, *Australia*, 20–21, 41, 58.

46   Dawson, *Australia*, 58.

47   Dawson, *Australia*, 76.

48   See, for example, Dawson, *Australia*, 84–6.

49   Dawson, *Australia*, 79–80.

50   Dawson must have reported McDonna's subsequent death to the authorities: Forbes CJ later wrote that the father of the murdered boy had slain the first white man he came across, 'according to the rite of his countrymen, which demands blood for blood'. Forbes to Horton 15 May 1827, cited in *R v Ridgway*, note 5. No Sydney newspaper reported McDonna's death.

51   Dawson, *Australia*, 84–91.

52   See Russell, *Savage or Civilised?*, 91–99.

53   Docker, *Origins of Violence*, 218.

54   *R v Ridgway et al.*

55   Tina Loo, 'Savage Mercy: Native Culture and the Modification of Capital Punishment in Nineteenth-Century British Columbia', in Strange, ed., *Qualities of Mercy*, 116–20.

56   Bannister, *Humane Policy*, ccxl–ccxlii.

57   Francis Forbes CJ to Horton, 15 May 1827, cited in *R v Ridgway*, Note 5.

58   *R v Ridgway et al.*; *Gazette*, 20 April 1827.

59   *R v Ridgway et al.*

60 NSW Executive Council Minute Books, 4/1515 No. 19 reel 2436, AONSW; Governor Ralph Darling to Earl Bathurst, 8 October 1826, *Historical Records of Australia (HRA)*, Series 1 Vol. 12, 632.

61 *Monitor* (Sydney), 29 September 1826.

62 *Monitor*, eg 9, 16 March 1827.

63 *Australian* and *Gazette*, 13 December 1826, 10 and 16 February 1827.

64 Amid prolific commentary, see in particular *Australian*, 23 February, 1, 10 and 13 March 1827; *Gazette*, 24 and 27 February, 3, 6, 13 and 29 March 1827; *Monitor*, 24 February, 2 and 16 March 1827.

65 NSW Executive Council Minutes, 5 March 1827, cited in David Plater and Sue Milne, '"The Quality of Mercy is not Strained": The Norfolk Island Mutineers and the Exercise of the Death Penalty in Colonial Australia 1824–1860', *ANZLH E-Journal*, Refereed Paper no 1, (2012): 28. http://www.anzlhsejournal.auckland.ac.nz/pdfs_2012/Plater-Milne-Piracy-and-mercy.pdf, accessed 8 May 2013. See also Erin Ihde '"Bold, manly-minded men" and "sly, cunning base convicts": The Double Standard of Escape', *Journal of Australian Colonial History*, 7 (2005): 123–38.

66 See, for example, *Australian*, 13 March 1827; *Gazette* 13 March 1827; *Monitor*, 16 March 1827. On scaffold statements, see Kathy Laster 'Famous Last Words', *International Journal of the Sociology of Law*, 22 (1994): 1–18. See also Karen Halttunen, *Murder Most Foul: The Killer and the American Gothic Imagination* (Cambridge: Harvard University Press, 1998).

67 William Cowper to Alexander McLeay, 19 March 1827, NSW Executive Council Minutes Number 29 4/1515 reel 2438, AONSW.

68 *R v Ridgway et al.*

69 *R v Ridgway et al.*, note 5.

70 *Gazette*, 14 October 1826.

71 *Gazette*, 7 October 1826; Darling to Bathurst, 8 October 1826, *HRA* Series 1 Vol. 12, 632; *Australian* 25 November 1826, 6 March 1827.

72 *HRA* Series 1 Vol. 13, 858.

73 Dawson, *Australia*, 231–3.

74 Fletcher, *Ralph Darling*, 186.

75 *Australian*, 3 April 1827.

76 *Australian*, 11 April 1827.

77 Forbes to Horton, 15 May 1827. Although Darling obtained confirmation of the pardon from the king, he was rebuked for failing to explain adequately the delays that had made it necessary. Darling to Bathurst, 13 May 1827, *HRA* Series 1 Vol. 13, 300–01; Right Hon W Huskisson to Gov Darling, 29 November 1827, *HRA* Series 1 Vol. 13, 625–26.

78 Bannister, *Humane Policy*, ccxl–ccxliv.

79 See the essays by Greg T. Smith and Simon Devereaux in *Qualities of Mercy*, ed. Strange, 21–76.

80 *Gazette*, 20 April 1827.

7

Of clubs and whiskers: Young men, honour and violence in the backlands of Northeast Brazil, 1865–1889

Martha S. Santos

One October afternoon in 1883, a 32-year-old day labourer named Alexandre Rodrigues and a 25-year-old farmer, Luís Pereira de Sousa, engaged in a fight outside a residence in the rural northeastern town of Santa Cruz, province of Ceará, Brazil. According to witnesses' depositions in an assault trial against Alexandre, he arrived at Anastácio Pontes's house armed with a machete and immediately began ridiculing Luís. The older man invited the farmer to a physical confrontation by saying: 'Luís does not have any whiskers.' Moreover, he referred to an old feud between the two men due to their contested claim over a club by asking, 'hadn't you been saying that you were going to take my club from me?' At this point, Luís and Alexandre went outside the house to exchange blows. According to his declaration in the subsequent criminal proceedings, Luís felt compelled to respond to such a personal offence and 'to defend his honour, as it was natural'.[1]

A superficial perusal of this fight for honour between two illiterate combatants, as described in a criminal court case, would seem to affirm one of the most enduring tropes of Brazilian literature, history and popular culture – the idea that the *sertanejos*, or free poor male inhabitants of the semiarid hinterlands of the Northeast, have possessed exaggerated sentiments of honour and natural impulses towards violence since time immemorial.[2]

Indeed, characterizations of the *sertanejos* produced by state authorities, foreign travellers and contemporary observers during the nineteenth and early twentieth centuries portrayed them as men driven by 'hot passions, strange hatreds, and the spirit of revenge'. Even more, by invoking dichotomous understandings of the Brazilian nation as divided between civilization, concentrated in coastal cities, and barbarism, located in the rural hinterlands, these mostly elite, urban and coastal observers qualified the apparent lack of self-restraint of the *sertanejos* in matters of honour as symbolic of their unrefined and anachronistic culture and, ultimately, of their inferiority.[3] In recent years the stereotype of the belligerent *sertanejo* has been challenged, but only by focusing on its rhetorical repetition by northeastern elites with specific political agendas during the twentieth century.[4] Similarly, both popular and much scholarly literature continues to maintain the implicit, and often explicit, view that a culturally mandated *machismo* characterizes men and masculinities in Latin America, and that 'Latin' men are particularly prone to honour-related violence due to the weight of seemingly inescapable cultural prescriptions.[5]

By contrast, this chapter historicizes the reproduction of aggression and the concern with sentiments of honour among free poor men from the cattle-ranching and agricultural hinterlands of Ceará. Long-held representations of these men as driven culturally towards the violent defence of honour put inordinate emphasis on discourse, detached from analyses of practice. Focusing instead on the experience of young rural men involved in violent disputes over reputation, I examine the meanings of honour, honour-related violence and the emotional states associated with honour within the context of shifts in power relations between different groups of men and among men and women that characterized the *Cearense*[6] backlands during the second half of the nineteenth century.[7] As Eiko Ikegami emphasizes, 'political dynamics' are central to 'the process of navigating and cultivating sentiments'.[8] Thus, this chapter demonstrates that the young *sertanejos*' seemingly constant preoccupation with maintaining honourable reputations, displaying courage and avenging personal offences through violence should be seen as strategies used to assert authority and power over other men within a milieu of broad-ranging upheavals that destabilized the survival strategies and gender politics of free poor communities and families. Likewise, the strategic defence of manly honour by young and mostly racially mixed *sertanejos* represents an attempt to negotiate gendered status and power from within the marginalized positions that those who lacked powerful patrons and were poor, illiterate and of mixed ancestry occupied in the hierarchical social and racial order in place in Brazil during the imperial period.[9] This analysis underlines Pierre Bourdieu's argument that 'even the most strictly ritualized exchanges', such as the violent defence of honour – often identified as residing only at the level of emotion – 'have room for strategies'.[10] In broader terms, this chapter maintains that in order to understand masculine violence, even that committed in the name of cultural notions such as honour, it is necessary to consider the material circumstances and specific historical conditions that circumscribe the reproduction of honour-related violence and the emotional states connected to it.

Through analysis of the ways in which the performance of violence in service of honour was explained, justified or belittled by young *sertanejos*, local elites and the criminal justice system in Ceará, this chapter also deconstructs the representation of *sertanejos* as 'naturally' violent and passionate. Here, I show how the rhetorical repetition of a discourse regarding the *sertanejos*' belligerent 'nature' and inability to control their emotions contributed to its diffusion and shaped the ways in which rural poor men were perceived by others and perhaps even understood themselves. Discourse, Stuart Hall reminds us, does not passively transmit meaning, but is productive, or constitutive, of meaning. In the words of David Parker, discourse and figures of speech, 'when widely diffused ... become culture'.[11] Thus, this chapter unveils some of the ways in which the discourse on the *sertanejos*' supposed inherent capacity to fight for honour produced meanings such as the renewed cultural sanction and naturalization of the unrestrained use of violence in service of masculine honour, which in turn legitimized a violent form of masculine domination.

Men among men: Claims of honour and questions of violence

An extensive body of scholarship on the topic of honour and violence in Latin America and the Mediterranean has demonstrated that men, both from elite and subordinated groups, took affronts to their honour seriously, especially when they occurred in public, although lower-class males were more likely to use violence in defence of honour. The apparent reliance of these men on face-to-face, and often aggressive, challenges and affirmations of honourable manhood has been explained in the literature by the structure of honour and its interaction with subordinate men's social and class position. According to classic formulations, honour encompasses a man's evaluation of his own worth as well as the social validation of that estimation. Honour functions through an interplay between virtue (socially valued conduct) and precedence (a right to social esteem or status). Because the social recognition of a claim to honour is pivotal in attaining it, a man's honour is always insecure – as it can be contested – and requires constant renewal. These contests always occur in public, since public opinion serves as the ultimate tribunal that asserts or revokes a man's honour. Nevertheless, according to this scholarly view, because plebeian men could not easily access the public forums that local male elites throughout the region used to settle their disputes of honour – namely the print media and the courtroom – they were more likely to resort to violence, insult and riposte as means to maintain and protect personal honour.[12]

Recent scholarship (including the chapters by Jonas Liliequist, Penny Russell and Nigel Worden in this volume) has revealed that the masculine defence of honour and its emotional connotations are also often associated with the assertion of male power and prestige in a range of public forums.[13] In his study of gender and honour in late colonial Mexico, Steve Stern has shown that men from the subordinate groups forged their manhood and ratified the connection between masculinity, honour and power within public spheres of plebeian male sociability. As he explains, 'in this horizontal arena, men created cultural spaces to affirm their valor and competence, their honour and importance as men'.[14] In the *Cearense* backlands, cultural spaces that provided opportunities for poor *sertanejos* to interact socially with men from the same colour and class group, and to build what Stern calls the 'status as a man among men' were parties, card games, markets, festivals and the *desafios*, or oral poetic contests, in which *cantadores*, or popular bards, asserted and questioned honour through verse.[15] Crucially, in all these forms of masculine socialization, the logic that publicly conferred this sense of honour was competition and the emotionally charged display of daring and physical prowess. For instance, cards games – often accompanied by the consumption of alcohol – tested a man's boldness. The winners could publicly claim a momentary social superiority or form of power over other men. Free poor men also appear to have used betting as a way to measure daring. In several criminal cases, *sertanejos* declared that they had attended parties where they won items ranging from *violas*,[16] clubs and occasionally dogs in their bets with other men. Even within the oral realm of the *desafio*, *sertanejos* demonstrated stamina and inventiveness – so as not to become entangled in complicated rhymes – but also bravery.[17]

Yet, just as in other regions of Latin America, these forms of plebeian gendered affirmation, reliant as they were on the principle of masculine competition and on the display of bravery, often led to violence, especially when a man publicly insulted another man's courage, his assertions of daring and fearlessness or his masculine competency. Such challenges invited violent retribution because, as Ana Alonso has argued, the aspects of masculine honour that are constructed as 'natural', such as virility, bravery and valour, are also 'considered to be the natural foundations for [male] power and honour-precedence'. Within that context, not responding to words or acts of defiance would be tantamount to accepting one's weakness, powerlessness and inability to exercise masculine dominance.[18]

It is possible to observe the values, behaviours and emotions associated with defending honour through criminal trial records, especially of assaults, aggravated assaults and homicides, which detail aggressive encounters between *sertanejos* and their peers. For instance, according to a legal

complaint of assault against the 30-year-old illiterate farmer Francisco
Alves Bezerra, he had used a hoe to wound two teenagers who had disputed
his tale of valour during a *derrubada da vaca*, a contest that consisted of
overturning cattle. As the complaint noted, the two youngsters had been
questioning 'whether he really had skills in handling cattle or he had enjoyed
a streak of luck'. Implicit in this violent response was the assumption that
if Francisco had not retaliated to the insult, he would have conceded that
he did not possess manly valour. According to another assault trial, on the
night of 29 July 1874, the illiterate farmers Francisco Gonçalves da Silva,
José Vicente da Silva and José Alexandre da Silva attended a *samba*, or
dance party, at the house of another illiterate farmer, Félix Pereira de Souza,
in the Lugar São Tomé, municipality of Itapagé. According to eyewitnesses,
a fight ensued after Francisco Gonçalves, a 30-year-old man, began taunting
and insulting José Vicente's competence as the lover of a woman named
Ana. Under these circumstances, José Vicente, who was 26 years old, and
his brother, José Alexandre, also in his twenties, confronted this taunt by
taking out their knives and initiating a fight that resulted in the wounding of
Francisco Gonçalves and the arrest of the three men.[19]

Criminal trial transcripts inevitably accentuate the importance of physical
aggression in the assertion and defence of honour. Yet, it is noteworthy that
an examination of a sample of criminal cases featuring violent acts through
which free poor *Cearense* men displayed strength in public contests, no
doubt, for honourable status reveals that age was a factor in the reproduction
of honour-related violence. I selected the cases that detail insults, physical
challenges and public brawling for reasons of honour – acts that appear in
the criminal record as assaults, aggravated assaults and homicides – from
a larger pool of 200 criminal suits featuring masculine violence committed
for a variety of reasons in the municipalities of Jucás and Tamboril between
1865 and 1889. From a total of 46 men who appear as perpetrators and
victims in 28 criminal cases of honour-related violence, three quarters were
illiterate. Given the overall lack of access to education for the majority of
the rural poor in Ceará, these men's illiteracy signals their location in the
bottom ranks of society.[20] Moreover, an equal proportion of men featured in
these cases were not only poor, but young. This profile powerfully contrasts
with the age of those men involved in physical assaults related to disputes
for landed property. From 42 men described in 37 criminal cases of this type,
two – thirds were older than 30 years old, and the remainder were between
the ages of 16 and 30. These figures point to a link between differential
degrees and qualities of masculine honour or status according to age and
the reproduction of violence in the *Cearense* backlands. They also parallel
Robert Muchembled's and Pieter Spierenburg's conclusions regarding the
reliance on duelling and ritualized violence to establish male respect among
urban and rural youths in Northern France and Amsterdam during the early
modern and modern periods.[21]

Gender and age in a time of transition

Nevertheless, social and economic conditions, including employment patterns, demographic make-up and racial and class categories, also contributed to a more volatile culture of honour among youths than among older men, as Lyman Johnson has noted in his study of honour and violence among plebeian men in late colonial Buenos Aires. There, many young men entered the labour force during their early teens and lived away from their families. As day labourers and apprentices in the artisan trades, these young men occupied the lowest ranks within workplace hierarchies marked by seniority, age and strength. In addition, Buenos Aires's working class was highly fluid in nature, and many of the young men who made their way into the city were in transition to jobs in other towns or the agricultural frontier. In terms of race and ethnicity, this population of workers was not uniform. The labour market in colonial Buenos Aires relied heavily on native workers, as well as large numbers of Portuguese and Italian immigrants, and also slaves. Because of these conditions, Johnson argues, fewer older men could exercise a restraining influence on youths, while at the same time young men were encouraged from their early years to 'act like men'.[22]

In looking at the *Cearense* hinterlands after the mid-1860s, several socio-economic and demographic characteristics similar to those pointed out by Johnson appear to have influenced the place of young men within the masculine culture of challenge and riposte and their willingness to take physical risks as a way to establish masculine power and prestige. Most cities and towns in the cattle-ranching and agricultural hinterlands of Ceará were not as large or ethnically diverse as late-colonial Buenos Aires. Nevertheless, a series of broad-ranging upheavals brought intense hardship and even social disorganization to these rural communities, which, in turn, led to the loss of masculine status for young rural men, especially those who had lived by means of small-scale agriculture and cattle grazing. Families of small farmers and ranchers, who had experienced a brief moment of prosperity and autonomy as the economy of the drought-stricken interior of Ceará became increasingly diversified since the 1840s, saw their tenuous economic and social gains eroded beginning in the 1860s.[23] Changes in the international cotton market that had favoured the free poor, the decline of slavery in the region, which caused the loss of access to slave labour for small-scale slave-owners, the conscription of poor men to fight in the Paraguayan War (1864–1870) and then the Great Drought of 1877–1879, which brought food scarcity, famine and even death, especially to the rural poor, transformed the material conditions of families of small farmers and ranchers. Indeed, these shifts disrupted the ability of free poor *Cearenses* to eke out their survival from land and animal husbandry as they faced increasing indebtedness, dispossession, downward mobility and geographic dislocation. Even more, young rural families as a group experienced the greatest difficulties in setting up and retaining viable and autonomous agrarian households for themselves during these calamitous years. Facing these conditions, *sertanejo* men and women adopted wage labour as a means to supplement the increasing void of agricultural production in their household income, while families resorted to alternative modes of survival that often required men to be absent from home. Many young men also spent time away from their families when they hid from recruiters and press gangs during the most intense years of impressment for the Paraguayan War or when they adopted banditry, an activity that attracted mostly men, as a means of survival.[24]

These reversals of fortune, in turn, undermined the ability of young men to display the social manifestations of honour, including access to property ownership, effective provision for family members and guardianship of the sexuality of female kin, that had served free poor men as the means to establish social prestige and power, and even to negotiate access to resources during the years of prosperity. As *sertanejo* families contending with sustained deprivation faced increasing dependence on wage labour – an activity that for *Cearense* men symbolized lack of autonomy and honour – and even the humiliation of becoming *retirantes*, or drought refugees, who moved about the backlands in search of food and shelter, free poor men experienced their poverty and destitution as sources of dishonour and shame. Indeed, these years also witnessed the presence of a significant stratum of free poor women who remained behind in hinterlands locations and who earned their own living and that of their families independently of family men.[25] The increased visibility of free poor women who lived outside of familial patriarchy, in turn, challenged the gender politics of *sertanejo* communities and families, according to which men were the legitimate household heads and guardians of female kin.[26] It is also worth bearing in mind that the social hierarchies in place in the backlands classified those *sertanejos* who did not have economic autonomy, regular employment or powerful patrons as dishonourable, and ranked their masculinities as deficient, vagrant and criminal.[27] Given that the factors that brought hardship to the rural poor during these very difficult years targeted young families especially, and that young *sertanejos* were increasingly unable to establish themselves or remain as independent small farmers and ranchers, it is exceedingly likely that the category of free poor males who experienced the highest degrees of physical mobility, degradation by their social superiors and complete destitution were young men.

Ridicule and riposte in the backlands

Unconstrained by family obligations and facing itinerancy, humiliation and impoverishment, some young *sertanejos* evidently attached a special emotional sensitivity to expressions of ridicule and were more willing than their older counterparts to take risks and enact violence in their competitive

interactions with their peers. It is telling that 62 per cent of the men involved
in violent acts associated with honour in the criminal cases from Jucás
and Tamboril were not originally from the communities where they had
engaged in fights and had been arrested. These emotionally charged acts of
aggression, in turn, would serve to prove that even if poor, and therefore
in lack of the material signifiers of honour, men possessed the 'natural'
attributes that guaranteed a form of masculine power and social dominance
over a defeated rival, whether he was a newcomer or a more established male
figure in the community. For example, Lourenço Alves Bezerra, a 21-year-
old, illiterate farmer from Jucás, allegedly attacked Antônio Francisco
Gomes with a machete in a cane field in the Lugar Areias. According to a
witness, Lourenço Alves arrived at a field one morning in August of 1875,
whereupon he saw Antônio – who did not regularly work in the Lugar
Areias – with an unconcealed knife ready to cut canes. He said that 'he was
not afraid of Antônio's knife', and that 'he, Lourenço, was not afraid of any
man'. Lourenço then wounded Antônio in the head and hand.[28]

In the backlands and elsewhere in slaveholding Brazil, plebeians of mixed
ancestry who occupied a marginal social standing used racial insults and
even violence against slaves and other free poor people of colour to establish
the importance of respect for racial hierarchies. Interacting in a slaveholding
society where African men and women and their descendants were held
as human property and therefore as dishonourable, free people of mixed
descent and whites alike used racial stereotypes to mark their presumed
social superiority. Moreover, in the racial hierarchy of the hinterlands,
nonslaves thought themselves entitled to ridicule slaves and commit acts of
violence towards them and all others constructed as such by virtue of their
race or lowly status, without the expectation of retribution. Such challenges
came with the expectation of impunity, since those who had no honour
were not expected to defend it.[29] The importance of racial hierarchy, status
and honour for free poor *sertanejos* can be illustrated in the following 1875
case in which a low-level court officer named Gonçalo de Carvalho insulted
and attacked two male slaves. Due to a lack of sufficient personnel to fulfil
police duties in the hinterlands, free poor civilian men often performed law
enforcement tasks including making arrests, breaking up fights, transporting
prisoners and manning jails. Thus, the court officer Gonçalo had been
charged with patrolling the town of Tamboril on Christmas Eve, 1875. As
the slave Cipriano declared in a criminal assault trial in which he and the
slave Gregório featured as defendants, they had been singing and dancing
in a *samba* on 24 December, when the court officer arrived and ordered
the party to end by saying 'tonight the blacks are going to pay for their
sins'. Cipriano mentioned that at that particular moment he asked, 'who
had issued that order', and Gonçalo replied that 'he himself was the one who
issued that command'. After this exchange, the court officer struck Cipriano
in the head. The legal complaint presented Gonçalo's version of the events.
According to this narrative, he had ordered the end of the party 'because the

slaves were fighting among themselves', and then they attacked him with clubs. Here, it appears as if Gonçalo was asserting the racial hierarchy and his racial superiority over the slaves, as well as his authority to terminate their party. But crucially, the slave Cipriano's statements show that even for a slave, the authority of a lowly paid, probably racially mixed, court officer was questionable. Even more, the slaves' action of fighting with Gonçalo demonstrates that they challenged the presumed prerogative of the court officer to insult them due to their race and servile status. Crucially, the slaves' anger-fuelled fighting reaction to the insult, which might superficially appear as the simple enactment of a *macho* cultural script, should be understood as an emotional response which, following Robert Solomon's insights, did not preclude but rather involved 'reflective appraisals and evaluations', or 'judgments', in this case of comparative status and of the importance of race in the negotiation of status.[30]

Criminal cases demonstrate that during their fights, brawls or other physical attacks, young men not only engaged in violence but also articulated a discourse that clearly defined courage as the emotion through which a man's superior manhood and status could be affirmed. This is observable in the fight between the 21-year-old illiterate day labourer José Francisco da Costa and the 22-year-old farmer Trajino Gomes Guedes. According to a witness who testified in the assault trial against José Francisco, he (Francisco) had told Trajino to 'stay away' from a woman named Inés – who allegedly had suffered a beating at the hands of Trajino – or otherwise, 'the one who would receive a beating would be him'. To this remark, Trajino had responded by holding his knife, saying that 'no man is more *macho*, or brave, than another', and by daring José Francisco to a physical fight.[31] According to these understandings, the fight would determine who the bravest man was and, in consequence, the one whose orders would be obeyed, in spite of any other shortcomings in his life. Such assertions made sense within hierarchical communities in which class, colour, economic autonomy and connections with powerful patrons determined the rank of poor men as either honourable or dishonourable. Yet, they also reveal that some young *sertanejos* interposed their claims to honour based on personal courage into the social ranking of masculinities and in that way asserted a form of power over others, especially among their peers.

In this discourse of masculinity, fear – as the opposite of courage – was shunned as an emotion that real men did not feel, and the performance of violence was required as the most visible sign of a man's lack of fear, or bravery. This was put in evidence when, in 1871, the 30-year-old illiterate farmer José Ferino de Moraes, from the town of São Francisco, exchanged blows with José Francisco de Sá. According to a witness, the fight started one afternoon because José Ferino had insulted José Francisco by asking him (after gunshots had startled the man), 'What are you running from, *cabra*?[32] Are you afraid?'[33] The significance of José Merino's insinuation that José Francisco was a coward, or less than a man because he became startled, and of the insulting use of *cabra* as half-caste, lies in the fact that they required an aggressive emotional response in order for a man to stop the ridiculing of his character as passive, fearful and obviously emasculated, and to challenge the assertions of racial subordination.

Clearly, some young men used violent assertions of masculine valour as a way to establish honour and reputation within relationships of power with their peers. Socio-economic factors such as the itinerancy of poor young men, the fluidity in their employment arrangements and the large numbers of men who lived outside family relationships injected a degree of danger and a sharp potential for physical aggression into the competitive culture of male sociability among young *sertanejos*. Moreover, because this culture of male interaction sanctioned risk-taking, rivalry and physical daring as privileged avenues to demonstrate possession of the 'natural' attributes of masculinity and honour, young *sertanejos* maintained that the violent defence and protection of honour was a 'natural' necessity.[34] In this sense, the young *sertanejos*' concern with honour, the means through which they asserted that honour and the understandings about the seemingly instinctive drive to violently avenge honour correspond to what several scholars, including Nigel Worden in this volume, describe as plebeian, popular or horizontal codes of honour that emphasized the right to respect within a community of equals.[35] Nevertheless, it was not only poor rural men, acting within a plebeian culture of honour that authorized violence, who construed and legitimized their aggressive emotional responses to insult as 'natural'. Indeed, as we will see below, the criminal justice system in imperial Brazil – managed and controlled by national and local elites – played a part in strengthening the discourse according to which men, including those who were young and poor, enjoyed a gender-specific right to validate their honour through violence.

Honour, violence and the criminal justice system

The second half of the nineteenth century witnessed the expansion of the state into the farthest corners of the Brazilian empire, including the hinterlands of Ceará. For the planter class that constituted the ruling elite at the imperial and local levels, a larger, effective and centralized bureaucracy that controlled police administration and the criminal justice system figured prominently in the imposition and maintenance of order throughout the country. Imposing order expressed an effort to safeguard the social, racial and gender hierarchy in Brazil and the agrarian basis of the export economy, with its need for disciplined labour, whether slave or free.[36] Within this context, at least some young *Cearense* men who participated in drunken brawls or knife fights as well as those who murdered other men for reasons of honour – actions that according to public prosecutors and police authorities occurred due to 'frivolous' motives – were arrested, indicted and even put to trial. Yet, the workings of local criminal courts in these cases were loaded with contradictions. In several instances, juries – made up of local male elites – absolved young men who were indicted for physically assaulting other men in fights and parties, in accordance with the determinations of criminal laws with regard to crimes of honour that, in fact, sanctioned some forms of honour-related violence.

In nineteenth-century Brazil, as in the cases of Germany and France discussed by Robert Nye in this volume, newly created and self-consciously 'modern' legal codes accommodated older notions of honour that justified certain acts committed in order to avenge personal honour. According to the Brazilian Imperial Criminal Code of 1830, causing physical injuries, cuts and wounds on the body of another person, with the objective of insulting and hurting, constituted a crime against the security of life and of personhood, punishable by incarceration for one month to eight years. Yet, at the same time, engaging in an act *em desafronta*, or vindication, of 'an insult or dishonour against the delinquent, his or her ancestors, children, spouses, or siblings' constituted an extenuating circumstance in deciding the sentence of any crime. Moreover, the Criminal Code established in an ambiguous manner that 'crimes committed in defence of a person and his or her rights', and 'in defence of the delinquent's family', were justifiable, and therefore not punishable.[37] Thus, as we will see in the *Cearense* cases, the courts legitimized the practice of private vengeance among young men, and reinforced a cultural discourse that justified masculine aggression in defence of honour.[38]

Even if formally condemning the use of male aggression to maintain masculine reputation, the courts often proved lenient in sentencing young *sertanejos* who engaged in violent disputes over points of honour. This is visible through the experience of the illiterate young brothers José Vicente and José Alexandre, from the Lugar São Tomé, Itapagé, who were absolved from a charge of aggravated assault, even after a police investigation based on witnesses' depositions and a physical exam established that the brothers had indeed assaulted and wounded the victim, Francisco Gonçalves da Silva. According to the jury, José Vicente and José Alexandre had committed the crime 'in self-defence and in defence of their honour', which had been offended by Francisco Gonçalves' insinuations that José Vicente was impotent in his sexual relations with his lover Ana. The legal basis for this decision rested upon two extenuating circumstances established in the Criminal Code that allowed juries to determine lesser punishments or even exonerate offenders when they could prove that they had perpetrated a crime in defence of honour.[39] This case parallels Leandro Kierszenbaum's conclusions for twentieth-century Uruguay, where the reduced sentences granted to lower-class men who participated in creole or plebeian duels point to ways in which the law and criminal courts 'recognize[d] and respect[ed] the reputation and dignity of the person who had killed or wounded' in accordance to plebeian notions of honour.[40]

In addition, criminal courts contributed to the recirculation of shared cultural assumptions regarding men's seeming innate tendencies to aggression and the inevitability and acceptability of violence in defence of honour. For instance, in his deposition in the aggravated assault trial of Alexandre Rodrigues, who had wounded Luís Pereira de Sousa in a fight, Alexandre emphasized that 'it was natural' for him to defend himself violently from the insults launched by Luís, who attacked his honour by saying that he did not have any whiskers. This argumentation obviously achieved the goal of gaining the sympathies of male jury members in favour of Alexandre, as he was acquitted, despite the fact that the indictment, based on depositions by witnesses, had proven that Alexandre had committed the crime. Some of the rhetorical strategies that young *sertanejos* and their lawyers or public defenders used to obtain exoneration or shorter sentences from jury tribunals included appeals to the idea that a 'provocation' or insult launched against a man's honour necessitated an automatic emotional and violent response. The 30-year-old farmer, Vicente Luís dos Santos, for instance, argued in his defence from charges of aggravated assault that the reason why he hit Manoel Alves with a club in the market of São Mateus was that 'he had been provoked by Manoel, who was insulting and attacking him', and he 'only wanted to defend himself'. According to witnesses, Manoel Alves had violently shooed Vicente Luís' dog, an action that resulted in a fight during which Manoel Alves called Vicente Luís 'a liar'. The justification of his actions as in agreement with a code of honour worked effectively in Vicente Luís's case. Although in June of 1875 the municipal judge charged the defendant with aggravated assault and argued that 'a disapproved motive compelled him to commit the crime', the jury sentenced Vicente Luís to a minimum prison term of six months because, in their view, 'he did perpetrate the assault, but not due to a censured motivation'.[41]

According to the Criminal Code, juries needed to take into account 'superiority in sex, force, and weapons' as an aggravating circumstance in judging all crimes.[42] Nevertheless, in several cases in which poor men physically assaulted poor and unprotected women as a way to defend their honour, the courts either absolved or were exceedingly lenient with the male perpetrators of these acts.[43] Such judicial decisions, in turn, show that all-male local criminal courts were often unwilling to interfere in the perceived right of men, even if poor, to violently avenge honour. They also point towards a cross-class agreement among men regarding the acceptability of using extra-legal violence to defend honour and enforce gender hierarchy. Thus, for instance, in January of 1883 the farmer Bernardino Dias do Nascimento was formally accused of physically injuring Maria Lucina, a 38-year-old laundress, with a knife. According to the official complaint, Bernardino had come to the house where Maria Lucina was staying one night in São Miguel, a *fazenda*, or rural estate, where he tried to force her to go into another room and engage in sexual relations with him. She resisted and got the help of her sister Luzia to physically restrain Bernardino, at which point he brandished a knife and wounded Maria Lucina. As witnesses noted, Maria Lucina had said to Bernardino that he was 'shameless' by trying to force her into a sexual relation. The criminal investigation determined that Bernardino had indeed assaulted Maria Lucina, through depositions from several witnesses, the defendant and the plaintiff and through a physical examination. Yet the jury absolved Bernardino, arguing that three extenuating circumstances that were established in article 18 of the Criminal Code applied in this case: first, that the defendant had committed the crime in self-defence and in defence of his rights. Through the deployment of this legal notion, the jury justified Bernardino's violent act as one executed in vindication of his wounded honour, a deed that, in turn, served to restitute his social precedence. After all, he had been called 'shameless' in public. The second extenuating circumstance that applied in this case, according to the jury, was that the aggression had been initiated by the offended person, in this case Maria Lucina (this, despite the fact that, according to the records, neither Maria Lucina nor her sister threatened Bernardino with any weapon). Finally, the defendant had been inebriated when he had committed the crime, and was thus less culpable than a sober man.[44]

This clause from the Criminal Code, which was often invoked in the sentencing of honour-related crimes, also helped to perpetuate the cultural discourse regarding men's inability to judge their emotional state or their capacity to inflict pain when they engaged in physical contests to prove personal honour. For instance, the 24-year-old, illiterate farmer Felipe Gonçalves de Santiago was charged with the homicide of Francisco Benjamin, which took place at a party in the municipality of Itapagé in June of 1874. According to the witnesses' declarations, a 22-year-old man named Raimundo Vieira Venâncio was playing a *viola* in the *samba* when Felipe took it away from him and left the party. Benjamin got up and confronted Felipe, attempting to force him to return the *viola* so that the dance could continue. The witnesses noted that Benjamin attacked Felipe with a stick. Felipe then hit Benjamin with the *viola*, which ended up in pieces, and then wounded him with his knife. In his deposition during the proceedings, Felipe noted that 'he did not know whether he was indeed the author of these wounds, since he was completely drunk on that occasion'. In another section of the interrogation, the defendant explained that he did not remember much because 'his judgment was totally impaired, as he was extremely inebriated'. After testimony by several witnesses established that the defendant wounded Benjamin, the jury acquitted him, citing two extenuating circumstances stipulated in the Criminal Code. First, that 'the delinquent committed the crime in response to another person's attack', and second, that 'the delinquent perpetuated the crime in a state of intoxication'.[45] In this manner, both the Criminal Code and the local criminal court sanctioned the violent expression of certain types of anger as righteous, or at the very least, understandable.

This kind of appraisal made by local male elites as judges and juries and sanctioned by the clauses of the Criminal Code that accommodated the performance of violence in service of masculine honour, in all probability, contributed to strengthening the notoriety of poor young men who not only used violence as a way to assert masculine status but also got away with it, even if they were brought to trial. Moreover, although only a minority of men who committed acts of violence ever fell under the radar of the criminal justice system, reports concerning the reputation of those who were exonerated most likely spread like wildfire in backlands communities. As the *Cearense* author Domingos Olímpio described in his 1903 naturalist novel *Luzia-Homem*, townspeople followed closely the developments in criminal courts, and enthusiastically gossiped and embellished details of the depositions and results of criminal proceedings. Thus, in various ways, the criminal justice system contributed to the diffusion of discourses that justified the practice of masculine violence in service of honour and legitimized emotional states that brought about violence.[46]

Conclusion

During the verbal exchanges leading to the fight between Alexandre Rodrigues and Luís Pereira de Sousa that opened this chapter, both of these young men expressed what to contemporary readers might seem an absurd concern with whiskers – the physical embodiment of a confrontational manhood – and a club – a precious commodity whose possession was worth a deadly fight. Despite their own claims regarding their 'natural' impulses to defend honour through violence, the importance of clubs and whiskers for *sertanejo* males – even if shaped by cultural notions of honour – was not indicative of an essentialized violent masculinity. Instead, as this chapter has shown, the cultural value of weapons and of a man's strength in handling violence was reinforced within a context in which young male backlanders could rely only on aggression as the means to exercise a form of power or authority over others.

As we have seen, rapidly impoverished young men employed culturally sanctioned forms of masculine challenge and aggression to establish status and prestige among their peers, as the loss of land, slaves and livestock that affected their families since the 1860s had undermined their capacity to sustain honour claims contingent on economic success and property ownership. Through the young *sertanejos'* use of aggression and their retelling of the details of fights that took place in public, they reproduced a cultural discourse that exalted courage as the 'natural' endowment that guaranteed masculine honour. In this discourse of masculinity, those who displayed fear were perceived as the rightful targets of humiliation, since their fear exposed their lack of bravery and, consequently, of status and respectability. While these shared understandings regarding the importance of violence to avenge honour corresponded to plebeian cultural values, police authorities at the municipal and provincial levels, and local male elites as judges and jury members in criminal courtrooms also played a role in the diffusion of a discourse that sanctioned aggression in defence of honour and legitimized emotional states that resulted in violence. Thus, far from being a timeless fixture, the culture of honour was, in fact, re-created through the everyday practice and discourse of *sertanejos* and other actors, within a context of unequal distributions of power based on gender, class, age and race.

Notes

1   Itapagé, Cr., 9, 32: 7, 1883, Arquivo Público do Estado do Ceará, Fortaleza, Brazil (hereafter, APEC).

2   Northeastern folk novels and popular poems have often celebrated the domineering character and the supposed obsession with honour of infamous manly backlanders. See Candace Slater, *Stories on a String: The Brazilian Literatura de Cordel* (Berkeley: University of California Press, 1988); several motion pictures produced within the 1960s *Cinema Novo* movement focused on the timeless violence of male *sertanejos*. See Glauber Rocha, *Deus e o Diabo na Terra do Sol*, 1963, and *Antônio das mortes*, 1969; Ruy Guerra, *Os fuzis*, 1964; for museum exhibits celebrating the courage of male *sertanejos*, see 'Vaqueiros', Centro Dragão do Mar de Arte e Cultura, Fortaleza, Ceará; for historical works that have emphasized the 'culture of aggression' of rural Brazil, see Maria Isaura Pereira de Queiroz, *O messianismo no Brasil e no mundo* (São Paulo: Dominus, 1965); Robert Levine, *Vale of Tears: Revisiting the Canudos Massacre in Northeastern Brazil, 1893–1897* (Berkeley: University of California Press, 1992); E. B. Reesink, *The Peasant in the Sertão: A Short Exploration of His Past and Present* (Leiden: Institute of Cultural and Social Studies, 1981); Antônio Candido de Mello e Souza, *Os parceiros do Rio Bonito*, 2nd ed. (São Paulo: Duas Cidades, 1971).

3   José Ernesto Pimentel Filho, 'A Produção do Crime: Violência, Distinção Social e Economia na Formação da Província Cearense' (Ph.D. diss, Universidade de São Paulo, 2002), 153–57. For contemporary depictions of honour-obsessed *sertanejos*, see Euclides da Cunha, *Rebellion in the Backlands*, trans. S. Putnam (Chicago: University of Chicago Press, 1944), 54, 77–79, 175; George Gardner, *Travels in the Interior of Brazil* (New York: AMS Press, Inc., 1970 [1846]),161–62; Ceará, *Falla* (A. F. Henriques: Assembléia Provincial, 1870), 7; 'Relatorio da Secretaria da Polícia do Ceará', in Ceará, *Falla* (D'Oliveira Dias:Assembléia Legislativa, 1883), 2; Tristão de Alencar Araripe Júnior, *Luizinha* (Rio de Janeiro: José Olympio Editora, 1980 [1878]),78.

4   See Durval Muniz de Albuquerque Júnior, '"Quem é frouxo não se mete": Violência e masculinidade como elementos constitutivos da imagem do nordestino', *Projeto História (PUCSP)*, 19 (1999): 173–88, and *Nordestino: Uma invenção do falo – uma história do gênero masculino (Nordeste, 1920–1940)* (Maceió: Edições Catavento, 2003).

5   For useful critiques of the unitary Latin American *macho* cliché and its political and academic uses, see Matthew Gutmann, ed., *Changing Men and Masculinities in Latin America* (Durham: Duke University Press, 2003), 1–25, and *The Meanings of Macho: Being a Man in Mexico City* (Berkeley: University of California Press, 1996), 221–42; see also Marysa Navarro, 'Against *Marianismo*', in *Gender's Place: Feminist Anthropologies of Latin America*, ed. Rosario Montoya, Lessie Jo Frasier and Janice Hurtig (New York: Palgrave Macmillan, 2002), 257–70.

6   The term *Cearense*, which is used throughout this study, refers to a resident of Ceará. As an adjective, the term also means having to do with or relative to Ceará.

7   This chapter builds on findings presented in Martha S. Santos, *Cleansing Honor with Blood: Masculinity, Violence, and Power in the Backlands of Northeast Brazil, 1845–1889* (Stanford: Stanford University Press, 2012).

8   Eiko Ikegami, 'Emotions', in *A Concise Companion to History*, ed. Ulinka Rublack (Oxford: Oxford University Press, 2011), 347.

9   According to the 1872 census of Ceará, *pardos*, or persons of mixed African and European descent, constituted 49 per cent of the free provincial population, while free blacks and *caboclos*, racially mixed individuals with Indian ancestry, accounted for 12 per cent; 39 per cent of the province's free inhabitants were white. Brazil, Directoria Geral de Estatística, *Recenseamento da população do Império do Brasil a que se procedeu no dia 1o de Agosto de 1872*, Vol. 4 (Rio de Janeiro, 1873–1876), 176. For analyses of the social and racial order operating in imperial Brazil, see Richard Graham, *Patronage and Politics in Nineteenth-Century Brazil* (Stanford: Stanford University Press, 1990); Emilia Viotti da Costa, *The Brazilian Empire: Myths and Histories* (Chicago: University of Chicago Press, 1985); and Roger Kittelson, *The Practice of Politics in Postcolonial Brazil: Porto Alegre, 1845–1895* (Pittsburgh: University of Pittsburgh Press, 2006). The Brazilian imperial period was inaugurated after independence in 1822 and ended with the collapse of the monarchy in 1889.

10   Pierre Bourdieu, *Outline of a Theory of Practice*, trans. Richard Nice (Cambridge: Cambridge University Press, 1977), 15.

11   Stuart Hall, ed., *Representation: Cultural Representations and Signifying Practices* (London: Sage Publications, 1997), 41–51; David Parker, '"Gentlemanly Responsibility" and "Insults of a Woman": Dueling and the Unwritten Rules of Public Life in Uruguay, 1860–1920', in *Gender, Sexuality and Power in Latin America since Independence*, ed. William French and Katherine Bliss (Lanham, MD: Rowman and Littlefield, 2007), 126.

12   Historical works on honour and violence among poor men in Latin America include, among others, Lyman Johnson, 'Dangerous Words, Provocative Gestures, and Violent Acts: The Disputed Hierarchies of Plebeian Life in Colonial Buenos Aires', in *The Faces of Honor: Sex, Shame and Violence in Colonial Latin America*, ed. Lyman Johnson and Sonia Lipsett-Rivera (Albuquerque: University of New Mexico Press, 1998), 127–51; John Charles Chasteen, 'Violence for Show: Knife Dueling on a Nineteenth-Century Cattle Frontier', in *The Problem of Order in Changing Societies*, ed. Lyman

Johnson (Albuquerque: University of New Mexico Press, 1990), 47–64; Leandro Kierszenbaum, 'Between the Accepted and the Legal: Violence in Honor Disputes in Uruguay (1945–1970)', *International Journal of Politics, Culture, and Society*, 25 (2012): 35–48. On classic conceptualizations of honour in contemporary Mediterranean societies, see Julian Pitt-Rivers, *The Fate of Shechem or the Politics of Sex: Essays in the Anthropology of the Mediterranean* (Cambridge: Cambridge University Press, 1977); J. G. Periastiany, ed., *Honour and Shame: The Values of Mediterranean Society* (Chicago: University of Chicago Press, 1966).

13 Bourdieu, *Outline*; Ana Maria Alonso, *Thread of Blood: Colonialism, Revolution and Gender on Mexico's Northern Frontier* (Tucson: University of Arizona Press, 1995); Steve Stern, *The Secret History of Gender: Women, Men and Power in Late Colonial Mexico* (Chapel Hill: University of North Carolina Press, 1995).

14 Stern, *The Secret History*, 171.

15 Stern, *The Secret History*, 177.

16 A *viola* is a small guitar, typical of the Brazilian northeastern hinterlands.

17 See Tamboril, Cr., 5, 8: 7, 1872; Tamboril, Cr., 6, 9: 14A, 1876, APEC; da Cunha, *Rebellion*, 102.

18 Alonso, *Thread of Blood*, 80–81.

19 Tamboril, Cr., 6, 9: 14A, 1876; Itapagé, Cr., 3, 26: 9, 1874, APEC.

20 In this study, I have used illiteracy as a proxy for poverty.

21 Robert Muchembled, *A History of Violence: From the End of the Middle Ages to the Present* (Cambridge: Polity, 2011), 46, 67–81, 284–97; Pieter Spierenburg, ed., 'Knife Fighting and Popular Codes of Honor in Early Modern Amsterdam', in *Men and Violence: Gender, Honor, and Rituals in Modern Europe and America* (Columbus: Ohio State University Press, 1998), 128–58.

22 Johnson, 'Dangerous Words', 127–51.

23 For an in-depth analysis of the period of prosperity and the changing fortunes of free poor families, see Santos, *Cleansing Honor*, chaps. 1 and 4.

24 Santos, *Cleansing Honor*, chaps. 1 and 4.

25 Santos, *Cleansing Honor*, chap. 5.

26 Santos, *Cleansing Honor*, chaps. 2. 4 and 5.

27 Santos, *Cleansing Honor*, chap. 2.

28 Jucás, Cr., 4, 15: 18, APEC.

29 On racial constructs in the backlands, see Linda Lewin, 'Who Was "o Grande Romano"? Genealogical Purity, the Indian "Past" and Whiteness in Brazil's Northeastern Backlands, 1750–1900', *Journal of Latin American Lore*, 19 (1996): 129–79; for an analysis of race, slavery, insults and violence elsewhere in Brazil, see Kittelson, *The Practice of Politics*, 105–08.

30 Tamboril, Cr., 5, 8: 18, 1843, APEC; on emotions as 'judgments', see Robert Solomon, 'I. Emotions, Thoughts and Feelings: What Is a "Cognitive Theory" of the Emotions and Does It Neglect Affectivity?', *Royal Institute of Philosophy Supplement*, 52 (March, 2003): 1–18, and Ikegami, 'Emotions', 337.

31 Itapagé, Cr., 11, 34: 19, 1888, APEC.

32 The word *cabra* (literally, 'the goat') refers to an individual of mixed-race, the product of a combination of Indian, white and African ancestry. In addition, it denotes indeterminacy in the racial categorization of a person of colour and can have the pejorative connotation of half-caste. *Dicionário eletrônico Houaiss da língua portuguesa* (CD-ROM, version 1.0, 2001), s.v. *cabra*.

33 Itapagé, Cr., 2, 25, 1871, APEC.

34 Itapagé, Cr., 9, 32: 7, 1883, APEC.

35 On plebeian codes of honour in Latin America, see Richard Boyer, 'Honor among Plebians: *Mala Sangre* and Social Reputation', in *The Faces of Honor*, 152–76; Johnson, 'Dangerous Words', 127–50; on popular codes of honour in Amsterdam, see Spierenburg, 'Knife Fighting', 115–18; on horizontal honour, see Frank Henderson Stewart, *Honor* (Chicago: University of Chicago Press, 1994), 148–49.

36 For an analysis of state formation in Ceará, see Santos, *Cleansing Honor*, chap. 2.

37 J. M. P. de Vasconcellos, *Codigo criminal do Império do Brasil* (Rio de Janeiro: Eduardo & Henrique Laemmert, 1859), 87–89.

38 See Jucás, Cr., 4, 15: 6, 1872; Tamboril, Cr., 2, 5: 13, 1862; Tamboril, Cr., 7, 10: 22, 1876; Itapagé, Cr., 3, 26: 9, 1874; Itapagé, Cr., 11, 34: 19, 1888, APEC; art. 18, nos. 3, 4, 6 and 8, Vasconcellos, *Codigo criminal*, 15–16.

39 Itapagé, Cr., 3, 26: 9, 1874, APEC; art. 18, nos. 3, 4 and 6, Vasconcellos, *Codigo criminal*, 15.

40 Kierszenbaum, 'Between the Accepted and the Legal', 44.

41 Itapagé, Cr., 9, 32: 7, 1883; Jucás, Cr., 4, 15: 13, 1875, APEC.

42 Vasconcellos, *Codigo Criminal*, 13.

43 For an in-depth examination of the prosecution of honour-related violence against unprotected women in the backlands of Ceará, see Santos, *Cleansing Honor*, chap. 5.

44 Itapagé, Cr., 9, 32: 10, 1883, APEC; Vasconcellos, *Codigo Criminal*, 13, 15–16.

45 Itapagé, Cr., 3, 26: 8, 1874; art. 18, no. 9, Vasconcellos, *Codigo criminal*, 16.

46 Domingos Olímpio, *Luzia-Homem* (Fortaleza: ABC Fortaleza, 1999 [1903]), 130–31.

8

Emotion, gender and honour in a fin-de-siècle crime of passion: The case of Marie Bière

Eliza Earle Ferguson

On 9 January 1880, mere steps from the Opéra Garnier, a singer named Marie Bière shot her former lover, Robert Gentien, three times as he strolled out for the evening accompanied by another woman. During Bière's subsequent trial for attempted murder in the Cour d'assises de la Seine, the defendant and her famous attorney, Charles Lachaud, complicated this familiar melodramatic story of vengeance when they contended that it was maternal love, not jealousy, that had inspired her violence. Bière blamed Gentien for the death of their baby daughter, who had perished while in the care of a wet nurse, to whom the callous father had demanded the baby be sent. Rather than legitimating the child and redeeming Bière's honour by marrying her, Gentien had claimed that his obligations as a 'gallant man' were fulfilled simply by giving Bière a monthly stipend. Whereas Bière hoped to parlay their love affair into marriage, Gentien had effectively converted it into an economic transaction. Through a skilful presentation of his client's emotions as an abandoned mother, in contrast to her paramour's lack of affect, the defence successfully upheld Bière's claim that the shooting was a legitimate outcome of her wounded feminine honour. Rejecting the clear-cut standards of the law, Lachaud called on jurors to consult their hearts in their verdict. Bière's acquittal – by the jury and the court of public opinion expressed in the popular daily press – validated her use of violence to restore her lost honour.

Recent work on the history of emotions has highlighted the ways in which emotions are implicated in structures of social organization and power.[1] New analyses of the public sphere have rejected its original theorization as a realm of strictly rational decision-making and explored its function as an "informal cultural arena mediating between private experience and the polity" where emotion is no longer banished to the private sphere.[2] In fin-de-siècle Paris, the cultural preoccupation with 'crimes of passion' presents an opportunity to explore how a private drama of love and violence became an urgent problem for public debate. Although never defined as a legal category, crimes of passion were popularly understood to be acts of violence that occurred between two people in an intimate relationship characterized by love, whether married or not.[3] Courtroom testimony exposed a dense nexus between individuals and their social milieu in their various expectations for intimate relationships, what Barbara Rosenwein has called an 'emotional community'.[4] In a typical trial for a crime of passion, the emotional community was personified by a dozen or more friends and neighbours, who testified about the couple's relationship and thus provided a clear basis for standards and judgements of their behaviour.[5] Bière and Gentien, however, did not live together and did not socialize as a couple, so very few people knew much about their relationship.[6] Instead, the three days of testimony constituted the assize court itself as a kind of provisional emotional community, where jurors and observers rendered judgements about the validity of Bière's and Gentien's emotions, and the actions they provoked. Vivid accounts of the trial in the popular press allowed readers to participate in this emotional community by proxy. Together they affirmed a system of values that validated Bière's love, rage and grief, and condemned Gentien's coldness. In this context, being an honourable woman or man required the transparent presentation of authentic emotions, sexual fidelity if not chastity and the fulfilment of conventional social obligations. Further, Marie Bière's acquittal provided an occasion for articulating protests against the sexual double standard and certain procedures and patriarchal privileges inscribed in French law, including Article 340 of the Penal Code, which prohibited paternity suits. The far-reaching repercussions of Marie Bière's trial underscore how compelling claims about emotion and honour animated debates in the public sphere concerning gender, power, sexuality and the family.

In a case like Marie Bière's the sources for analysing emotions are exceptionally rich, making it possible to cross-reference different accounts of the same phenomenon. The trial dossier preserves oral testimony of 44 witnesses deposed by the investigating magistrate, together with dozens of letters written by Gentien, and a journal and other documents written by Bière.[7] These documents offer a record of the display of emotions and motivations that both Bière and Gentien sought to manipulate. In addition, newspaper accounts gave detailed information about testimony given during the trial, the appearance and comportment of everyone who took the stand and the responses of the people present in the courtroom.[8] Press reports all confirmed that the courtroom was overflowing with spectators every day of the trial, including some notable society ladies and members of the demimonde, as well as several important literary figures like Alexandre Dumas *fils*.[9] Their outbursts of applause, shouts and murmurs were noted in press reports, which provide a sense of the trial's emotional register and the tenor of public opinion: overwhelmingly in favour of Bière. The jurors who acquitted Bière might well have felt as the audience did, though the only direct evidence about their judgement was their verdict. The legal question the jurors were called upon to answer was simply whether or not Bière had attempted to kill Gentien. Given that Bière herself readily confessed to the deed and had scrupulously recorded this intention in her journal prior to the attack, her acquittal can only be explained by jurors' recourse to extra-legal standards of emotion and honour. Ultimately, the perception of the protagonists' ability to feel and express apparently authentic and appropriate emotions was crucial to the outcome of the trial. For Bière, true love was the sign of true honour, and therefore, she could use violence legitimately in its defence. Her acquittal validated her action to rehabilitate her own honour through violence.

Appearance and authenticity

Observers of the trial placed a high value on a transparent correlation between what they perceived to be the protagonists' interior state and their exterior appearance. When Bière first appeared in the courtroom on 5 April, she was dressed modestly and simply, entirely in black. *La Presse* found her to be an 'energetic woman', with a 'calm and collected' expression.[10] Reports from *Le Petit Journal* and *Le Figaro* noted that her manner was anything but theatrical. 'She is not there "to pose," you can see at the first glimpse; she affects neither timidity nor fear.'[11] The noted legal chronicler Albert Bataille wrote in *Le Figaro* that those who expected a theatrical performance by Bière were disappointed. 'It is impossible to respond more simply, more sweetly, and also with more dignity than did the accused. Marie Bière was *true* [sic] from one end to the other. Those who heard her could not have been mistaken!'[12] Her apparent naturalness was reinforced by her appearance of faded beauty, indicating not only that she had suffered but that she had been beautiful enough to inspire love. *Le Petit Parisien* published a portrait in its weekly supplement, drawn from an earlier photo, perhaps so readers could judge for themselves.[13] *Gil Blas* reported: 'The unhappy accused first inspires interest by the traces of physical and moral suffering that she has endured and that ravaged a face that should have been beautiful, illuminated by the flame of her long-lashed black eyes, whose brightness, extinguished today, only reappears in flashes.'[14] Such traces of her suffering seemed to reinforce Bière's version of events, and the newspapers were unanimous in describing the response of the audience to her as 'sympathetic'. This term is highly significant in this context, suggesting a fellow-feeling with the accused.

If Marie Bière's features and manners won her the goodwill of the audience, Robert Gentien's had quite the opposite effect. *La Presse* and *Le Petit Parisien* both noted his stylish elegance, but implied a lack of manly vigour. 'Monsieur Gentien is a rather strong man, tall, with an elegant turnout; he has a rather long beard of a red color; his hair is blond; he expresses himself with a certain nonchalance; his voice is weak.'[15] *Le Petit Journal* noted that he took his oath 'with an attitude that was a little *cherchée*'.[16] Albert Bataille deployed his usual flair in *Le Figaro*: 'Well dressed, well groomed … Monsieur Robert Gentien is exactly what we said he was yesterday: correctness itself.'[17] On subsequent days, he was variously described as bored, cold, irritated or indifferent. He seemed little able to experience or perhaps even to inspire strong feelings. Overall, the impression was of a man of stylish and correct surface appearances, but with no strength of character, and no deep emotions. His emotional style was that of an impassive man of the world, not an impassioned lover.[18]

Love and sex

Bière's appearance of emotional authenticity in court drew on the familiar narrative she and her lawyer sought to establish of the honest, virgin girl dishonoured by a wealthy seducer.[19] Bière's age and profession cast doubt on her claim of being a guileless victim, however. Nearing the age of 30, Bière had spent almost a decade as a modestly successful opera singer before she met Gentien. While she had been born into a middle-class family in Bordeaux, he was the heir to the Château de Tustal, southwest of the same city. Said to have an income of 80,000 francs, he amused himself with hunting, gambling and traveling.[20] They were introduced by a mutual acquaintance in Biarritz, and initially it seemed they observed every propriety, carefully chaperoned by Bière's mother. Matters took a different turn when they left Biarritz and started exchanging secret letters, culminating in Bière accepting an assignation at Gentien's bachelor apartment in Paris.

Could an honest woman be seduced in this manner? Bière and her attorney insisted that sex could be part of a courtship leading to marriage. When Bière and Gentien confronted each other in the office of the investigating magistrate Guillot before the trial, her first question to him concerned her virtue. The transcript of their exchange was read in court. 'When I came to your place for the first time', she asked, 'was I an honest woman, and did you consider me as such'? Gentien replied coolly, 'The question is embarrassing, a young woman who accepts a rendezvous and who comes to a young man's house is at least exaggerating when she tries to pass for an honest woman.'[21] According to *Le Petit Parisien*, this comment provoked 'a murmur of reprobation from one end of the chamber to the other'.[22] Far from defending the woman he once loved, as an honourable man should, Gentien was now ready to attack her virtue. The public prosecutor, Lefebvre de Viefville, echoed Gentien's doubts in his closing argument. He asserted that 'her fall was free, voluntary … Furthermore Monsieur Gentien did not have to do with an ingénue, a girl of eighteen who was unaware of the danger; she was 27, with experience given by a life in the theater'.[23] Quite simply, Bière should not have expected anything but a passing affair with Gentien.

In the analysis of defence attorney Lachaud, Gentien's love letters to Bière indicated that he had given her more to hope for. They confirmed Bière's assertion that she had been an honest woman and that Gentien was pursuing a legitimate courtship, or at least that he wished her to believe so. Lachaud read Gentien's first love letter in its entirety, especially highlighting this passage:

> You are, without the least flattery, the most adorable woman that I have ever met. Everything in you is honest, sympathetic, and generous…. So with what joy will I meet with you again on the sixteenth! With you I feel I am better and I am raised up in my own eyes.[24]

Lachaud then turned to the courtroom audience, and asked:

> Are we here in the world of gallantry where Monsieur Gentien could be, as he always says, such a 'gallant man?' There he makes a declaration of love to an honest young girl. He loves her for her honesty, for her generosity. He is better since he has known her; he is elevated in his own eyes. This letter is not the only one. No, Mademoiselle Bière did not believe that in this liaison there would be nothing but pleasure.

Lachaud went on to read another letter, where Gentien spoke of 'the huge sacrifice you are about to make for me', describing himself as a 'man of heart', who was 'not an ingrate'. 'It is very clear, isn't it?' asked Lachaud, '… they love each other with a love that is serious, honest.' She goes to the rendezvous, Lachaud continues. 'He takes her, brings her to his house; she belongs to him. There was no violence; this woman was seduced, that's all. She gave her whole heart, all her passion, all her ardor.'[25] Bière thus appeared as a trusting and inexperienced young woman, who had made the mistake of giving her heart and her body to an unworthy man who 'belongs to a class of men who only like fleeting liaisons; love, for him and his ilk, is the material possession of a woman'.[26] For Bière, sex was an expression of love, while for Gentien, it was merely a physical encounter.

Motherhood, money and madness

Whatever implicit promises Gentien's letters may have contained, he never actually offered marriage, not even when Bière bore him a child. She discovered her pregnancy in January 1878, after she had left Paris for a lucrative singing engagement in Brussels, and Gentien had embarked on a long Mediterranean tour. Initially, neither parent welcomed the pregnancy. Bière admitted to using special baths and purgatives, and alleged that Gentien sent her to consult a Dr. Rouch, who offered to end the pregnancy.[27] This was hardly an auspicious beginning for Bière's maternity. Her baby Juliette-Claire Bière was born on 4 October 1879, with 'father unknown' listed on her birth certificate; six months later she died of bronchitis. Not only did Gentien fail to acknowledge his legal paternity, but he also refused ever to see the baby. In court he explained that he did not want to have to go to the Parisian suburb Saint Denis or subject himself to 'wet nurses' gossip', implying that he wanted the relationship to remain secret.[28] It would have been understood in this era that the tacit purpose of Gentien's requiring a wet nurse was to end Bière's lactation so that he could continue to have sex with her. Bière visited her child frequently, as might be expected of a doting mother, and she often asserted that she would have preferred to care for the child herself. Reportedly she was so distraught at her baby's sudden death that she was unable to attend the infant's funeral, and she had a portrait made of the cadaver before the interment. Yet perhaps the most impressive evidence of her maternal love was her demonstration of grief when she spoke about the baby in court. 'Marie Bière stood up, her eyes wet with tears, raised to heaven, her voice broken with sobs. She speaks in a shaking voice, she is gasping; the memory of the poor little dead being suffocates her.'[29]

In spite of this performance, the prosecution did not take Bière's claims about her maternal feelings at face value, complicated as they were by Bière's continued affair with Gentien even after the baby's death, as well as her demands for money. When the presiding magistrate asked her why she continued to have relations with Gentien, she asserted that she wanted to have another child. 'That's the way you hoped to hold onto the father?' the judge asked.[30] 'Oh! My God! No', she exclaimed. 'He still could have left me; but at least I would have had the love of a child which would have reminded me of the one I lost. All mothers will understand me.'[31] The judge was unconvinced by her explanation. 'Perhaps you believed it', he conceded, but he pressed the accused:

> it is even the charitable hypothesis of Monsieur the Investigating Magistrate. He wondered if, to justify in your own eyes the criminal act that you meditated, you sought justification of the true motive in a more elevated feeling. You invoked the memory of your child to give satisfaction to your personal sentiments.

To the presiding magistrate, Bière appeared to be motivated by greed and a desire for revenge rather than maternal love.

The question of money was indeed a thorny one for Bière: she may have started the relationship as a virgin in love, worthy of marriage, but she soon became a kept woman, in the very dishonourable position of exchanging sex for money. Bière had been supported entirely by Gentien ever since her mother discovered their affair and expelled her from the family home in the fall of 1878. Her attempt to return to her singing career was cut short by her pregnancy and subsequent loss of her voice. Bière's maid Madame Husson affirmed that Gentien sent Bière 300–500 francs every month.[32] In the fall of 1879, Bière went so far as to demand the sum of 3,000 francs from Gentien (under threat of exposing the affair to his family) for the purpose of establishing herself as a voice teacher. 'I want to be and I am a proper woman, not a kept woman. I want to rehabilitate myself through work and I want you to help me', she wrote Gentien, in a letter read aloud by the presiding magistrate.

While Bière raged over being a kept woman, Gentien insisted that there was nothing wrong with the transactional nature of their relationship. *Le Figaro* reported his testimony, and also noted the emotional responses of the audience: 'I always conducted myself as a *perfect gallant man* (explosion of murmurs) and my conscience reproaches me nothing, since in leaving her I gave her a pension. (Oh! Oh! Long agitation.)'[33] It was quite conventional for a wealthy man to keep a mistress, yet by the standards of his milieu, Gentien was a stingy lover. In addition to the allowance, he had installed Bière in an apartment with a paltry set of furniture, and there was no mention of his ever taking her out to restaurants or the theatre, or giving her other presents.[34] He encouraged her to take another lover – as he did himself by 1879 – but doing so would have cemented her status as a fallen woman.

Bière became increasingly distraught in the summer and fall of 1879, to the point where her sanity was in doubt. She saw Gentien for the last time on 30 June, when she staged a suicide attempt to frighten him. In the evaluation of the famous alienists Émile Blanche and Auguste Motet, this signalled the development of an increasingly extreme state of emotional distress. These alienists were summoned by the investigating magistrate to assess Bière's mental health because it was essential for the prosecution to establish that she was not, in fact, insane at the time of the crime.[35] A person whose rational capacity was impaired could not be held legally responsible for committing a crime, as provided in Article 64 of the French Penal Code, which exempted anyone 'constrained by a force which he could not resist', or in the state of *démence* (madness). This term specifically designated an impairment of reason, 'the incapacity to direct one's acts and to foresee their consequences'.[36] Yet an extreme emotional state did not necessarily entail an impairment of reason, as the doctors who evaluated Bière determined. At the trial, Blanche testified that he found evidence of madness in her family: one uncle died in an insane asylum, a 'very eccentric' brother was seeking his fortune in the Argentinean pampas and Bière's mother was found to be 'very disturbed' after an arrest for shoplifting.[37] Not only did the mental illness of close family members suggest a hereditary predisposition to madness, but Bière herself also had a history of extreme emotions.[38] According to Dr.

Blanche, these predispositions were exacerbated by her becoming a mother: 'ever since she felt her child move, the maternal feeling in turn engulfed and dominated her in excessive measure'. The official indictment concluded that doctors 'had determined that the disturbance of her mind had not caused her to lose awareness of her acts and that she should be considered responsible for them'.[39] From a legal standpoint, this opinion meant that the court could reduce the possible penalties for her in case of conviction; however, it did not mean that the doctors advocated her acquittal.

Emotion and honour in the assize court

Jurors were no more immune to powerful emotions than the defendant, or at least this was the hope of Bière's attorney Lachaud. Whereas earlier in the century, attorneys had appealed to the cool reason of professional judges,[40] Lachaud made a career of persuading jurors with his dramatic emotional pleas. Dubbed the 'attorney of the passions' by Léon Gambetta, Lachaud's special gift was 'to enter into the living flesh of the situation of the trial, to experience the passion of the accused, to feel all his angers … and to cry for mercy with the desperate energy of the unhappy man himself'.[41] The power of an expressly emotional appeal was quite troubling to many observers of the fin-de-siècle assize court. As the jurist Louis Proal despaired, 'An eloquent attorney, who knows how to move the hearts of the jurors and to put their reason to sleep … can make them forget the suffering of the victim and the necessity of social defense.'[42] Lachaud's 3½-hour closing argument was a masterpiece of this genre.[43]

He began with a direct appeal to the jurors' hearts: 'I have never known a more unhappy woman, more worthy of pity than my client! She had the most correct feelings, the most generous passions; she loved what is good. And here she is on the defendants' bench, devastated, fallen, without a single hope in the world.'[44] The question he posed for the jurors was how such a sweet young woman could have come to such a pass. 'I will show you where all this unhappiness came from, who caused it, and I hope that after hearing me, you will hold out your hand to this young woman to help her lift herself up!'[45] The cause of her unhappiness of course was Gentien, whom Lachaud portrayed as a cold-hearted manipulator. 'Ah! The odious cowardice of this man! His heart did not beat; his eye remained dry. Let him go laugh with his friends about this whole adventure! I am sure that all the honest people have judged him!'[46] According to Le Figaro, the response of the audience was, 'Bravo! Bravo! Long emotion (longue émotion)'.[47] Those who cheered expressed their affiliation with an emotional community of 'honest people' ready to condemn Gentien.

Though enhanced by Lachaud's rhetorical flair, Bière's own account was central to the defence. The core of Lachaud's speech was a long exposition of Bière's journals and the letters the two exchanged, comprising nearly two-thirds of his text.[48] His selections were faithful copies of the documents in the trial dossier, and gave an accurate impression of the overall body of written material, albeit emphasizing the passages least flattering to Gentien. It is plausible that Bière wrote her journal as a record of her emotions and intentions in view of her potential suicide, or an exercise in 'effortful self-shaping',[49] but the prosecution suspected more cynical motives. As the presiding magistrate noted during his interrogation of Bière, 'The investigating magistrate told you – and it has been thought – that you drafted all this to colour your crime and to make it more interesting.' But Lachaud treated the documents as if they would give transparent access to her innermost feelings. 'The woman's heart is going to open before you', he promised his listeners,[50] a heart that was true and honourable.

Bière's journal dramatically depicted her increasing desperation and resolve to kill Gentien, and Lachaud skilfully used it to draw the jurors to sympathize with her. By the middle of December 1879, she wrote that she was actively seeking an opportunity to attack Gentien, stalking him at public events. The last entry was dated 6 January, where Bière reported that she spent seven hours waiting for him parked in an unheated cab. Lachaud summed up:

> The state of mind of this unhappy woman is well established: it is delirium…. She is at the mercy of the passion that dominates her…. This man had neither love nor humanity; he never wanted to see his daughter. He was implored in vain by the unhappy woman I defend; by this unhappy woman, she who had the madness of maternal love![51]

Such a woman did not deserve condemnation but sympathy, Lachaud concluded.

> Messieurs the jurors, ask yourself this question. Is there not a limit to everything? Can we dominate all temptations? Ask yourselves…if, at certain moments, your will would not abandon you? You will say that there is a limit to human strength; you, men of the law, you will say that above the life of a man, there is something even more respectable: honour![52]

For Lachaud, the jurors' sense of honour was the ultimate standard by which Gentien and Bière should be judged. 'Let those who want to live à la Gentien know that, when they have dishonoured and lost a woman, she may avenge herself and face the law without fear, and face those who apply [the law] with respect and confidence.' Bataille reported that the audience responded with 'Prolonged emotion, yes, yes!'[53] The jury must have been persuaded, for they rendered a negative verdict in less than a quarter hour, and the news was greeted by a cheering crowd of thousands on the Place Dauphine.

It was crucial that Lachaud deployed the theme of honour at the climax of his argument, for it was the key to Bière's innocence. The index of Gentien's and Bière's honour was their respective capacity to feel the appropriate emotions. They were both in love, but his love was merely sensual, while hers was true. When their baby was born, Gentien showed not the slightest twinge of paternal love, while Bière doted on Juliette-Claire. Neither one of them upheld bourgeois standards of honourable behaviour – after all, it was an affair between an opera singer and a playboy – but this was not a case where the standard rules applied. Rather, the guarantor of Bière's honour was her honest heart, just as Gentien was condemned by his heart of stone. As Lachaud instructed the jurors, their justice was to be found in their own understanding of how willpower can buckle under temptation. They could understand how the rational mind might be overcome by other forces. And in such circumstances, Lachaud argued, honour was the most important value, a lodestar to guide them in their judgement. Honourability and sensibility were thus deeply interconnected, not just for the protagonists in the case but for the jurors as well. It was their sympathetic response to Bière that showed them that honour and justice should be hers.

Consequences in the public sphere

As jurors responded positively to the call to judge with their hearts, so too did the wider public that avidly followed her trial, appropriating her very private story of love, sex and abandonment for a variety of political purposes. Most notably, her story helped frame demands for increasing women's political and civil rights. 'If you want women to obey your laws, make laws that protect them!' Jean Frollo argued in *Le Petit Parisien*.[54] Bière would never have attacked Gentien, he argued, if she had been able to make him recognize the baby as his own. A commentator in *Gil Blas* named 'Renée' agreed. If Bière could have verified Gentien's paternity legally, then such a man 'would sooner resign himself to chastity than run the risk of being a father following a *partie fine*'.[55] Two editorials in the feminist periodical *Le Droit des femmes* also demanded legalizing paternity searches. 'If it is understood that a woman of 28, honest until then, knows what she is doing in giving herself, doesn't the man who takes her know just as much as she?' asked Léon Richer.[56] Even the notorious misogynist Alexandre Dumas *fils* professed a change of heart after assiduously attending Bière's trial. Having once endorsed a husband's right to kill his unfaithful wife,[57] he now advocated better laws for women's protection, especially the right to search for paternity and the right to divorce. If women could vote, he argued, they would bring about these legal changes, and crimes of passion would be superseded by legal action.[58] Divorce would become possible in France in 1884, while paternity suits would not be legalized until 1912.[59]

Discussion of Bière's case and others like it helped to focus public attention – and eventually the efforts of legislators – on these issues.[60]

Bière's case crystallized fears of women's violence while setting a precedent for women's acquittal in similar cases. The name of Marie Bière became a kind of shorthand for women's vengeance against men. One editorial sarcastically predicted that she would become a saint, and that seduced women would pray for her to bless their revolvers;[61] another envisioned that 'all the little belles of the boulevard will soon go out with revolvers hanging from their necklaces'.[62] The press continued to describe numerous women who attacked their lovers as being 'in the mold' or 'school' of Marie Bière.[63] Her name was frequently invoked over the years together with that of Madame de Tilly (acquitted for burning her husband's lover with acid in 1880)[64] in cases of apparent imitators, such as Adèle Pautard[65] and Rosa Vélay.[66] The acquittal of these women seemed to confer impunity on women who sought revenge against their faithless partners, prompting further critiques of the leniency of the assize court jury. The high rate of acquittal in the assize court would finally be reined in with the 1941 institution of *échivange*, where jurors decide the verdict in the company of a professional judge.

Bière's case also had an immediate effect on assize court procedure, in the abolition of the presiding magistrate's *résumé*.[67] Given between the final arguments of the defence attorney and the deliberation of the jury, the résumé summarized the case for the prosecution, and was meant to provide guidance for the jurors on the legal points they had to consider. In his résumé, the presiding magistrate Bachelier had alluded to the possible punishments that Bière might incur in the event of conviction. Lachaud vehemently objected, because the jury was not meant to consider the penalty in their deliberations; they were only to decide the question of guilt.[68] This highly publicized incident helped tip the balance against the résumé, which was eliminated in 1881. Partly for his efforts to bring about this reform the Paris city council recognized Lachaud in 1933 by erecting a plaque in his honour.[69]

Conclusion: Gender, emotion and honour in the public sphere

Bière's acquittal was a rejection of the licentiousness of a 'gallant man' and the legal code that condoned it. The ideas about honour deployed in Bière's trial offer an implicit critique of aristocratic debauchery in favour of a permanent union based on affection and reproduction. To borrow Rosenwein's term, the emotional community that vindicated Bière's aspirations for an honourable union rejected the standards of the emotional community of the gallant world to which Gentien belonged. Sexual continence was a key component of bourgeois honour, as was the use of sex for legitimate procreation only.[70] Gentien, of course, did not live up to these standards, and neither was Bière a bourgeois lady. Yet Bière's aspiration to convert their affair into a love match was validated by her successful self-presentation as an honest woman and aggrieved mother. A love match of this kind was not impossible in practice, but it certainly would have challenged prevailing social standards.[71] If Gentien had indeed married her, he would have affirmed her honour as a woman and his as a man. Without a marriage, Bière was no longer a respectable mother, but a kept woman, and her violent retribution punished Gentien as much as it restored her honourable status. Observers of the trial could assess the relative merits of the protagonists by using their affective faculty – what a nineteenth-century alienist might have called *sensibilité morale*. Their intuitive assessments of how Gentien and Bière experienced and expressed their emotions provided the basis for Bière's absolution. In other words, judgements grounded in emotion made it possible to expand the notion of honourability even to include Bière's attempt at murder.

Such close yoking of honour and emotion provided a surprisingly flexible way of judging the protagonists. In a context of strict law codes, restricted access to formal politics and a burgeoning sphere of mass communication, honour provided a way to navigate the shifting shoals of intimate relationships. Fin-de-siècle juries were notorious for acquitting the authors of crimes of passion precisely because they could sympathize with justifications of violence based on honour. The result was a more permissive attitude towards the use of violence in the name of honour than the law alone would allow, even violence used by women.[72] In other national and historical contexts, honour codes and law codes have interacted with different results in adjudicating violent conflict between intimate partners, sometimes reinforcing and sometimes undermining traditional patriarchal privileges.[73] During the French Third Republic, jury trials, public courtrooms, a free press and a high rate of literacy helped facilitate a collective negotiation of what honour might mean.[74] In this case, the honour of an aggrieved mother – even the unwed mother of an illegitimate child – finally trumped the honour of an elite man whose sexual adventures were no longer deemed excusable.

Marie Bière's case had an enduring legacy in political, legal and social terms. It demonstrates the extent to which 'diverse publics can contribute to the more general formation of public opinion on a scale sufficient to influence the state and other social institutions'.[75] To be sure, only men enjoyed all the rights of citizenship in the Third Republic, but many women – not least of whom was Bière herself – actively framed a variety of problems posed by her case: seduction, paternity and violence. Her trial provided the rhetorical occasion for a vigorous public discussion where truth was produced through the heart, not rational analysis. It was not necessary to be a trained expert in law or psychiatry to participate in judgements about Gentien's or

Bière's guilt; it took a true heart to perceive that a disgraced opera singer had more honour than her aristocratic lover. Her case demonstrates how an emotionally charged private conflict could matter politically, and indeed how a sensational crime of passion could matter in framing problems for the public good.

Notes

1   Robert A. Schneider, ed. 'AHR Conversation: The Historical Study of Emotions', *The American Historical Review*, 117, 5 (December 2012): 1487–1531; Barbara H. Rosenwein, 'Worrying about Emotions in History', *The American Historical Review*, 107, 3 (June 2002): 821–45; William M. Reddy, *The Navigation of Feeling: A Framework for the History of Emotions* (Cambridge: Cambridge University Press, 2001).

2   John L. Brooke, 'Reason and Passion in the Public Sphere: Habermas and the Cultural Historians', *Journal of Interdisciplinary History*, 29, 1 (Summer 1998): 48. See also Susan Dewey, '"Dear Dr. Kothari … ": Sexuality, Violence against Women, and the Parallel Public Sphere in India', *American Ethnologist*, 36, 1 (2009): 124–39; Jane Haggis and Margaret Allen, 'Imperial Emotions: Affective Communities of Mission in British Protestant Women's Missionary Publications, c. 1880–1920', *Journal of Social History*, 41, 3 (Spring 2008): 691–716; Lynn M. Voskuil, 'Feeling Public: Sensation Theater, Commodity Culture, and the Victorian Public Sphere', *Victorian Studies*, 44, 2 (Winter 2002): 245–74.

3   For a crime of passion between two male partners, see the case of Vaubourg and Boutry, Archives de la Ville de Paris et du Département de la Seine (AVP), D2U8/289, 20 February 1892.

4   To analyse an emotional community, Rosenwein invites the researcher 'to uncover systems of feeling: what these communities (and the individuals within them) define and assess as valuable or harmful to them; the evaluations they make about others' emotions; the nature of the affective bonds between people they recognize; and the modes of emotional expression that they expect, encourage, tolerate, and deplore'. Rosenwein, 'Worrying about Emotions in History', 842.

5   For an analysis of more typical cases of crimes of passion in the context of their urban social milieu, see Eliza Earle Ferguson, *Gender and Justice: Violence, Intimacy and Community in Fin-de-Siècle Paris* (Baltimore: The Johns Hopkins University Press, 2010).

6   Witnesses in Bière's case included no neighbours, only a handful of friends, Bière's concierge and maid, a few people she knew through her profession and several expert witnesses (doctors, alienists and a firearms expert).

7   AVP, D2U8/96, 7 April 1880.

8   The six daily newspapers surveyed for this study range from the very conservative *Le Figaro* and *Le Journal des Débats*, to the more popular *La Presse* and *Gil Blas*, to the truly mass-oriented *Le Petit Parisien* and *Le Petit Journal*, which was particularly noted for its sensational coverage of *faits-divers*.

For the larger context of the popular press and crime reporting, see Dominique Kalifa, *L'Encre et le sang: Récits de crimes et société à la Belle Époque* (Paris: Fayard, 1995).

9   'Le Drame de la rue Auber', *Le Petit Journal*, 7 April 1880.

10   'Affaire Bière', *La Presse*, 6 April 1880.

11   'Le Drame de la rue Auber', *Le Petit Journal*, 7 April 1880.

12   Albert Bataille, 'Gazette des tribunaux', *Le Figaro*, 6 April 1880. Bataille's articles on Bière are collected in his *Causes criminelles et mondaines de 1880* (Paris: E. Dentu, 1881), 13–51.

13   *La Vie Populaire, Édition hebdomodaire du Petit Parisien*, 11 April 1880. Women who admired Bière might have wanted to buy the 'costume Marie Bière' advertised for 270 francs, featuring a vest in the shape of a heart, and a belt pierced with a sword of justice. Adèle de Chambry, 'Le Monde et la mode', *La Presse*, 11 April 1880.

14   El Cadi, 'Le Drame de la rue Auber', *Gil Blas*, 7 April 1880. See also 'Le Drame de la rue Auber', *Le Petit Parisien*, 7 April 1880 and Bataille, 'Gazette des tribunaux', *Le Figaro*, 6 April 1880.

15   'Le Drame de la rue Auber', *Le Petit Parisien*, 7 April 1880.

16   'Le Drame de la rue Auber', *Le Petit Journal*, 7 April 1880.

17   Bataille, 'Gazette des tribunaux', *Le Figaro*, 6 April 1880.

18   On masculinity in fin-de-siècle France, see Christopher E. Forth, *The Dreyfus Affair and the Crisis of French Manhood* (Baltimore: The Johns Hopkins University Press, 2004) and Annelise Maugue, *L'Identité masculine en crise au tournant du siècle, 1871–1914* (Marseille: Rivages, 1987).

19   Ann-Louise Shapiro frames her discussion of Bière's story as a melodramatic narrative. See *Breaking the Codes: Female Criminality in Fin-de-Siècle Paris* (Stanford, CA: Stanford University Press, 1996), 37–38. Ruth Harris discusses Marie Bière's story in terms of the self-representation of a romantic heroine, but not in terms of honour, in *Murders and Madness: Medicine, Law, and Society in the Fin de Siècle* (Oxford: Clarendon, 1989), 218–25.

20   Cited in Lachaud's closing argument. Charles Lachaud, *Plaidoyers de Lachaud, recueillis par Félix Sangnier*, Vol. 1 (Paris: G. Charpentier, 1885), 434.

21   AVP, D2U8/96.

22   'Le Drame de la rue Auber', *Le Petit Parisien*, 8 April 1880.

23   'Le Drame de la rue Auber', *Gil Blas*, 9 April 1880.

24   Lachaud, 436.

25   Lachaud, 437.

26   Lachaud, 433.

27   As abortion was illegal in France, Dr. Rouch denied the allegations. On abortion in nineteenth-century Paris, see Rachel Fuchs, *Poor and Pregnant in Paris: Strategies for Survival in the Nineteenth Century* (New Brunswick, NJ: Rutgers University Press, 1992).

28   'Le Drame de la rue Auber', *Le Petit Journal*, 7 April 1880.

29 Bataille, 'Gazette des tribunaux', *Le Figaro*, 6 April 1880.

30 El Cadi, 'Le Drame de la rue Auber', *Gil Blas*, 7 April 1880.

31 Some observers took this as an oblique reference to Marie Antoinette, who said something similar in her trial.

32 'Affaire Bière', *La Presse*, 7 April 1880.

33 *Le Figaro*, 7 April 1880 (emphasis in the original). See also *Le Petit Journal*, 7 April 1880.

34 Cadi, 'Le Drame de la rue Auber'. Commenting on the acquittal in *Gil Blas*, 'Renée' mocked Gentien's parsimony. 'Thirteen hundred francs of furniture! Here are the amorous follies of a man of our day, almost twice a millionaire!' Renée, 'Lettre d'une parisienne à une provinciale', *Gil Blas*, 10 April 1880.

35 In Ferguson, *Gender and Justice* (Chapter 5). I found no correlation between an alienist's evaluation of the accused and a jury's verdict.

36 Paul Dubuisson, 'De l'Évolution des opinions en matière de responsabilité', *Archives de l'Anthropologie criminelle* (1887): 103.

37 'Affaire Bière', *La Presse*, 7 April 1880. Dr. Blanche contacted the investigating magistrate after reading Marie Bière's name in the paper.

38 Even Émile Zola commented on Bière's fateful inheritance. He saw her case as a real-life illustration of the hereditary principles that underlay his Rougon-Maquart novels. 'It was such a decisive example of the experimental novel!' he wrote. '[H]ere is where the experiment begins: Marie Bière, of a peculiar temperament, product of a heredity that was debated in court, shoots her lover; and thus, this pistol shot is like the drop of sulfuric acid that the chemist pours into a funnel, for as soon as the story decomposes, the precipitation occurs, the primitive elements appear. Isn't it marvelous?' Émile Zola, *Oeuvres complètes illustrées d'Émile Zola*, Vol. 31 (Paris: E. Fasquelle, 1906), 285.

39 AVP, D2U8/96. The official indictment (*acte d'accusation*) was also published in full in *Le Journal des débats* ('Bulletin Judiciaire', 6 April 1880), *La Presse* ('Affaire Bière', 6 April 1880), *Gil Blas* ('Le Drame de la rue Auber', 7 April 1880) and *Le Petit Journal* ('Le Drame de la rue Auber', 7 April 1880).

40 Reddy, *The Navigation of Feeling*, 272.

41 Léon Gambetta, 'Maître Lachaud' *Le Figaro, Supplément littéraire du dimanche*, 18 April 1880. Originally published in the *Cour d'assises illustrée* in 1862.

42 Louis Proal, *Le Crime et le suicide passionnels*, Paris: Félix Alcan, 1900, 285, 287.

43 Long excerpts of Lachaud's argument appeared in *Gil Blas* ('Le Drame de la rue Auber', 9 April 1880). It was summarized in *Le Petit Journal* ('Le Drame de la rue Auber', 9 April 1880), *Le Petit Parisien* ('Le Drame de la rue Auber', 9 April 1880), *La Presse* ('Affaire Bière', 9 April 1880) and *Le Figaro* (Albert Bataille, 'Gazette des Tribunaux', *Le Figaro* 8 April 1880). The concluding argument made by the prosecution [*réquisitoire*] reportedly lasted 1 ½ hours, but received much shorter shrift in the press.

44 Lachaud, 430.

45 Lachaud, 430.

46 Lachaud, 444.

47   Bataille, 'Gazette des Tribunaux', *Le Figaro*, 8 April 1880.

48   This estimate is based on the full text of Lachaud's speech published in *Plaidoyers de Ch. Lachaud* (op. cit.).

49   The phrase is from William Reddy in 'AHR Conversation', 1497.

50   Lachaud, 445.

51   Lachaud, 456. Bataille reported that the audience responded to this crescendo with 'sensation' ('Gazette des Tribunaux', *Le Figaro*, 8 April 1880).

52   Lachaud, 457.

53   Bataille, 'Gazette des Tribunaux', *Le Figaro*, 8 April 1880.

54   'Jean Frollo' was the pseudonym for Charles-Ange Laisant, editor of *Le Petit Parisien*, 'Marie Bière', *Le Petit Parisien*, 9 April 1880. Part of Frollo's editorial was reproduced by Léon Richer in 'Marie Bière', *Le Droit des femmes: Revue internationale du mouvement féminin*, 12, 186 (1880): 77.

55   Rénée, 'Lettre d'une parisienne à une provinciale', *Gil Blas*, 10 April 1880.

56   Richer, 'Marie Bière', 76–78.

57   Alexandre Dumas *fils*, *L'Homme-Femme: Réponse à M. Henry D'Ideville*. 4th ed. (Paris: Michel Lévy, 1872). In 1872, Dumas was responding to the trial of an aristocrat named Du Bourg, who was acquitted for killing his wife when he discovered her *en flagrant délit*.

58   Alexandre Dumas *fils*, *Les Femmes qui tuent et les femmes qui votent* (Paris: Calman Lévy, 1880).

59   On debates surrounding divorce in fin-de-siècle France, see Jean Elisabeth Pedersen, *Legislating the French Family: Feminism, Theater, and Republican Politics* (New Brunswick, NJ: Rutgers University Press, 2003). On paternity suits, see Rachel G. Fuchs, *Contested Paternity: Constructing Families in Modern France* (Baltimore: The Johns Hopkins University Press, 2008).

60   Andrea Mansker has analysed how professional women and feminists deployed notions of honour in demands for status and rights in *Sex, Honor and Citizenship in Early Third Republic France* (Houndsmills, Basingstoke, Hampshire and New York: Palgrave Macmillan, 2011).

61   Albert Millaud, 'Sainte Marie Bière', *Le Figaro*, 9 April 1880.

62   Pie Borgne, 'Chronique Parisienne', *Gil Blas*, 10 April 1880.

63   See, for example, 'Échos de Partout', *La Presse* 3 May 1880; 'Le Drame de la rue de Douai', *Le Figaro*, 20 August 1880; and the story of Eugénie Perrin recounted in 'Nouvelles Diverses', *Le Figaro*, 25 November 1887.

64   For an account of Madame de Tilly's trial, see Bataille, *Causes Criminelles et mondaines de 1880*, 174–93. For a comparison of Tilly's and Bière's cases, see 'La Loi qui permet de tuer', *La Presse*, 19 August 1880.

65   'Chronique', *Le Droit populaire*, 18 December 1880. For the dossier of Pautard's case, see AVP, D2U8/109. Pautard had been abandoned in destitution by her husband, whose new mistress was pregnant. For anxieties about Bière inspiring imitators, see also Albert Millaud, 'Les Graveurs sur chair', *Le Figaro*, 2 September 1880; Albert Bataille, 'Gazette des Tribunaux', *Le Figaro*, 7 November 1885.

66 'Tribunaux: Mlle Rosalie Vélay', *Le Droit de femmes: Revue internationale du mouvement féminin*, 13, 203 (1881): 157–58. For the trial dossier, see AVP, D2U8/120.

67 Albert Bataille, 'La Cour d'assises', chap. 6 in *Le Palais de Justice de Paris: son monde et ses moeurs, par la Presse judiciaire parisienne… préface de M. Alexandre Dumas fils* (Paris: Librairies-Imprimeries réunies, 1892), 281.

68 Albert Bataille, 'Gazette des Tribunaux', *Le Figaro*, 8 April 1880. See also: 'Affaire Bière', *La Presse*, 9 April 1880.

69 'Inauguration de la plaque apposée, à la mémoire de Lachaud, sur l'immeuble portant le no 11 de la rue Bonaparte', *Supplément au Bulletin Municipal Officiel* (3 February 1933): 761–67.

70 On nineteenth-century bourgeois honourability, see Robert A. Nye, *Masculinity and Male Codes of Honor in Modern France* (Berkeley: University of California Press, 1993).

71 One such love match was the case of Emilie Muller, wife of Edouard Genuyt de Beaulieu, acquitted of shooting him in 1884. She was an opera singer from humble origins. Although her aristocratic in-laws had opposed the match, they esteemed her so highly that they took her side against Edouard (AVP, D2U8/162).

72 In my larger study of crimes of passion, I found that the acquittal rate for men was 28 per cent, while for women it was 64 per cent, though men far outnumbered women as defendants. Ferguson, *Gender and Justice*, 9.

73 For some contexts where state justice worked to curtail violence between intimate partners, see Astrid Cubano-Iguina, *Rituals of Violence in Nineteenth-Century Puerto Rico: Individual Conflict, Gender, and the Law* (Gainesville: University Press of Florida, 2006); Barabara Alpern Engel, 'In the Name of the Czar: Competing Legalities and Marital Conflict in Late Imperial Russia', *Journal of Modern History*, 77 (March 2005): 70–96; Martin Wiener, *Men of Blood: Violence, Manliness, and Criminal Justice in Victorian England* (Cambridge: Cambridge University Press, 2004). Historians of Latin America have been particularly attentive to the ways that women could deploy notions of honour within and against patriarchal social and judicial structures. See Steve J. Stern, *The Secret History of Gender: Women, Men, and Power in Late Colonial Mexico* (Chapel Hill: University of North Carolina Press, 1995); Kimberly Gauderman, *Women's Lives in Colonial Quito: Gender, Law, and Economy in Spanish America* (Austin: University of Texas Press, 2003); Arlene J. Diaz, *Female Citizens, Patriarchs, and the Law in Venezuela, 1786–1904* (Lincoln: University of Nebraska Press, 2004).

74 A comparable study on fin-de-siècle Argentina is by Sandra Gayol, '"Honor Moderno:" The Significance of Honor in Fin-de-Siècle Argentina', *Hispanic American Historical Review*, 84, 3 (2004): 475–98.

75 Craig Calhoun, 'The Public Sphere in the Field of Power', *Social Science History*, 34, 3 (Fall 2010): 328.

9

Deeper than the death: Chaste suicide, emotions and politics of honour in nineteenth-century Korea

Jungwon Kim

In 1904, in the final years of the Chŏson dynasty, the Bureau of Ritual Administration ordered that a memorial arch be erected in honour of Madam Kim (1883–1904), who had committed suicide after the death of her husband, Sim Chaedŏk (1887–1903). The widow, born of an illustrious Sŏhŭng Kim family and a distant descendant of a prominent Confucian scholar,[1] had married Sim, a man from another elite family, at the age of 17. Although younger than his bride, Sim died from illness soon after their marriage. It is not clear how Madam Kim killed herself, for her biographies and the other documents about her death claim that she took her life without the use of any tool or poison.[2] What is clear, however, is the tremendous effort taken by her in-law family, as well as Confucian scholars in her community, to obtain official government recognition of Madam Kim's death as an honourable action that expressed her chastity (*yŏlhaeng*).[3]

In Chosŏn Korea (1392–1910)[4] many accounts were produced to highlight such actions as chaste suicides prompted by women's commitment to follow their deceased husbands into death. Male literati connected individual suicides to the ideal of the 'chaste wife' (*yŏlbu*) who had fulfilled the utmost Confucian virtue required of women. Although loyalty (*ch'ung*), filiality (*hyo*) and chastity (*yŏl*) were the three cardinal human relationships in Confucian morality, which carried distinct duties for subjects, children and women, the seeking of formal endorsement for chaste suicide was also linked to social and economic anxieties of elites in the Chosŏn state. These fears grew as their status declined over the nineteenth century.[5] In earlier periods of crisis, such as the Imjin Wars of 1592–1598 and Manchu invasions of 1623 and 1636, Chosŏn officials had made explicit connections between female chastity and male loyalty to the state.[6] Wifely fidelity was equated with political loyalty, and the performers of chastity and filial devotion were praised for demonstrating their passion for these values through self-sacrifice, self-mutilation and suicide – even though these practices violated the Confucian admonition against children harming the physical body given them by their parents.[7]

Thus, neither the practice of widow suicide nor its praise was consistent or uncontested, and both were connected to political and social conditions that shifted over the long history of the Chosŏn dynasty. By examining biographies of chaste women in the late nineteenth and early twentieth centuries in combination with evidence produced through legal inquiries into their deaths, we can see clearly that the virtuousness of self-destruction was a strategic construction of an elite in decline towards the dynasty's close. Being a faithful wife in earlier times had had little to do with the violent action of bodily harming or killing. In the early years of the Chosŏn dynasty, a widow who never remarried but committed herself to lifelong service to her deceased husband's family was recognized for devotion and wifely virtue. The deepening of Neo-Confucianization from the seventeenth century rendered the ideal of chaste women more prominent and instrumental, and the concept of women's fidelity became gradually enmeshed with the idea of bodily self-sacrifice, which appeared as the ultimate proof of chaste widowhood and criterion for wifely virtue. By the eighteenth century, Confucian scholars drew a clear status distinction between a widow who simply did not remarry (jŏlbu, or 'principled wife') and a widow who chose to commit suicide (yŏlbu, or 'chaste wife').[8] Although a widow's maintenance of fidelity without remarrying continued to be valued, male authorities no longer acknowledged it as a sufficient expression of genuine commitment to chastity.

The increased value and concern placed on chastity during the eighteenth and nineteenth centuries produced an outpouring of chaste suicide narratives. Whereas only a few records of faithful wives had appeared in the early Chosŏn years, Confucian literati produced numerous biographies of chaste women in final centuries of the dynasty. These 'violent tales of dead widows', depicting women as martyrs to marital loyalty and extolling them as exemplary heroines, have been used by subsequent scholars to examine the culture of chastity in late Chosŏn Korea. The conventional explanation within Korean historiography for the cultivation of the chaste suicide ideal is the Neo-Confucian transformation of Korean society, which strengthened the patriarchal lineage system of the elite group in the second half of the dynasty. It is certainly true that, with the development of Confucian patriarchy and patrilineality by the late Chosŏn period, filiality had become gendered: a daughter was supposed to be married out into another patriline at an early age and to redirect her filial duties away from her own parents and towards her parents-in-law as an important marital responsibility. However, such explanations analyse Neo-Confucian institutions and practices without considering the emotional dynamics of these shifts.

An alternative approach to understanding how the chastity ideal was sanctified by Confucian elites can be taken by analysing biographies of widows who committed suicide alongside the writings of women who recorded their motivations in intimate terms. These remarkable texts have been preserved because women's notes were used as evidence in state legal investigations into their deaths. Consequently, a range of emotions that might otherwise have been invisible in the practice of widow suicide can be interpreted through the insights introduced by historians of emotion. The honouring of women's voluntary deaths occurred at a moment when a community 'holding various values and ideas, practicing various forms of sociability, and privileging various emotions and styles of expression' took shape in tandem with the rise of Neo-Confucianism.[9] By considering widows' interpretation of their decision to kill themselves as well as Confucian writers' instrumental articulation of the values and feelings connected to chaste suicide, we can highlight 'the social and relational nature of emotions'.[10]

In this chapter I focus on petitions and circular letters which were collected and produced by Confucian literati in a bid to obtain official recognition of women's chaste deaths. I ask how and why these elite scholars represented women's acts of suicide, performed in the name of the chastity ideal, as honourable and virtuous. In addition, I examine women's deathbed notes and letters, drafted before taking their own lives, to examine how they described their own motives. These rare sources allow us to elucidate how individual emotional expression compared with prescriptive norms and to explore the fissures and bridges between social norms and individual women's experience.[11] 'The multiplicity of emotional modes and styles co-existing in social life'[12] served as an impetus for the honouring of chaste suicide as well as its practice. At the individual level, although moral stricture influenced their behaviour, widows' acts of suicide were not dictated by the political and moral agendas of Confucian moral strictures or government recognition. At the collective level, although emotional control was considered the key to self-cultivation in Confucianism, and emotion otherwise took on negative connotations among the Confucian literati,[13] they validated violent acts of suicide when they could present them as sincere emotional expressions of Confucian virtue. Thus, honour became implicated in chastity discourse and practice – in relation to the manifestation of widow's integrity and to the consolidation of the reputation and status of elite families.

The following examination of two widow suicide cases – Madam Kim's in 1904 and Madam Yu's in 1898 – interrogates how the motives and emotions associated with chastity suicide were interwoven and reinforced in late-Chosŏn Korea. Madam Kim, a young widow who took her life upon her husband's death, left death bed notes, which I read to map out the competing ideologies between chastity and filiality, and the complex boundaries between values and emotions. Moreover, her suicide's commemoration reveals how family members and Confucian scholars rallied wider communities to support official endeavours to honour chaste suicide in nineteenth-century Korean society. The second, contrasting case concerns a woman's resort to suicide as a means to protest against her unjust treatment. Madam Yu took her life after a villager slandered her reputation by impugning her sexual integrity. In both cases, however, family members and Confucian literati managed to mobilize petitions and circular letters to shore up the chastity ideal, by honouring Madam Kim's chaste death, and to ward off accusations against Madam Yu's morality and, by extension, her family's. Yet, there were some who questioned the motives that lay behind such public endeavours, both from Confucian moralists, who regarded them as venal, and from family members, who privately expressed their love, sorrow and bitterness. Thus it is possible to uncover and historicize the different emotional styles that circulated within shared Confucian values.[14]

Confucian communities and the making of chaste women

Although some examples of virtuous women had appeared during the previous Koryŏ (918–1392) dynasty, the foundation of the Chosŏn state marked a turning point in attitudes towards and discourse about the concept of chastity. Unlike the Buddhist Koryŏ society, the Chosŏn dynasty was established under Neo-Confucianism, which became the state ideology.[15] In particular, Confucian statecraft in early Chosŏn Korea viewed Koryŏ customs of marriage and women's engagement in activities outside the home as threats to both familial and social order. Chastity was seen not only as the orthodox core of female virtue but also, most importantly, as ensuring social morality based on the patriarchal and patrilineal family system.

Neo-Confucian reformers worked to impose juridical and social sanctions on widows who remarried and to reward those who did not. Not only was a legal stipulation enacted prohibiting a widow's remarriage and specifying that the sons of remarried women were prohibited from taking the civil service examinations (the main avenue to enter the bureaucracy throughout the dynasty),[16] but the government also endeavoured to spread the chastity values to the broader female population by publishing handbooks on virtuous womanhood.[17] Moreover, a system emerged during the Chosŏn period of granting rewards to exemplary people, such as loyal subjects, filial-minded sons and daughters and women who remained faithful after their husbands' deaths, all of whom were publicly honoured in both material and symbolic ways. Regardless of her social status, the rewards bestowed on any woman included goods such as rice, cloth, land and houses; exemption from taxes and corvée labour; upgraded official positions for the sons of chaste wives; the release from their social class of women of the lowest status; and the erection of memorial arches or tombstones.

The process of identifying and honouring chaste widows was bureaucratic, though largely based on community-based recommendations. In most cases, family members or local Confucian scholars prepared a biographical petition documenting a virtuous woman's exemplary behaviour, and then submitted it to the local office. Once the local magistrate verified the accuracy of the submitted petition, he sent the materials up to the provincial officials, who in turn submitted it to the central government in the capital. After the government reviewed and approved the candidate's merit, the request for a reward was sent to the Ministry of Rites, the office with the authority to issue awards based on outlines written in the law.[18] Awards for chaste women were granted at the beginning of every year, and the same procedure continued until the end of the dynasty. While material awards and tax advantages were most attractive to nonelites, receiving a commemorative arch for an exemplar's household or her native town was considered the highest honour for an elite family.[19] The arch was regarded as a symbol of the family's moral achievement, and here the collective actions of families and Confucian scholars in the town where a virtuous woman had resided played a central role in making the case for her having been a chaste woman.

This trajectory was followed in the case of Madam Kim, who committed suicide in 1904. In addition to a family petition drafted and signed by 10 male members of the Sim family (Madam Kim's in-law family), 32 scholars in town signed and submitted another petition to the local court. Moved by both petitions attesting to Madam Kim's virtuous life and suicide, a local magistrate reported her case to a higher officer (the provincial governor), who was also deeply touched by her exemplary life and death. Soon, a district-level petition signed by 40 Confucians reached the provincial governor, followed by a provincial-level one signed by 580 scholars-officials who resided in South Kyŏngsang Province. Emphasizing Madam Kim's moral family background and extraordinarily virtuous life, these petitions all requested the erection of an arch to commemorate Madam Kim's heroic death and inspire people with her moral behaviour. Praising Madam Kim's sincere heart that had resulted in her righteous death,[20] the governor of South Kyŏngsang Province recommended her case to the central government for review. In the tenth month of the same year in which Madam Kim had died, the government finally approved the appeals and directed the Bureau of Ritual Administration to award the Sim family a memorial arch in honour of Madam Kim.[21]

The Sim family also compiled a three-volume work, which contains various documents, including the petitions, reports by the provincial governors and official orders handling the reward, as well as 15 biographies, eulogies and epitaphs written by male scholars in the Sim family and other Confucian scholars in Madam Kim's town and beyond. This campaign demonstrates the lengths families and communities had to go to before a widow who took her life could be recognized as chaste. As local elites, Confucian scholars involved in the campaign attempted to direct the government's vision towards their significant role in society, and they also intended that their writings on Madam Kim's behalf would transmit Confucian values to the community at large. Because these values and ideals served as important indicators of male literati's moral reputation, their endorsement of chaste widow suicide was an indispensable component in maintaining their social status in late Chosŏn Korea.

In fact, the growing difficulty of securing governmental posts towards the end of the dynasty led more and more families to turn to other means to consolidate their membership among the elites, including the veneration of widows who committed suicide. After the Manchu invasions, many elites began returning to and settling in their local hometowns due to the limited number of official positions available in the central government. The numbers of local elites thus grew greater than ever,[22] and they participated in a broad range of local administration through their local Confucian association. These exclusive organizations were closed to those without the required family background. Although local elite families were politically marginalized from the centre of power, having an exemplary family member was a powerful method of proving to the public the honourable standing of a family. Petitioning for the recognition of a chaste suicide could also glorify a local community in which people with the same surname lived near one another, mostly connected through marriage and scholarly networks. The collective actions of several 100 male scholars, culminating in the petitions on behalf of Madam Kim, thus highlight the process by which an individual woman's suicide could be made to serve public ideals of honour.[23]

The Confucian literati's collective efforts to receive government-sponsored honours and their commitment to the chastity ideal can be connected to similar efforts in mediaeval Europe, in which scholars defined and assessed what was 'valuable or harmful to them'. By analysing how they evaluated others' emotions, we can discern 'the modes of emotional expression that they expect, encourage, tolerate, and deplore'.[24] All four petitions, signed by a total of 662 Confucian scholars in South Kyŏngsang Province, opened by noting the fact that Madam Kim was a descendant of Kim Kwaengp'il (1454–1502), one of the most eminent and respected early Confucian scholars. Because she was born and raised in 'a family which had been time-honoured by the government for having the tradition of Confucian education',[25] Madam Kim had, as the petitions clearly imply, an innate moral foundation that ultimately influenced her decision to die for the Confucian ideal. The petitions also point out that Madam Kim's husband was a descendant of a loyalist, Sim Chagwang (1592–1636), whose true heart was always trusted by King Injo (r. 1623–1649) and who died carrying out the monarch's orders during the Manchu invasion in 1636.[26] The petitions describe the Sim family as 'a family known for its loyalty and filiality', inferring that Madam Kim's virtuous character was magnified after her marriage by her husband's family tradition of loyalty and filiality.

The petitions place greatest emphasis on Madam Kim's attitude towards her destiny of *chongsa*, or 'following-in-death'. In eighteenth- and nineteenth-century Korea a small minority of scholars questioned such claims by condemning widow suicide after a husband's peaceful death. Chŏng Yagyŏng (1762–1836) stressed that such acts were irresponsible, as they were undertaken without consideration for surviving in-law parents and children.[27] In Chŏng's lengthy essay, 'Yŏlburon' ('A Thesis on Chaste Wives'), he criticized the extremes of virtuous behaviour praised by most of his contemporaries as a dishonourable way of gaining social recognition for elite families, and as a means to secure material awards for members of nonelite groups.[28] Witnessing the increasing practice of chaste suicide out of vulgar motivations during his time, he distinguished the excessive expression of virtue that ended in death (improper suicide) from its proper expression, namely out of a righteous heart and a widow's sincere feelings. To endorse widows' suicides indiscriminately would encourage women to take their lives lightly. As Chŏng argued, there was nothing commendable or canonical about widows making this sacrifice. Such *chongsa* was uncontrolled action and therefore unacceptable.

Brushing aside such criticism the scholars who petitioned to honour Madam Kim took care to acclaim the fact that she had showed no hesitation or fear about following her husband into death. She was remarkably calm facing her husband's death, 'without showing any trace of frustration about her life (by beating her chest out of deep resentment)'.[29] Madam Kim's exceptional rectitude made her case even more deserving of official commemoration as exemplary. The provincial-level petition proclaims, 'Alas, how chaste it is! Dying itself is difficult, yet quietly following the decision to die is far more difficult. How difficult [is what] Madam Kim has accomplished!'[30] Madam Kim was able to carry out such a quiet, resolute death because 'she always observed rituals carefully and did not do things derived from her selfish emotion or affection (K. *chŏng*; Ch. *qing*)'.[31] Whereas the thought of Wang Yangming (1472–1529) valorized an emotional response to grief in late Ming China, as Alison Bailey notes in her chapter, Madam Kim's promoters emphasized her commitment to ritual propriety, avoiding any suggestion that her action was driven by grief. The prominence placed on Madam Kim's 'following-in-death' was so critical to her posthumous identification that the three-volume work dedicated to her suicide was entitled *Chongyongnok* (A Record of Following the Path).

Indeed, close analysis of the petitions – circulated, approved and authorized by the Confucian scholar communities – illuminates the complexity of shared feelings and perceptions towards chaste suicide; equally, it reveals the emotional strategy by which the Confucian literati legitimated women's acts of violence performed in the name of chastity. Communities of scholars bonded together through their shared interest in Madam Kim's case and through their declared belief that chaste suicide was the highest moral action possible for a woman to perform. While Confucian scholars ardently praised the restraint of sentiment displayed by Madam Kim, their petitions served as emotional textual spaces. Hundreds of scholars joined to authorize the petitions and to legitimate the violent action by providing language that codified, formed and evoked these Confucian men's unified feelings about Madam Kim's choice of death.

Madam Kim, filial daughter and chaste wife?

Whereas scores of petitions, biographies and eulogies beatify Madam Kim for her quiet yet indomitable attitude towards her destiny of following her deceased husband in death, her own writings are full of distress and despair about her fate. In her own notes, left before she committed suicide three months after her husband's death, she deplores the fact that her life of 20 years has been transient, like an empty dream.[32] She writes poignantly that no one would ever have expected her life (as the wife of an elite man) to be so miserable that it can hardly be expressed. Using the phrase 'How resentful' (wŏnt'ong) in line after line, she states, 'It is best to die if I have to live as a fool who can neither see the world nor listen to anything.... Who would ever know my thoughts inside? Where can I write down the layers and layers of resentment that rankle in my heart?'[33] Also, in short notes discovered in a crevice in the wall of her room, she describes how her life is hopeless, and she assumes that it will be unremittingly agonizing and useless if she remains alive as a widow.

Thus, the Confucian scholars' descriptions of Madam Kim as a fearless woman who met her death calmly appear at odds with her own testimony. Madam Kim's notes show her contemplating the kind of life that she would face as a young, childless widow, rather than conveying a sense of firm commitment to the normative chastity ideal. 'My remaining life will be nothing but futile', she judged: 'being imprudent, I only follow the Great Path; but how pitiful I am. How pathetic, how resentful!'[34] The 'Great Path' of following her deceased husband into the ground was, then, not a step that Madam Kim embraced because she was committed to the ideal of chastity. Rather, she was ambivalent and desperate. Her writings reveal mixed emotions and express her indecision and bitterness over the need to follow an ideal as a preferable fate. She would be honoured for her moral integrity if dead; if she remained alive she would confront a fate worse than death.

Although Madam Kim left no word that we know of for her in-law parents, except a brief note on the generosity they had shown her during her short marriage, she did leave a letter to her father, which expresses her guilt at dying before her parents and asks him to forgive an unfilial daughter for this grave sin.[35] Though married into a new family, Madam Kim's letter shows more concern about failing to repay her own parents' affection than about performing her marital and filial duty towards her parents-in-law. Moreover, in the eulogy that Madam Kim's father subsequently dedicated to his daughter, he said nothing about any virtuous trait in the suicide his daughter had carried out. To her father Madam Kim was a beloved and loving bride, rather than a heroine who exemplified Confucian virtue. His worries began even before her death, as he wrote: 'I was anxious about a woman being affectionate (yŏja yakjŏng) [and so was my daughter].'[36]

This paternal account, distinct from the petitioners' descriptions of Madam Kim's motives, raises questions about the relation between her emotions and her decision to take her life. Madam Kim's writings are filled with dejection about her situation, casting doubt on whether she was, as petitioners claimed, 'ready to take the path [of suicide] and showed not even slight sign of resentment upon death'.[37] Her writings indicate multiple considerations, including her conjugal affection for her dead husband and despondency about a life without him:

For about six years [of marriage], we did not even have one leisure moment to drink together [due to his illness]. Because [I believe] my affectionate husband returned to Heaven [i.e., he died], I try not to be sorrowful. [Yet] if I had known this would happen, I would have done better. How hardhearted I was! Now, realizing that I was heartless, my remorse is eternal and my bitterness is infinite. How most regrettable! In this world, whom can I rely on [if I continue to live]?[38]

Although Madam Kim spent her short marriage taking care of her husband, who fell ill directly after the wedding took place, she was not reticent in articulating her conjugal attachment in emotional terms. Departing from the teaching of the Confucian ritual handbooks, which discouraged reference to conjugal relations, her note emerges as a place of both marital intimacy and obligation.[39]

The only person who appreciated the conflicted emotions contained within Madam Kim's decision to die was perhaps her father. A Confucian scholar himself, he acknowledged the grand meaning of chaste suicide as the ultimate expression of a wife's loyalty to her husband, yet had hoped his beloved daughter would not have to face it: 'A wife following her deceased husband is a completely righteous thing. Nevertheless, how can a father [not] wail upon a child's death? What kind of logic is this? ... I only try to suppress heartbreaking sorrow.'[40] In anguish, he continued: 'If I say you should die, I am a heartless [father]; but [even] if I do not want you to die, will your life be a happy one?' In this question he conveys his own turmoil, but he also authorizes the sincerity of his daughter's despair at the hardships and constraints that awaited her as a young, childless widow.[41] Thus, the intimate evidence in Madam Kim's case further illustrates how the virtue of chastity could conflict with equally potent ideal of filiality.

Confucianism saw filiality as the foundation of the familial and social orders, placing it at the centre of virtuous emotions. With the entrenchment of Confucian patriarchy during the late Choson period, a married daughter was supposed to render her primary filial devotion to her parents-in-law, meaning that a daughter's filial duties to her natal parents were 'transferable' to her husband's parents as a core part of her marital obligations. This expectation made a daughter's filial piety subordinate to a wife's fidelity.[42] In general, historians concur that the 'filial devotion of officials for their parents would be transformed into loyalty to the ruler'.[43] Accordingly, the 'wifely way' is considered the analogue of the 'subject's way', meaning that the idea of chastity operated as the female counterpart to male loyalty to the state. Within this framework, proper spousal relations could be realized and sustained only by a wife's chastity, and what might have been considered an unfilial act of chaste suicide in regard to a woman's natal parents could be regarded as a married daughter's fulfilment of marital fidelity.

Nevertheless, the child–parent relation evoked the most universal of reciprocal human emotions, including deep filial love for parents who provided life and nurturing, even when the family relation was framed in terms of duty and rites outlined by Neo-Confucian rituals. While some scholars have acknowledged the potential conflict of chastity with another essential Confucian norm of filiality, they have not considered the emotional basis of a woman's choice of suicide over her filial attachment to her parents. They presume that the archetypal form of Confucian family proprieties required the ritual subjects to control their emotions so as to uphold the proper hierarchical relations within a family, regardless of family members' feelings for each other. Yet Madam Kim's decision to die was emotionally devastating for father and daughter alike. Her letters to her father and his eulogy for her clearly indicate that the Neo-Confucian ritualism based on obligation and discipline could neither silence individual feelings nor rule out intimacy in family relations.

Whether a married daughter's filial emotion was completely transferred to her in-laws or merely extended to them (while remaining active towards her own parents as well), these feelings could be seen to serve the values delineated by the patriarchal family system in a Confucian society. This Confucian vision of social harmony resolved the conflict between filial emotion and marital fidelity in favour of a woman's husband and in-laws, though it also flagged the potential tension between the two virtues. As JaHyun Kim Haboush points out, however, it was not simply a question of a married daughter's ability to transfer her filiality to her husband's family for the sake of wifely virtue, but of 'how filial values and filial emotions

could still be seen as being in harmony when social norms ran counter to
the exclusivity of filiality', an observation that underlines the complexity
of emotional life within social norms.[44] 'Although emotions and values are
made to remain in harmony in a Confucian society',[45] as Haboush notes, the
emotions expressed in Madam Kim's death bed notes and her father's eulogy
posed a counterpoint to the moral order prescribed in Confucian literature.

Madam Yu, chaste widow and vengeful woman

The tone of the intimate texts associated with Madam Kim's suicide points
to the painful existence she would have faced had she remained alive.
Significantly, the texts provide compelling evidence of the lowly status
of widows in Chosŏn society, despite the Confucian state's readiness to
honour those who remained faithful to their deceased husbands by refusing
to remarry. In choosing to remain unmarried widows affirmed the hold
of classic models of chastity; yet, widows of all classes were marginalized
socially and vulnerable to accusations of immorality. Women who remarried,
especially elite women, faced social prejudice and a possible decline in
status, because their sons and grandsons would lose the eligibility to sit
for the civil service examination due to the stigma of having an unchaste
mother or grandmother. Even those who chose not to remarry were exposed
to various sexual attacks (both verbal and physical) from outsiders: once a
husband died, the position of a widow became not only ambiguous within
her husband's family (for a childless widow like Madam Kim in particular)
but a potential source of scandal within the community as well, as the case
of Madam Yu illustrates.

Maintaining chaste widowhood, then, depended largely on the effort
of a widow's family members to confirm her virtue. Unless her in-law or
natal family could provide her with moral and, even more critically, material
protection, it was almost impossible for a widow to perform the expected
duty of remaining secluded in the women's quarters of the house and
entirely devoted to the family of her late husband. For impoverished women,
sexual loyalty and property were even more closely tied to the feasibility of
widowhood, since they had to engage in a variety of economic activities
outside the home if they were to survive, and they frequently became the
targets of various rumours as a result. Even the widow of an elite family of
limited means could find herself the victim of groundless rumours, damaging
not only to herself but to the entire family, if neighbours and community
members chose to make her chastity an issue.

The suicide of Madam Yu and its protracted adjudication demonstrate
the impossible position in which widows often found themselves. The
records of her case do not indicate how long she had been widowed before
she committed suicide at the age of 47 in 1898, but it is clear that Madam
Yu did not have a surviving son to succeed her husband's line. Instead, she

was raising an adopted son on her own in the small Pudan village of South Ch'ungch̆ong Province after her husband died. In Confucian patriarchy, only a son could succeed a patrilineal line, though couples without sons could adopt one from among the husband's male relatives.[46] One night, on the twelfth day of the ninth month,[47] her adopted 12-year-old son informed his maternal uncle that his sister, Madam Yu, was suffering from severe stomach ache.[48] The pair rushed to her room where they discovered an earthenware vessel containing traces of poison lying near her body. They fed her diluted rice water to try to revive her but she died. The incident was reported by her adopted son, first to his father (a cousin of her late husband) and then to the local court.

Madam Yu's natal family and husband's family apparently held elite status, but neither was sufficiently wealthy to manage a scholarly life. This situation meant that most of the men were engaged in farming rather than the study of Confucian classics. Towards the latter part of the dynasty, many elite families struggled economically, especially if they had not produced civil service exam passers for a long time. Madam Yu's families, like many others, had to pursue 'profit', an activity despised by Confucians.[49] Because of her straightened economic circumstance she could not remain deep within the women's quarters to sustain the image of virtuous widowhood; in fact, she engaged in numerous economic pursuits, even renting a room in her house to a man of an outside family. Madam Yu's enterprise and initiative, which ensured her survival, also left her vulnerable to rumours about her chastity.

In recognition of her family's status an autopsy was not performed. Instead, the cause of her death was determined through the physical evidence around Madam Yu's body and through witness testimony. After examining the earthenware vessel containing poison, the local magistrate (accompanied by a retinue of clerks, medical specialists and military officers) confirmed that she had died as a result of 'suicide by poison', and testimony from her son and brother provided a sense of her motive.[50] Together, this evidence led to the finding that Madam Yu had committed suicide after a man named Im Ch'ungho had spread malicious gossip that disparaged her reputation. Because his allegations also cast a shadow over family honour, efforts were made by her family and members of her village to call for an investigation. All who spoke to the investigators agreed that Im had concocted a rumour that Madam Yu had behaved immorally, and that he had repeated his allegations in a circular letter he sent to leading Confucian scholars in town. Upon learning about Im's attack, Madam Yu had indignantly declared, 'I will live or die at Im's house', and ran there to confront him with a sickle.[51] Neighbouring women dissuaded her from attacking him and she was forced to return home. Deterred from defending her honour and resentful over having to endure ill fame and disgrace, she died by suicide later that night.[52]

The full details of the rumour and Im Ch'ungho's motivation for circulating it remained unclear until a second round of testimony was taken after Im had run away.[53] This exposed the fact that Im had specifically claimed that Madam Yu and her remote male relative, Yu Ch'igŭk, were engaged in an improper sexual relationship.[54] A 30-year-old who made a living by farming, Yu Ch'igŭk dwelled near Madam Yu's home. According to the family's testimony he had observed that the lonely widow struggled to manage her life, with only her young son to help, so he sometimes took care of farming and gathering firewood for Madam Yu out of sympathy. But after he had quarrelled with Im in a dispute over a bamboo field, the latter set about to expel Madam Yu's supporter from the village.

The angered Im proceeded to involve other villagers in his cause and enlist the aid of local Confucian scholars. In a circular (*t'ongmun*) he sent out to men of the village, he claimed that there was a licentious relationship between Madam Yu and Yu Ch'igŭk, and he underlined its worrying moral implications for the village:

> From the past, distinction between men and women was clear; a boy and girl should not sit together after they have reached the age of seven.... Previous sage-kings instructed that a man should not wish to indulge in [sexual] passion, and a woman should not desire private relations. In case this was violated, the previous kings instituted laws [to punish such criminals] which are written in the law book. Now, [moral] spirit is very chaotic and people do not know ritual and propriety.... [Since this case of Yu Ch'igŭk and Madam Yu happened in this town] how can it be said that the country has law and this town has [Confucian] propriety? ... Alas, out of my blood-boiling wrath, I cannot help but take this way to issue a circular. On the thirteenth day of this month, members of the [Confucian] association should all gather in town and admonish Yun Ch'igŭk and the woman [to whom he is] related. Then let's destroy Yu's house and kick him out [of this town] so that we can rectify the custom and [moral] spirit of the village.[55]

Madam Yu committed suicide just before the date Im had set for taking the collective action against Yu Ch'igŭk.

For Confucian scholars throughout the Chosŏn dynasty, circular letters served as a means to build social networks, and a textual space where individuals could coordinate, publicize and mobilize their opinions.[56] Because Im's letter was copied by an official at the court and attached to the end of legal testimonies as evidence in Madam Yu's death reports, we do not know how many local scholars actually signed the circular. However, he clearly appealed to his targeted audience in the village by invoking Confucian gender norms, which condemned the violation of male and female separation as well as the danger of subjective passions. Moreover, by linking chastity to the reputation of the village, he urged his audience to recognize the seriousness of a case that challenged the ideal of chastity, stressing individual chastity as an essential part of the shared notion of community honour. Im's voicing of his own frustration – his fear for the reputation of the village if the problem were left unsolved – indicates how emotions were brought into play through the circular as they were negotiated, expressed and conceived of in the context of a community where honour embedded in Confucian moral values stood at the heart of governing both individual and collective behaviours.

Im, the accused slanderer, was not the only individual who mobilized the politics of honour. The investigative report into Madam Yu's suicide arrived at the court about a month after it happened, hinting that her in-law family had hesitated before they decided to register this case. Although they evidently knew that it was a criminal offence to pressure or cause any person to commit suicide,[57] they could not be certain of the eventual outcome if Madam Yu's case was submitted to the local court of Sŏsan district. If they won, it would restore honour to Madam Yu's affinal family as well as to her in-law family; however, this decision also invited further disgrace by airing the very rumour that had caused Madam Yu to take her life.

Ultimately, the magistrate found Im's rumour to be false. Moreover, in his postscript to the case he praised Madam Yu's death, declaring that her suicide derived from 'her adamant [will to uphold] chastity'.[58] According to the official record, there was no question of Madam Yu's real motive. The testimonies of her family members and neighbours had convincingly painted her as a faithful widow who had always upheld the supreme virtue, and whose only reason to die was the damage caused to her moral reputation, and the shame this had brought to her families.[59] The court's and family's construction of her action as moved by chastity concerns was an essential rhetorical manoeuvre used to portray her death in the most sympathetic light possible. Madam Yu took her life, but in death she affirmed the status of a vulnerable elite in the eyes of the wider community.

But was the magistrate correct in his assumptions concerning Madam Yu's emotional state? Before poisoning herself, Madam Yu's had left a testament of her own which made no mention of chaste widowhood; instead, the document boldly asserts her sense of personal integrity and her conviction that she had suffered an injustice that ought to be avenged:

> Upon writing [this testament], how sorrowful it is…. Dying is not a sad thing at all; yet dying with ill fame and disgrace is extremely vexatious…. I have never done anything to harm other people, yet who could revenge me after I die in dishonour? How bitterly mortifying it is that I have been unjustly charged and have gotten into this situation in the course of life! Please investigate [who has done this to me] and punish him on my behalf….[60]

Just as her families were concerned with their own honour, so Madam Yu was keenly aware of what it would be like to have a licentious rumour follow her around as she continued to lead her life in the village. It would mean the destruction of her public image and loss of her moral self and dignity that, once ruined, would be difficult to restore through living. Committing suicide was not a matter of enacting the chastity ideal or preserving an indicator of her elite family status; rather, she considered it a way to fulfil her passion to reinstate her lost honour.

Madam Yu may have been one of the many Koreans at the time who saw the act of suicide as admirable, and as effective in expressing fidelity, in bringing attention to an unjust situation and in seeking revenge against one's oppressors. Explicitly asking in her testament that she be avenged, Madam Yu chose a form of death that would magnify the emotional impact of her cry for justice, thus shaping the meaning and significance of her death as much as she could, while also making herself exemplary of chastity. And as she had wished, her death was ruled to be a chaste action, ritually sanctioned and officially recognized during the late Chosŏn dynasty.

Conclusion

In Confucian Chosŏn society, where one's personal virtue extended to the public good, the notion of women's chastity was politically salient. Because a wife's loyalty to her husband was deemed to be equivalent to a man's loyalty to the king, both were considered essential for social order. Although some Confucian scholars spoke against valuing widow suicide over staying alive to serve the surviving family, most literati esteemed it as the highest expression of wifely duty. Female chastity worked to guard the social position of families and individuals, particularly elites, keenly aware of its power to reinforce or undermine status. Confucian beliefs in Korea confirmed emotions only as elements in social hierarchy and only when expressed through ritual form. Widow suicide was therefore memorialized as the product of a calm and unemotional resolve to follow proper practice, not as an expression of grand emotion. Only a few Confucian scholars portrayed widow suicide as a selfish – and thus antisocial and un-Confucian – act taken to enhance individual reputation and family fortunes.

The suicide notes left by women who took their lives provide a reminder that however much ideological valuations define the moral world of individuals, they cannot fully account for individual emotion and action. Madam Kim's writings indicate that she despaired over the miserable life she faced as a young childless widow, and she struggled over her enduring affection for her family, a love her father reciprocated. Similarly, Madam Yu, who committed suicide long after her husband died, provided little indication that she was motivated by the Confucian ideal of following her husband into death. A member of the elite class, though lower in social status than Madam Kim, she nonetheless faced the same vulnerability since suspicions of infidelity could ruin her reputation. Her decision to kill herself arose from her loss of dignity within the community, and it also offered a means to seek revenge against a tormenter who could otherwise operate with impunity.

Thus complex emotions surrounded the formal acknowledgement of social obligations and political recognition of widow suicide.

Confucian scholars' collective efforts of petition writing and the circulation of letters defining and extolling the chastity ideal illuminate the emotional connection among a group that shared the same values and their tendency to adhere to the same norms of emotional expression in achieving their goals. The emotions that they evoked were calm dutifulness on the part of widows and, for their own part, righteous pride that womenfolk had followed the proper path. The two cases examined in this chapter powerfully illustrate diverging emotional styles for opposing objectives, which converged in terms of hegemonic Confucian values. They also highlight the need for historians to revisit the practice of chaste suicide by examining evidence from both the individual and the collective point of view. Chaste suicide cannot be separated from historical and intimate circumstances and shifting social, economic and political tensions that prevailed as individuals reconfigured the way they understood their own bodies, cultural values and emotions.

Notes

I would like to thank the editors of the volume for their insightful comments and precious suggestions on various drafts of this chapter. This project was supported by the Academy of Korean Studies Grant funded by the Korean Government (Ministry of Education) (AKS-2010-DZZ-2101).

1 As one of the most eminent and representative early Chosŏn Confucian scholars, Kim Kwaengp'il (1454–1502) particularly valued the importance of the Confucian text *Elementary Learning* (*Sohak*) for educating children.

2 A likely explanation is that she starved herself to death. This form of suicide is recorded in broadly similar circumstances in Korea. See JaHyun Kim Haboush, *The Memoirs of Lady Hyegyŏng: The Autobiographical Writings of a Crown Princess of Eighteenth-Century Korea* (Berkeley: University of California Press, 1996), 41.

3 Sim Chonghwan, ed., *Chongyongnok* (A Record of Following a Path) was published in three volumes in 1909 by one of Madam Kim's in-laws, Sim Chonghwan, and includes Madam Kim's own handwritten deathbed letters. I used a copy stored in the Kyujanggak Archive in Korea (ko 4655–4694/ sangbaek ko 920.7–G429s–v.1/3).

4 Founded in 1392, Chosŏn was the last dynasty in Korean history and endured for more than 600 years, until the country was colonized by Japan in 1910. For transliteration, I use the McCune-Reischauer system for Korean terms and Pinyin for Chinese.

5 Chosŏn Korea was hierarchically structured based on a hereditary status system that was divided into elite aristocrats, commoners and the lowborn. The elites, known as the *yangban*, consisted of a small group of governing

aristocrats at the top of the society and enjoyed most of the political, social and economic privileges, such as tax exemption. While formal education of female elites was limited, most male elites were trained in the Confucian classics so as to pass the civil service examination. Throughout this chapter, I use the term 'elite' to refer to this group.

6   Yi Sukin (Lee Sook-in), 'The Imjin War and the Official Discourse of Chastity', *The Seoul Journal of Korean Studies*, 22, 2 (December 2009): 137–56, 148.

7   Although harming one's body violated the core value of Confucian filiality, various acts of self-inflicted violence, such as flesh sacrifice, were widely practised as other forms of filial devotion. For a study of filial slicing from the perspective of Chinese religious life, see Jimmy Yu, *Sanctity and Self-Inflicted Violence in Chinese Religions, 1500–1700* (Oxford: Oxford University Press, 2012), 62–88.

8   See Yi Tŏkmu, '*Sasojŏl' (Small Matters for Scholars), Vol. 6 Kukyŏk ch'ŏngjanggwan ch'ŏnsŏ (Complete Literary Collection of Ch'ŏngjanggwan*, Korean translated) (Seoul: Minjok munhwa ch'ujin wiwŏnhoe, 1980), 126.

9   Barbara H. Rosenwein, 'Worrying about Emotions in History', *American Historical Review*, 107, 3 (June 2002): 821–45, 842–45, passim.

10 Frank Biess, Alon Confino, Ute Frevert, Uffa Jensen, Lyndal Roper and Daniela Saxer, 'Forum: History of Emotions', *German History*, 28, 1 (March 2010): 67–80, 70–71.

11 Although copious amounts of writing on women's chaste suicide were produced by male literati, almost no record on suicide was written by women themselves. I have introduced two testaments left by widows before their suicide in *Epistolary Korea: Letters in the Communicative Space of the Chosŏn (1392–1910)*, ed. JaHyun Kim Haboush (New York: Columbia University Press, 2009), 375–89.

12 Susan J. Matt, 'Current Emotion Research in History: Or, Doing History from the Inside Out', *Emotion Review*, 3, 1 (January 2011): 117–24, 118. In this passage Matt credits Barbara Rosenwein for this insight.

13 Because disciplining oneself through repression of emotion was a vital step to becoming an ideal man (K. *kunja*; Ch. *junzi*) who achieved a superior moral position, emotional rhetoric was repressed in the writings of Confucian literati in Chosŏn Korea. Ch'oe Kisuk, 'Discourses of Emotions and Their Metaphysics during the Joseon Period: Focusing on the Joseon Literati's Writings Written in Hanmun (Chinese script)', *Tongbang hakji*, 159 (2012): 3–52.

14 For a study of community-based diverse emotional styles and practices that were performed within a larger sociocultural context, see Benno Gammerl, 'Emotional Styles – Concepts and Challenges', *Rethinking History: The Journal of Theory and Practice*, 16, 2 (2012): 161–75.

15 For an important study on the Confucianization of Korean society, see Martina Deuchler, *The Confucian Transformation of Korea: A Study of Society and Ideology* (Cambridge, MA: Harvard University Press, 1992), 82.

16 A regulation on remarriage was legalized in 1485. *Kyŏngguk taejŏn (The Great Code of Administration), Vol. 3* ed. Han'gukhak munhŏn yŏn'guso (Compiled 1485, Reprint, Seoul: Asea munhwasa, 1983), 1b.

17 For example, *The Illustrated Guide to the Three Bonds* (Samgang haengsil to 三綱行實圖), compiled in 1432 by the government, devotes a section to biographies of virtuous women, targeting female audiences.

18 *Kyŏngguk taejŏn, Vol. 3*, 40a.

19 *Kyŏngguk taejŏn, Vol. 3*, 40a; *Taejŏn hoet'ong, Vol. 3*, 43a (Comprehensive Collection of Dynastic Code) (Compiled in 1865, Reprint Seoul: Pogyŏng munhwasa, 1990).

20 Sim Chonghwan, ed., 'Cheŭm' (Written Judgment), *Chongyongnok, Vol. 2* (A Record of Following the Path) (Kangnŭng: Naksan chŏngsa, 1904), 23b.

21 The official approval was granted several months after Madam Kim died. Whether the actual memorial arch was built or not is untraceable. However, the Bureau of Ritual Administration sent out an official order that wood and builders for the memorial arch should be supplied by the local office (where the petitions had been filed). It also noted that a list of slaves mobilized in the erection must be submitted after the construction. See Sim, *Chongyongnok, Vol. 2*, 24a–26b.

22 For the growth of the elite population during the late Chosŏn dynasty, Sun Joo Kim proposes two factors: 'Natural population growth and the perceived definition of elite – by which all descendants of a prominent ancestor were qualified to claim elite status'. Sun Joo Kim, *Marginality and Subversion in Korea: The Hong Kyongnae Rebellion of 1812* (Seattle: University of Washington Press, 2007), 29.

23 In discussing the evolution of Japanese honour culture, Eiko Ikegami terms this collective action in the pursuit of honour through competition a matter of 'honorable collaboration'. Eiko Ikegami, *The Taming of the Samurai: Honorific Individualism and the Making of Modern Japan* (Cambridge, MA: Harvard University Press, 1995), 18.

24 Rosenwein, 'Worrying about Emotions in History', 842.

25 Sim, 'Yuhyangjang' (Petition by Local Confucians), *Chongyongnok, Vol. 2*, 18b; 'Munjang' (Family Petition), *Chongyongnok Vol. 2*, 12b.

26 Sim Chagwang (1592–1636) was a military officer who was born in the year the Imjin War began and passed a military examination in 1625.

27 In Imperial China, which also witnessed the cult of chastity and a dramatic number of chaste suicides, officials and scholars voiced opposition to excessive and wasteful expressions of chastity. Janet Theiss, 'Managing Martyrdom: Female Suicide and Statecraft in Ming-Qing China', in *Passionate Women: Female Suicide in Late Imperial China*, ed. Paul S. Ropp, Paola Zamperini and Harriet T. Zurndorfer (Leiden, Boston, Köln: Brill Publishing, 2001), 47–76.

28 Chŏng Yagyong, *Tasan nonch'ong (Literary Collection of Tasan)* (Seoul: Ŭryu Munhwasa, 1972), 111–17.

29 Sim, 'Toyujang' (Petitions by Confucians Residing [South Kyŏngsang] Province), *Chongyongnok, Vol. 2*, 17a–17b; 'Yuhyangjang', *Chongyongnok Vol. 2*, 19a–19b.

30 Sim, 'Toyujang', *Chongyongnok, Vol. 2*, 22b.

31 Sim, 'Toyujang', 22b–23a. The meaning of *chŏng* is difficult to capture or translate in English as it carries different meanings, such as concepts of sentiment, emotions and passions. For a study on the sentiment of *qing* (*chŏng*) within the context of the Neo-Confucian discourse of self-cultivation, see Maram Epstein, *Competing Discourses: Orthodoxy, Authenticity and Engendered Meanings in Late Imperial Chinese Fiction* (Cambridge, MA: Harvard University Press, 2001), 64–65.

32 Madam Kim left four writings in Korean script: one testament, two short notes and a letter to her own father. Madam Kim, 'Pyŏksangsŏ' (Notes from the Wall), in Sim, *Chongyongnok, Vol. 1*, 6a.

33 Madam Kim, 'Yuhansŏ' (A Testament Resentfully Written), in Sim, *Chongyongnok, Vol. 1*, 5a–6a.

34 Madam Kim, 'Pyŏksangsŏ', in Sim, *Chongyongnok, Vol. 1*, 6b. 'Great Path' (*taeŭi* 大義) refers to what Confucian prescriptive literature outlines as a married woman's fidelity to her husband.

35 For the complete letter, see Jungwon Kim, 'Daughters' Letters of Farewell to Their Fathers', in *Epistolary Korea: Letters in the Communicative Space of the Chosŏn (1392–1910)*, ed. JaHyun Kim Haboush (New York: Columbia University Press, 2009), 382–89.

36 Kim Hŭiyŏn, 'Chemyomun' (A Eulogy), in Sim, *Chongyongnok, Vol. 3*, 27a.

37 Sim, 'Toyujang', 22a.

38 Madam Kim, 'Yuhansŏ', in Sim, *Chongyongnok, Vol. 1*, 5b.

39 For example, *Family Rituals*, the essential Confucian ritual handbook throughout the Chosŏn dynasty, outlines that it is inappropriate for a widow to wail for her deceased husband at night, since this might imply the couple's intimate marital relations. Patricia Ebrey, trans., *Chu Hsi's Family Rituals* (Princeton: Princeton University Press), 91n. For a superb study on the problematic nature of conjugal love as a deviation from the ideal of Confucian marriage, see Janet Thiess, 'Love in a Confucian Climate: The Perils of Intimacy in Eighteenth-Century China', *Nan Nü*, 11 (2009): 197–233.

40 Kim Hŭiyŏn, 'Chemyomun', in Sim, *Chongyongnok, Vol. 3*, 26a.

41 Kim Hŭiyŏn, 'Chemyomun', in Sim, *Chongyongnok, Vol. 3*, 27a.

42 Susan Mann, 'Widows in the Kinship, Class, and Community Structures of Qing Dynasty China', *Journal of Asian Studies*, 46, 1 (1987): 37–56.

43 Norman Kutcher, *Mourning in Late Imperial China: Filial Piety and the State* (New York: Cambridge University Press, 1999), 2.

44 JaHyun Kim Haboush, 'Filial Emotions and Filial Values: Changing Patterns in the Discourse of Filiality in Late Chosŏn Korea', *Harvard Journal of Asiatic Studies*, 55, 1 (1995): 129–77, 134. In this outstanding study of filiality, Haboush argues that while prescriptive literature reinforced filial values, popular discourse was constructed on the premise of the invariability of filial emotion through a dynamic resistance to social norms, celebrating the supremacy of emotions.

45 Haboush, 'Filial Emotions and Filial Values', 138.

46   Deuchler, *The Confucian Transformation of Korea*, 10.

47   All dates in the original legal report are recorded by the lunar calendar, as was conventionally done in the official records of Chosŏn Korea.

48   'Ch'ungch'ŏng namdo sŏasan-gun tongam-myŏn pudan-li ch'isayŏin yussi oksa munan' (An investigation report of a dead woman, Madam Yu of Sŏsan district, Ch'ungchŏng Province; hereafter 'Madam Yu's Case'). Kyujanggak Archive, Kyu 21648 (1899).

49   In the testimonies of Madam Yu's male family members, they all replied that their job was farming when the magistrate asked, 'How do you make a living?'

50   The condition of Madam Yu's dead body was described as 'her hair all messed up; body being yellow; and both eyes open'. Yu Tŏksu's testimony, 'Madam Yu's Case', 8b.

51   Yu Tŏksu's testimony, 'Madam Yu's Case'.

52   Yusŏ (A Deathbed Letter), 'Madam Yu's Case', 34b–35a.

53   It seems Im was not arrested until two rounds of legal testimonies and investigations ended. On the front page of the report where the final verdict is usually recorded, it is written, 'The victim is Madam Yu; the accused Im has fled; the actual cause of death is poisoning.' 'Madam Yu's Case'.

54   Yu Ch'igŭk was a fourth cousin of Madam Yu. Yu Tŏksu's testimony, 'Madam Yu's Case', 25b.

55   'Madam Yu's Case', 34a–b.

56   For a detailed discussion on the role of circular letters in Confucian scholar communities, see Hwisang Cho, 'The Community of Letters: The T'oegye School and the Political Culture of Chosŏn Korea, 1545–1800' (Ph.D. diss., Columbia University, 2010).

57   For example, the law prescribed that 'In all cases of cursing others, the offenders shall be punished by ten strokes of beating with the light stick'. If the circumstances of cursing led to more violent results, such as injury or death, heavier punishment was applied. Jiang Yonglin, trans, *The Great Ming Code/ Da Ming lü*, Laws on Penal Affairs, Section 4, Article 347; Section 3, Article 325 (Seattle: University of Washington Press, 2005).

58   'Madam Yu's Case', 30b–32b.

59   Han Sasŏk's testimony, 'Madam Yu's Case', 5b; 23b.

60   Yusŏ (A Deathbed Letter), 'Madam Yu's Case', 34b–35a. Written in Korean script, this rare testament appeared along with a hand-drawing of the earthen vessel found in her room.

10

How the duel of honour promoted civility and attenuated violence in Western Europe

Robert A. Nye

Historians and anthropologists have both documented a close connection between violence and honour in a diversity of cultures and societies. From the late Middle Ages through the nineteenth century, European honour cultures flourished in regions where state power was weak, and disputes were settled more frequently in personal confrontations than by recourse to legal authority. Historians have regarded the aristocratic duel as the emblematic social ritual of that era, and social theorists in the tradition of Norbert Elias have traced the frequency and forms of the duel for indications of the retreat of violence and the growing control of unruly emotional impulses. Although the number of duels oscillated according to time and place, there is no disputing the decline and eventual disappearance of the duel in the first third of the twentieth century.

However, the history and social functions performed by the duel have often been ignored in favour of using duelling as an exemplar of an archaism whose degeneration enabled the advance of civilization, the rule of law and the rise of personal dignity.[1] In this chapter I wish to argue that the history of the duel reveals that the codes and practices associated with affairs of honour not only diminished the violence of duelling encounters but governed the structures of male social interaction in social and professional life in ways that made violent confrontations less rather than more likely. Though an historic function of the duel was to differentiate between men eligible to participate in its rituals and thus to perpetuate social hierarchy, in the long run the duel exercised a levelling influence in society by stimulating the production of formal honour codes that appealed to upwardly mobile men. I also argue that these codes were sufficiently exigent to influence both law and custom as they applied to the place of women in democratizing societies.

Elias's account of the pacification of violence depends upon two principal mechanisms. One was the imposition of the rule of law and the monopolization of violence by the state, which made spontaneous violence more dangerous, eliminated the fear of falling under the power of another man and established mechanisms in individuals for self-restraint.[2] The second is the increasing complexity of society, which reinforced these affective changes and spread them to more individuals. In the account Elias offers, the shifts from emotional spontaneity to restraint and from vertical to more horizontal social orders occurred in tandem. The prestige of this model encouraged some historians to place the duel of honour and the decline of the aristocracy together among the casualties of modernization.[3] In the account below, I discuss how the codes that disciplined and restrained duellers were present from the outset in the duel of honour. They complemented, not undermined, the rule of law, and schooled generations of men in the advantages of civility. The 'primal' emotions that Elias believed inspired unregulated violence before the advent of the 'civilizing impulse' never had a place in the duel of honour.

If we consider a lengthier time line for the duel, decouple it from an exclusive class affiliation with irascible warrior elites and expand the domains governed by its rules, we will see that an exclusive association of honour cultures with violence and archaic social structures, although certainly accurate for particular times and places, has distracted historians from considering the contributions that honour and its practices have made to the modern world and to the development of human rights. Honour codes prospered with the rise of industrialization and urbanity and benefited from the complex psychological dynamics of social integration. With respect to late medieval and early modern Europe, it seems fairly uncontroversial to argue that honour was a jealous monopoly of Europe's noble military class, but in several domains the emulative practices of non-nobles had already begun. Nor were the practices or sentiments associated with honour incapable of surviving in centralized states with a monopoly of police power; modern Germany and France both give the lie to that generalization. In what follows I will consider some of the legal, ethical and sociocultural influences honour has engendered in Great Britain, France, Germany and Italy.

The dominant theme of this chapter concerns the evolution of the rules governing disputes and differences between men. Over hundreds of years, these rules developed from rough and ready codes of combat into quasi-legal statutes designed to adjudicate disputes, contain and minimize violence and preserve the honour and personal dignity of disputants. The forms these codes assumed in the modern west gave them authority in a range of conflicts relating to personal, familial and corporate honour. They held men who aspired to honourability to ethical standards understood by everyone in good society, and subjected them to scrutiny and to judgements that could offset the legal and cultural privileges they enjoyed as men, heads of families or professionals. However daunting it might have been to face an opponent's bullet or steel, proper adherence to the rules prescribed by honour codes protected men against the far more crushing shame endured by those who either sought to avoid confrontations or who yielded to spontaneous or violent reactions to affronts. William M. Reddy has characterized such 'effortful self-shaping' as bringing substantial emotional rewards, in this case a new dimension of personal understanding about the value of self-mastery, and the respect of those for whom this was an admired trait.[4] Reddy has emphasized elsewhere the suffering such constraining emotional regimes inflict on individuals, but I wish to indicate here the positive features of a system that enabled men, and eventually women, to improve their social status.[5]

It is important to recognize that though these codes originated in aristocratic milieux, they were in fact available to all worthy aspirants. No man or class of men controlled the codes; rather, it was the codes that made the men. Class, bloodlines or titles of nobility did not confer on elite men a permanent right to honour, nor irrevocably exclude men on the margins. Honour cultures were inherently unstable; who was in and who was out depended on changing social and economic fortunes and on the credible performance of what contemporaries took to be a right to honour. This point has been made at some length by social theorist Roger V. Gould. He has argued that honour cultures have invariably sought to regulate conflict in times of social change by insisting on solidarity and discipline within different, if overlapping, social milieux.[6] Vengeance and retribution are necessary features of such fluid situations, but the threat of violence mitigates conflict by containing it at the margins of contested social boundaries where individuals engage in negotiations over claims or rejections of inclusion. Contested claims of this kind would not arise at all if individuals did not already resemble one another in significant ways. Thus, though it is social mobility that produces occasions for conflict over status, it is social symmetry that establishes the warrant for resolving it.[7] Sociologist Georg Simmel, whose life was coeval with the nineteenth-century resurgence of German duelling, urged us to consider conflict not as a disruptive but as an integrating force. The expression of opposition gives us 'inner satisfaction, distraction, relief', and 'thus gives vitality and reciprocity' to relations we might otherwise avoid. Conflict 'is not only a *means* for preserving the relation but one of the concrete functions which actually constitute it'.[8] Simmel wishes to say that these moments of opposition and emotional resolution have been a dialectical aspect of conflict from the origins of human societies.[9]

Group discipline and the negotiation of honour claims enforce egalitarian codes of civility in two ways: by shaming or expelling group members who bring the group into disrespect through dishonourable behaviour, and by sanctioning methods for resolving such claims by violence only if negotiations fail. Both methods operate according to similar notions of the honour/dishonour binary that governs time and place. When there is sufficient agreement within the greater honour culture on these criteria, there will be a smooth cycling of the unworthy out and the newly worthy in, and a minimization of unpredictable violence or collective disorder. As I will show in the following sections, duelling codes managed to establish quasi-legal procedures that were amenable to rigorous codification. They were consequently adapted to the organizational needs of male professional groups, and also served as a model for more gender-inclusive forms of civility.

The characteristic criteria for inclusion in honour cultures – wealth, blood and lineage relations – are always open to challenge. When these are in doubt, the chief personal evidence for honourability has been sensitivity to insult, certainly to a direct physical affront, but particularly to the accusation that one has lied, though more trivial forms of disrespect were also important, as Jonas Liliequist's and Martha Santos's chapters affirm. To gain entry to or remain in an honour culture, the recipient of an insult had to be prepared to engage in a potentially dangerous duel to neutralize its stigma. However sceptical one is of a system that decides matters of truth with violence, there are complicated feelings underlying such rituals. According to the great French essayist Michel de Montaigne, 'I find that it is natural to defend ourselves most for the defects with which we are most besmirched. It seems that in resenting the accusation..., we unburden ourselves to some extent of the guilt; if we have it in fact, at least we condemn it in appearance.'[10] However, Montaigne did not doubt there existed 'laws' of honour, nor did he doubt that our words and our willingness to stand by them constituted the basic bond of human society. To be given the lie was to stand accused of betraying both society and one's own identity; the charge had to be refuted and some way found to adjudicate it.

The development of duelling jurisprudence from the sixteenth to the twentieth centuries

The duel originated, of course, as a judicial instrument. In France, until the last 'judicial duel' was fought in 1547, noble duels were judged by God, presided over by the sovereign, and often ended in death.[11] The royally sanctioned duel between Jarnac and La Châtaigneraye was the last of this kind; henceforth duels would be private affairs between individuals, in which comportment mattered more than outcome.[12] The popularity of the duel throughout the following 150 years was coterminous with the civil and religious upheavals of those years and the efforts of French monarchs to extend their authority over warring factions. These royal and religious factions took the form of honour cultures led by noble warriors exceedingly jealous of their monopoly of the point of honour.[13] Nonetheless, beginning in the late sixteenth century, French monarchs established a number of institutional procedures that sought to adjudicate differences between noblemen in the general interest of civic order. The act of offering or accepting a challenge was not a public criminal offense, but lèse-majesté, a personal offense against the sovereign. A Tribunal du Point d'Honneur staffed by gentlemen of the realm served as an appellate court through the reign of Louis XIV, and, together with lesser arbitrators, was successful in reducing the number and violence of private affairs. The sources of legal authority for weighing and judging these affairs derived from the aristocratic oral culture with which judges and appellants were entirely familiar.[14]

However, neither repression nor arbitration was as influential in curbing the excesses of honour violence as was another Italian import, which, along with the duelling rapier, arrived in Northern Europe in the sixteenth century: civility. Baldassare Castiglione's *The Courtier* (1529) and other texts on etiquette and courtly deportment circulated widely, schooling generations of European courtiers well into the next century.[15] But lessons in civility and resort to the duel, far from being incompatible, were indissociable qualities of noble gentlemen in this era. In France, young noblemen were taught the rules of civil comportment from an early age by parents who wished them worldly success.[16] In England, contemporaneous Italian *Codes Duello* were regarded as complementary to an education in refined manners, not a contradiction to it. As Markku Peltonen has explained for the English case, the duelling codes taught courteous behaviour, emphasizing that 'civil behavior was the norm and that recourse to the duel was strictly limited to certain cases. But for those cases the theory provided a precise ritual of procedure, from the initial injury to the final outcome of violence'.[17] Fencing enjoyed great popularity everywhere, both as a way of gaining familiarity with weapons and as a school for grace and politeness.[18] There was thus no decisive break with a military vocation for this class; honour and the civil virtues of honnêteté were equal components in a gentleman's armamentarium. As Kristen Neuschel has written of this period, 'Courtesy remained important to the warrior-gentleman of the seventeenth century; in fact, now that courtesy constrained violence more effectively, it was even more highly charged.'[19]

The emotional self-regulation of gentlemen in this era was thus a complex matter. Violence was never excluded as an option, but the anger which might provoke it, and which was no doubt deeply felt, was constrained by a set of rules acknowledged by antagonists that governed its expression. Indeed, the obligation to conceal open displays of anger was intrinsic to the negotiation of differences between gentlemen, and, should it come to that, to their performance in duels. The absence of references to strong emotions in the discourse on duelling by participants and observers alike might seem puzzling in light of the terrible wounds or death such encounters could provoke, but in fact the focus of attention in affairs of honour was on the comportment of the antagonists. Displays of anger, or, worse, fear, were far more important indications of weakness or unworthiness in a man than being bested by his adversary. It is therefore a mistake to simply equate the violence of the duel with the expression of primal emotions when a principal goal of the duellists was to conceal their feelings from the world. Expressions of relief at the outcome, or gloating, were similarly disdained. The duel was a forcing-house of self-discipline.

The civilized manners of city or court provided the context for the differences that arose between gentlemen. The man who had thoroughly mastered the precepts of civility was best prepared to attain justice from an affront, even if violence was ultimately unavoidable. In anticipation of that eventuality, there was accordingly a physical dimension to this kind of self-discipline, as Georges Vigarello has shown in his study of French seventeenth-century fencing manuals. These instructed men in an economy of bodily movements that emphasized restraint, grace, respect for one's personal space and that of an opponent, a corporeal analogue to politesse.[20] The historical fact that civility took flower alongside the duel of honour suggests that mechanisms for social conciliation evolved alongside the violent alternatives which were still very much a part of noble culture, thus challenging the notions of Elias and his followers that violence and civility were characteristics of separate and successive phases of historical development.[21]

The foundation of duelling jurisprudence lay in duelling manuals which proliferated in two historical waves throughout Western Europe. The first of these waves coincided with the importation of Italian fencing techniques and civility books in the sixteenth century, serving gentlemen as guides to comportment for the next two centuries. The second wave began in the first half of the nineteenth century and reached a kind of floodtide in the 1880s in Germany, France, Italy and Austria-Hungary, by which point the duel had been abandoned in the United States and in the British Isles and its colonial domains. The 200-year gap between these publishing cycles may be explained by the fact that the duel of honour was a new phenomenon in the sixteenth century and the first wave provided some necessary ground rules for regulated combat; but since the duel in the early modern West was still an almost entirely aristocratic practice, its rules were then conveyed in elite oral culture for the next two centuries, eliminating the need for new publications. By the 1820s, especially in Great Britain and France, an embourgeoisement of the duel had begun, which stimulated the production of modern codes to instruct new men in the rules of affairs of honour. The most important of these modern codes appeared in 1836 and was a model for many subsequent publications: *Essai sur le duel* by the Comte de Chateauvillard.

Chateauvillard's code was co-signed by peers of France and other eminent gentlemen and designed for use by 'qualified' men. Because the Criminal Code did not mention the duel, Chateauvillard believed his code merited legal status, 'because honour is no less sacred than governmental law'.[22] In the same year Chateauvillard's code appeared, it was cited in an assizes court case involving a fatal duel, with the effect of exculpating the survivor, who was judged to have adhered to the 'law' of the code. The political radical Adolphe Crémieux, who was the survivor's lawyer, conceded that any duel could become an occasion for premeditated murder, but, citing Chateauvillard, insisted an offender merited the death penalty 'not because he has engaged in a duel but because he has violated the laws of honour on the very terrain he had sworn to defend them'.[23] Throughout the rest of the century, the codes of Chateauvillard and his successors served as the basis for a 'private' jurisprudence that was regarded in civil and criminal law as the basis for both punishments and civil fines. His code outlawed 'extraordinary' duels, strictly regulated dangerous pistol duels and held that sword duels should cease with 'first blood'. The authors of all subsequent French duelling codes were accordingly able to present themselves as humanitarians committed to a decrease in violence, the enforcement of negotiated settlements where possible and as safeguards of the mutual respect of gentlemen in public and private life.

The driving forces for the duelling craze that swept Europe in the second half of the nineteenth century were both political and social: political regimes that put new voters and elites into play, and growth in the power, status and social pretensions of nonaristocratic notables. New duelling codes like Chateauvillard's acknowledged these changes by democratizing eligibility for the duel, detaching it from the class-based criteria that prevailed in most places until mid-century. Instead of an emblem of blood or *Stand*, honour was gradually transformed into the 'sense' of honour a man felt entitled to by virtue of his personal attainments and to which he laid claim as a right.[24] There was a certain self-confirming aspect to this process. Bruno de Laborie, author of one of the last duelling manuals published in France, attempted to explain that a man of honour felt a 'painfully nervous noble susceptibility' when insulted by an equal, but was oblivious to comparable slights from social inferiors.[25] Without directly acknowledging the emotional sources for these refined feelings, the new manuals simply assumed the unity of a man's class status and his emotional resources. The French sociologist Pierre Bourdieu has coined the term 'habitus' to describe the embodied gestural, emotional and cultural 'dispositions' of the members of classes or groups in order to explain how these individual qualities were experienced and perceived by others to be 'natural'. Bourdieu's conception of social practice nicely captures the feature of the new duelling manuals that regarded class and emotional sensibility as a unity, while acknowledging the reality of social mobility and personal transformation.[26]

Even in Germany, where the Kaiserreich continued to promote the exclusive prerogatives of the first estate, being regarded as capable of giving 'satisfaction' to another man (*satisfaktionfähig*) was expanded to vast numbers of middle-class men who were also reserve army officers or state bureaucrats.[27] In newly minted Republics like France and Mexico, regime loyalists considered eligibility for the duel to be the private dimension of their democratic citizenship, a right to be treated with respect by their social superiors. As was occurring elsewhere in Europe, these 'new' men also took special pains to school themselves in the art of fencing, where duelling skills, physical and emotional self-mastery and politeness could be readily acquired.[28]

By the 1870s the mobility that prevailed in industrializing nations made it increasingly difficult to identify a man's social status. The undifferentiated black dress of urban life gave few clues about origins or occupation, and the traditional class segregation of social and professional organizations had been considerably watered down. The new fluidity of social life produced uncertainty about hierarchy and thus occasions for disputes about precedence in matters great and small. However, this very uncertainty encouraged men to mind their words and gestures lest they provoke a stranger or a familiar sensitive in matters of the point of honour. The modern duelling manuals were designed to help men navigate situations of this kind.[29] Nonetheless, even the most passionate crusaders against duelling throughout Europe acknowledged the ameliorative effects achieved by regulating what they otherwise took to be a barbarous or sacrilegious vestige of the past.[30] Authors of duelling codes and antiduelling activists thus shared the common aim of lessening the frequency and violence of duels.

It was in Italy that the legal apotheosis of duelling regulations occurred. Progressive democratization, the perils of regional integration and social mobility combined to make duelling in Italy a particularly volatile and frequent phenomenon after mid-century. Thomas Hughes counts over 22 duelling manuals in print in 1914. The most successful of these was Iacopo Gelli's *Codice cavalleresco italiano* of 1892, which resembled the legal tomes on which it was modelled, including references to learned articles, precedents and glosses. It thus constituted, in Hughes' words, 'a living jurisprudence' of the duel. Unlike in France, the duel was formally illegal in Italy, but Gelli's book served as the legal basis for court rulings throughout Italy in which punishments and awards in civil suits were meted out for violation of the 'laws' of the duel.[31] Gelli also helped to establish regional honour courts, crowned by a *Corte permanente d'honore* in Florence which heard their appeals. He hoped his work would mitigate duelling violence, a goal shared by the antiduelling movement in his country.[32]

The importance of 'private' duelling jurisprudence was heightened in France, Italy and Germany by the relative weakness of libel laws. These punished public slander with risibly low fines and did not ordinarily consider the truth of an allegation, which left unresolved feelings and a cloud of uncertainty over the reputation of a slandered party who had surrendered his right to 'give the lie' to his antagonist by bringing legal action. In any case the laws of libel and defamation had no jurisdiction over private insults or physical affronts, or over breaches of the protection a man extended to the women in his household. For these matters, only a duelling challenge could testify to a man's unwillingness to entrust his honour to any power other than himself.[33] The neoclassical Zanardelli law code enacted in Italy in 1889 continued to criminalize the duel, but only punished severely departures from the established code. The code also exempted men who issued a challenge from the brief imprisonment and fine required by the law if they had done so following 'grave insult or serious disgrace'.[34] The distinction between honour and reputation was preserved in the 1931 Rocco code, in which 'The offence of insult protects one's subjective honour, the intrinsic value of the individual, while the offence of defamation protects the individual's objective honour or reputation, the idea that society has of a specific person'.[35] In Italy, and elsewhere, as we shall see, European legal codes acknowledged the existence of an indwelling essence of honour in individuals that enjoined respect and constituted the foundation of their personal identity.

Honour and professional ethics

The place of honour in the history of the professions was well established in early modern times. The Christian social humanism that was the basis for a noble education in the sixteenth century also guided would-be professionals in their preparation for the clergy, law and medicine, ideally stimulated by an inward 'calling that led them to their true vocations'.[36] But these early modern professionals were also emulating the aristocratic ethos that trained nobles for military service in the public interest. To preserve their collective reputations, early professionals attempted to discipline their members. Only the clergy had access to the courts to punish miscreants, but in order to advance the status of their professions, barristers, attorneys, doctors, surgeons and apothecaries discouraged behaviour that would bring shame to their corporations and collected fees in the form of voluntary honoraria to avoid the appearance of cupidity. By turning out the dishonourable, the honour of the group could be preserved.[37] Medieval corporations were replaced in nineteenth-century Europe by national versions of the 'free professions'. These professions submitted to varying degrees of government oversight, including educational standards and licensing, but were essentially free to regulate their memberships. Since the collective honour of the group depended directly on the honourability of its members, it made sense to modern European professionals to draw heavily on the rhetoric and practices of the honour codes that regulated civilian life.

The institutions that ensured professional self-discipline emerged differentially throughout Europe and North America. France had a national Ordre des Avocats as early as 1810, but in Italy and Germany networks of regional disciplinary chambers appeared only in the 1870s, culminating eventually in national organizations.[38] Germany established a formal honour court at Leipzig with jurisdiction over appeals in matters of professional discipline from regional chambers.[39] Ute Frevert relates that the concept of honour adopted by the German disciplinary chambers was modelled directly on that of government civil servants, who were frequent duellers and invariably *satisfaktionfähig*. The Supreme Honour Court in Leipzig did not officially endorse the duel, but was sympathetic with lawyers who were obliged to issue challenges on account of personal insult.[40] Engineers, secondary school teachers, dentists, veterinarians and other professionals followed suit with regional organizations in the twentieth century.

The medical profession followed a somewhat different path from the law. Physicians were later to gain government sanction to organize disciplinary institutions, or, as in the case of France, were denied it until the mid-twentieth century.[41] However, from the end of the eighteenth century, British and French doctors regulated their peers through local medical societies according to informal deontological principles established on gentlemanly codes of honour.[42] In Britain a General Medical Council (GMC) of senior physicians was created in 1858 to punish 'infamous conduct in a professional respect', and strike offenders from the medical register. There was no written code for judging offenders; as gentlemen, physicians were assumed to understand the unwritten code naturally. As Margaret Stacy has written, the GMC functioned much as a 'gentleman's club, concerned only that its members behave like gentlemen and that "bounders" should be evicted'.[43]

In rural areas in Britain, 'ethical' committees in the local British Medical Society followed a set of procedural rules designed to adjudicate professional disputes among members that were modelled directly on the point of honour. Thus, 'complaints must first be addressed by the complainant to the offender demanding his "explanation"'; only when this proved 'unsatisfactory' must the charge be forwarded to the committee. The committee 'mobilized a host of informal mechanisms ranging from inviting disputants to seek an "amicable resolution", where "amends" or "regrets" were expressed, to urging "ostracism" and extending censure to members who maintained professional or friendly relations with offenders'.[44] The patterns of personal friendships in professional groups were clearly affected by such procedures, if not directly determined by them. Mechanisms for re-establishing relationships were present, but it seems likely that wounded feelings would persist after an action was undertaken.

Being denied the opportunity to regulate the profession at a national level, French doctors organized local medical syndicates that were affiliated with national medical societies. In the course of the nineteenth and early twentieth century many of their deontological guides were published. These were not codes of medical ethics so much as panegyrics lauding the 'honour and dignity' of the profession and the 'courage' and 'generosity' of the physician. As one doctor wrote, 'We must follow the cult of honour. In its general character it is superior to both law and morality because one does not reason it out so much as feel it, as one does with religion.'[45] Such a sentiment reflects Simmel's contemporaneous observation of the emotional grounds of conflict resolution. The real aim of these guides was to remind medical men of the etiquette they must follow in consultations, competition for patients, the vacating and sale of medical practices, avoidance of advertising and fee-setting and in all matters of personal deportment.

When the 'loyalty' and 'courtesy' demanded of them by the code was violated, transgressors could be expelled from the syndicate and shunned by their colleagues. Although a medical license could only be withdrawn as a result of conviction for a criminal offense, collegial ostracism could effectively poison the practice of a man who violated the code. As William M. Reddy has argued with respect to government civil servants and journalists in the nineteenth century, the fear of humiliation and the emotional damage of public shaming not only encouraged the affability that smoothed relations among peers but promoted careers and protected the status of the profession.[46]

Occasionally, these internal mechanisms broke down, and an affair of honour intruded harshly into the professional sphere. At a meeting of the Paris Société de Biologie in 1857, the visiting Swiss scientist René-Edouard Claparède found himself in disagreement with a certain Dr. Rouget, a professor at the Paris Medical School, about whether the muscle structure of infusoria was composed of 'fibers' or 'folds'. When Claparède observed that Rouget's assertions were 'questionable', he came dangerously close to implying that Rouget had lied about what he had observed, and Rouget took immediate offense, raising his voice in indignation at the implication and challenging Claparède to a duel. He could find no seconds within the gathering to support him, and the affair ended there. However, the frequency of such incidents in all-male professional associations reminds us that the code of the duel was the natural extension and last resort of the ordinary rules of civil discourse.[47]

The rules in these early deontological codes served as the foundation for modern patient-centred ethical codes that emphasize patient rights together with the duties of doctors and medical personnel.[48] The honesty and discretion demanded of physicians by the older codes, their intolerance of shady practices like fee-splitting or unorthodox medical practices and their concern for the dignity and reputation of the profession ultimately redounded to the benefit of patients. A national code published by a union of medical syndicates in 1936 became the basis for a code promulgated by the newly founded Ordre des Médecins in 1947. The new order had the power to judge and expel licensed physicians for ethical lapses –a real police power – but the informal mechanisms of politeness, professional etiquette and ostracism that operated in earlier times continued to provide a reliable basis for professional discipline. Both the pleasant satisfactions of a scrupulous execution of honourable behaviour and the fearsome spectre of shame haunted every interaction between professional men.

What of professions in nations like the United States without a feudal past or tradition of chivalric honour? Robert Baker has shown that until recent times the ethical traditions of American medicine were borrowed from British texts and practices. The first written code anywhere in Western medicine was published by the American Medical Association in 1847 and derived largely from eighteenth-century British moral philosophy. The revised code of 1904, Baker writes, 'emerged from an ethos that looked back to ideals of gentlemanly honour, now reconceptualised as professional honour'.[49] In his history of the early American professions, Samuel Haber emphasizes that from the beginning of their corporate affiliations the clergy, lawyers, physicians and engineers sought to ingrain urbanity, politeness and mutual courtesy in their members and discourage naked competition and any public criticism of peers. Professions that developed later such as dentistry and veterinary medicine essentially emulated the codes that the core professions had fashioned for themselves out of the material of gentlemanly sociability.[50]

Gender, civility and the public sphere

The most conspicuous impact of the honour code in nineteenth and early twentieth-century Europe and North America was the effective exclusion of women from much of public life. Even where the law or convention did not bar them from voting, office-holding, club memberships or educational opportunities, women were discouraged from participation in domains of civil society dominated by an exclusive masculine sociability with its ever-present penumbra of polite tension, under which simmered resentments, rivalries and the permanent threat of violence. In France, the honour code reinforced Napoleonic legislation on the patriarchal family that treated women as legal minors under the protection of their husbands, requiring his approval for employment or travel. Because her only responsibility in the honour culture was to safeguard her sexual honour, the latitude for masculine hypocrisy and a sexual double standard was considerable, as Eliza Ferguson's discussion of crimes of passions indicates.

However, the demographic crisis which threatened France's great power status provided French women the opportunity to leverage their reproductive potential in behalf of greater civic equality. The new divorce law of 1884 was in part aimed at replacing sterile marriages with fertile ones; divorce courts provided women an opportunity to enlarge the sphere of their personal honour, much as women had been doing throughout the century in separation proceedings.[51] Andrea Mansker has tracked these divorce cases through 1914 and found that the most popular grounds in women's divorce suits was the 'injure grave', a term derived from the hierarchy of duel-worthy affronts, which essentially found fault with a man who failed to live up to his obligations under the honour code through sexual infidelity, abandonment of the domicile, failure to fulfil conjugal duties or behaviour that showed disrespect to his spouse, including physical violence. Of course, the woman who did the same received no mercy from the courts, but on the whole Republican judges narrowed the gap in the sexual double standard by finding fault with the dishonourable behaviour of husbands and urging a new standard of a mutual 'solidarity of honour' in French households. By holding a man's sexual virtue closer to the standard expected of women, Republican judges affirmed the dignity of a woman's marital status and offset some of the disadvantages she suffered in Napoleonic law.[52] By much the same logic, paternity suits, which had been forbidden in the civil code, were permitted after 1912, requiring men to acknowledge and support illegal liaisons.[53]

Frustrated in their efforts to obtain the vote, feminists in France mobilized in moral purity crusades against public vice, alcoholism and sexual perversions in the fin-de-siècle. Women were particularly indignant at the regime of legal prostitution that stigmatized women while excusing the shameful behaviour of their clients. As a symbolic representative of the 'gardiennes' of the 'foyer', the prominent feminist Avril de Saint-Croix was invited to serve on an extra-parliamentary commission on the 'venereal peril' where she argued that women had the right to control their own bodies, and ridiculed male 'gallantry' that justified visits to prostitutes at the risk of infecting their wives. Feminists were thus positioning women as defenders of the national health while exhorting men to adhere to the principles of respect, loyalty and sexual fidelity implicit in the code of honour.[54] A scrupulous adherence to honour earned French women legal equity and perhaps more civil equality as well, and both explained and justified the angry indignation of their protests.

With respect to the legal grounds for enforcing civility, there is an acknowledged difference between Anglo-Saxon and Roman-Germanic legal systems. Despite an early concern in English Common Law with the rights of powerless people to redress from personal insult, equitable penalties for insult remained more potential than real.[55] Anglo-Saxon law turned to mechanisms of civil compensation in libel and defamation statutes that put progressively greater weight on publicity and damage to reputation resulting in financial damage than to the wounding of personal dignity. Legal scholar James Q. Whitman has argued that American law has been unable to effectively prosecute hate speech because authorities prefer to punish abusive speech under obscenity statutes and because Americans consider First Amendment rights to be virtually limitless in the absence of potential violence.[56] When violence occurs, its punishment falls mostly under assault and battery law where either physical violence or its immediate threat, not offensive words or gestures, is the harm.

In France and Germany, by contrast, personal honour is a 'protectable legal interest' and has served as the legal foundation for European dignity and human rights law in the years since the Second World War. Frank Henderson Stewart's notion of honour as a 'claim-right' makes sense in this connection as the basis for enjoining the respect and civility of others, arising not from some abstract ideal of human rights, but, as Whitman argues, 'To the contrary, the European culture of honour and dignity reaches very deep into everyday social life, covering what to us seem astoundingly trivial matters of civility'.[57] German insult law falls into the category of a private criminal offense (*Privatklage*) on charges brought by the offended party, and punishes any gestural or verbal sign of disrespect, including incidents that occur in private and receive no publicity whatever. The statutes are vaguely worded and depend mostly on case law, but though penalties are not severe, convictions are taken seriously. In France, insults to honour and reputation, termed *atteintes à l'honneur*, are heard in correctional police courts and are judged according to the social and cultural context in which they were made, but, as in the German example, fines and jail sentences are mild but symbolically important.[58] Offended parties are not obliged to express indignation at an affront; the law assumes they feel it in their capacity as members of a democratic citizenry.

The concept of insult to personal honour was transported into the criminal law in Germany and France throughout the modern era, especially in the Kaiserreich. Elite concepts of honour and the sensitivity to insult, as we have seen, had begun to percolate through the social strata, a development that increased the likelihood of uncertainty over status and occasions for conflict.[59] Beginning in 1848, German liberal jurists and legislators sought to expand the sphere of private law to provide individuals a venue in which they might seek satisfaction from insult without resort to the duel. Judgements made in these courts appreciated the context and social origins of the parties in an effort to sustain social deference and acknowledge differing class concepts of honour and insult in the honour culture's hierarchy, but the end result, according to Ann Goldberg, was a progressive 'democratization' of honour throughout the social hierarchy. Indeed, one-third of the litigants in these actions were women, who, like their French counterparts, used the insult laws to bring men who had physically or verbally abused them to judgement.[60] In addition, Germany had a strong tradition of craft guilds, in which notions of corporate honour continued to flourish. These notions of the respect owed to labour lived on into the Nazi period in the form of laws protecting workers from capricious verbal abuse or other forms of disrespect from bosses.[61]

In their modern adaptation to the historic honour culture, the French have depended less thoroughly on legal concepts of insult and disrespect and more on cultivating the forms of sociability that mitigate occasions for conflict. Forms of democratic and Republican civility have been taught in the schools since the second half of the nineteenth century, and well before that a good upbringing included the inculcation of good manners in the young, exposure to adult society and illustrations of verbal witticisms and formulas that amuse but do not wound, or if they are meant to sting, not to the point of provoking violence.[62]

Whitman characterizes the retention of a socio-legal sphere of honour in contemporary France and Germany as a 'leveling up' in contrast to the 'leveling down' that constitutes American culture. As he writes, 'Egalitarianism in France and Germany is an egalitarianism that proclaims we are all aristocrats now; and in practice this has been an egalitarianism of widely generalized norms of civil respect.'[63] The duelling culture that flourished in the nineteenth century in both national societies thus prepared these modern democracies to incorporate into their citizenry the sensitivity to insult formerly felt by elite men punctilious on the point of honour. The preservation in the law in both countries of efforts intended originally to mitigate the inevitability and violence of the duel means that generations of their citizens have grown up in a legal regime punishing disrespect for others.[64]

The legacy of these histories for the emotional regimes of contemporary citizens is very possibly what a man 'eligible' for the duel must have felt in its heyday: a sense he was worthy of being treated with respect, feelings of indignation when he was not and a longing for justice to reaffirm what had been denied him. Modern laws punishing hate speech and defending human dignity are the product of the historic efforts by both abolitionists and proponents of the duel to contain its violence and unpredictability. What was once an exclusive quality of noble gentlemen who professed arms gradually expanded to include all men who sought honourability, and eventually women, who elevated their civil status by insisting that men live up to the ideals of honour to which they laid claim. The democratization of honour has not been without its setbacks, and we still acknowledge the honorific status of particular individuals and groups, but my aim here has been to show the debt that our modern democratic claim to be respected by others owes to a violent practice enacted to defend the respect of a powerful few.

Notes

1　For example, Kwame Anthony Appiah, *The Honor Code: How Moral Revolutions Happen* (New York: Norton, 2010).

2　Norbert Elias, *Power and Civility: The Civilizing Process*, Vol. II, trans. Edmund Jephcott (New York: Pantheon Books, 1982), 236–37.

3　Among these see Pieter Spierenburg, *The Broken Spell: A Cultural and Anthropological History of Preindustrial Europe* (New Brunswick, NJ: Rutgers University Press, 1991), 197–200; Malcolm Greenshields, *An Economy of Violence in Early Modern France: Crime and Justice in the Haute*

Auvergne, 1587–1664 (University Park, PA: Pennsylvania State University Press), 76, 174, 235–38. Among books on the history of the duel that have taken this perspective are V. G. Kiernan, *The Duel in European History: Honour and the Reign of Aristocracy* (Oxford: Oxford University Press, 1988); François Billacois, *Le duel dans la société française des XVI–XVIIe siècles* (Paris: Editions de l'École des Hautes Etudes en Sciences Sociales, 1986).

4   William M. Reddy, 'AHR Conversation: The Historical Study of the Emotions', *The American Historical Review*, 117, 5 (December 2012), 1497.

5   William M. Reddy, *The Invisible Code: Honor and Sentiment in Postrevolutionary France, 1814–1848* (Berkeley: University of California Press, 1997); *The Navigation of Feeling: A Framework of a History of Emotions* (Cambridge: Cambridge University Press, 2001).

6   Roger V. Gould, *Collision of Wills: How Ambiguity about Social Rank Breeds Conflict* (Chicago: University of Chicago Press, 2003), 17–22.

7   Gould, *Collision of Wills*, 66.

8   Georg Simmel, *Conflict and the Web of Group-Affiliations*, trans. Kurt H. Wolff (Glencoe, IL: The Free Press, 1955), 19.

9   Simmel, *Conflict and the Web of Group-Affiliations*, 29. Unlike Elias, Simmel almost invariably uses historical examples to make points to qualify transhistorical universals.

10 Michel de Montaigne, 'On Giving the Lie', in *Montaigne's Essays and Selected Writings*, ed. and trans. Donald M. Frame (New York: St. Martins Press, 1963), 285.

11 On the judicial duel see Eric Jager, *The Last Duel: A True Story of Crime, Scandal, and Trial by Combat in Medieval France* (New York: Broadway Books, 2004), 81–84. But Jager is premature about which duel was the 'last'.

12 Billacois, *Le duel dans la société française des XVI–XVIIe siècles*, 83–93.

13 See Brian Sandberg, *Warrior Pursuits: Noble Culture and Civil Conflict in Early Modern France* (Baltimore, MD: Johns Hopkins University Press, 2010).

14 Billacois, *Le duel dans la société française des XVI–XVIIe siècles*, 182–92, 195–209.

15 Norbert Elias, *The Court Society,* trans. Edmund Jephcott (New York: Pantheon, 1983).

16 See on the education of the early modern French nobility, Mark Motley, *Becoming an Aristocrat: The Education of the Court Nobility, 1580–1715* (Princeton, NJ: Princeton University Press, 1990); Jonathan Dewald, *Aristocratic Experience and the Origins of Modern Culture, 1570–1715* (Berkeley: University of California Press, 1993); Ellery Schalk, *From Valor to Pedigree: Ideas of Nobility in France in the Sixteenth and Seventeenth Centuries* (Princeton, NJ: Princeton University Press, 1986), 115–44.

17 Markku Peltonen, *The Duel in Early Modern England: Civility, Politeness and Honour* (Cambridge: Cambridge University Press, 2003), 52.

18 For the English case, see Jennifer A. Low, *Manhood and the Duel: Masculinity in Early Modern Drama and Culture* (New York: Palgrave Macmillan, 2003), 41–70.

19 Kristen B. Neuschel, *Word of Honor: Interpreting Noble Culture in Sixteenth-Century France* (Ithaca, NY: Cornell University Press, 1989), 206.

20 Georges Vigarello, 'The Upward Training of the Body from the Age of Chivalry to Courtly Civility', in *Fragments for a History of the Human Body, Part 2*, ed. Michel Feher, Ramona Naddaff, and Nadia Tazi (New York: Zone Books, 1989), 148–97.

21 On this argument, see Elias, *Power and Civility*, 235–47. Also see Pieter Spierenburg, 'Masculinity, Violence and Honor: An Introduction', in *Men and Violence: Gender, Honor, and Rituals in Modern Europe and America*, ed. Pieter Spierenburg (Columbus, OH: Ohio State University Press, 1998), 9; Wilbert Van Vree, *Meetings, Manners and Civilization: The Development of Modern Meeting Behavior*, trans. Kathleen Bell (London and New York: Leicester University Press, 1999), 6.

22 Comte de Chateauvillard, *Essai sur le duel* (Paris: Bohaire, 1836), 5.

23 On this incident and the details and assumptions of Chateauvillard's code, see Robert A. Nye, *Masculinity and Male Codes of Honor in Modern France* (New York: Oxford University Press, 1993), 140–45. The slightly later development of rules in sport followed a similar pattern: rudimentary notions of fairness became enforceable rules intended to limit and contain violence, the violation of which earned dishonour for participants. For an account of rule-making, violence and the civilizing process, see Norbert Elias and Eric Dunning, *Quest for Excitement: Sport and Leisure in the Civilizing Process* (Oxford: Basil Blackwell, 1986), 21, 150–90.

24 On honour as a 'claim-right', see Frank H. Stewart, *Honor* (Chicago: University of Chicago Press, 1994).

25 Bruno de Laborie, *Les lois du duel* (Paris: Manzi Joyant, 1906), 14–25.

26 Pierre Bourdieu, *Outline of a Theory of Practice*, trans. Richard Nice (Cambridge: Cambridge University Press, 1977), 80–82; see also *Bourdieu and Historical Analysis*, ed. Philip S. Gorski (Durham, NC: Duke University Press, 2013).

27 Ute Frevert, *Men of Honour* (Cambridge: Polity Press, 1995), 135–91.

28 Nye, *Masculinity and Male Codes of Honor*, 150–64; Pablo Piccato, *The Tyranny of Opinion: Honor in the Construction of the Mexican Public Sphere* (Durham, NC: Duke University Press, 2010). A similar phenomenon functioned in the Argentine public sphere in the same era. See Sandra Gayol, '"Honor Moderno": The Significance of Honor in Fin-de-Siècle Argentina', *Hispanic American Historical Review*, 84,3 (August, 2004): 475–98.

29 François Guillot, 'L'Honneur en partage: Le duel et les classes bourgeoisies en France en XIX Siècle', *Revue d'Histoire du XIX Siècle*, 34 (2007): 55–70; see also Jean-Noël Jeanneney, *Le Duel: Une passion française, 1789–1914* (Paris: Perrin, 2004): 123–36. For social mobility and the frequency of Irish duels, see James Kelly, *'That Damn'd Thing Called Honour': Duelling in Ireland, 1570–1850* (Cork: Cork University Press, 1995), 65–68. On the feelings aroused by social uncertainty, see Reddy, *The Invisible Code*.

30 See Andrew Mills, '*Satisfaktion* in Nineteenth-Century German Dueling Violence and Its Relevance for Literary Analysis', *The Germanic Review: Literature, Culture, Theory*, 86,2 (May, 2011): 134–52; also Frevert, *Men of Honour*, 94–97.

31 Steven C. Hughes, *Politics of the Sword: Dueling, Honor and Masculinity in Modern Italy* (Columbus, OH: Ohio State University Press, 2007), 177–90.

32 *Politics of the Sword*, 190, 205.

33 See on libel and the duel, Hughes, *Politics of the Sword*, 119–21; Frevert, *Men of Honour*, 144; Nye, *Masculinity and Male Codes of Honor*, 173–82.

34 Hughes, *Politics of the Sword*, 259.

35 Maria Gabriella Bettiga-Boukerbout, '"Crimes of Honour" in the Italian Penal Code: An Analysis of History and Reform', in '*Honour*': *Crimes, Paradigms and Violence Against Women*, ed. Lynn Welchman and Sara Hossain (London and New York: Zed Books, 2005), 231–32.

36 Rosemary O'Day, *The Professions in Early Modern England* (London: Pearson Education, 2000), 28–30. On expelling the dishonourable, see 270–71.

37 Georg Simmel writes about the intensity of intragroup conflict in which an individual's behaviour is seen to jeopardize the honour, integrity or security of the group in *Conflict and the Web of Group Affiliations*, 48–50.

38 Marie Malatesta, 'Introduction', in *Society and the Professions in Italy, 1860–1914*, ed. Marie Malatesta (Cambridge: Cambridge University Press, 1995), 10.

39 Konrad H. Jarausch, *The Unfree Professions: German Lawyers, Teachers, and Engineers, 1900–1950* (Oxford: Oxford University Press,1990), 13.

40 Frevert, *Men of Honour*, 129.

41 The dates were 1889 in Germany and 1910 in Italy. See Andreas Holger Maehle and Ulrich Tröhler, 'The Discourses of Practitioners in Nineteenth and Twentieth-century Germany', in *The Cambridge World History of Medical Ethics*, ed. Robert B. Baker and Laurence B. McCullough (Cambridge: Cambridge University Press, 2009), 432–34; Paolo Frascani, 'Between the State and the Market: Physicians in Liberal Italy', in *Society and the Professions in Italy, 1860–1914*, 145–74.

42 Mary Lindemann, 'The Discourses of Practitioners in Eighteenth-Century France and Germany in the Eighteenth Century', 391–93; Robert B. Baker, 'The Discourses of Practitioners in Nineteenth and Twentieth-Century Britain and the United States', in *The Cambridge World History of Medical Ethics*, 450.

43 Margaret Stacy, 'The British Medical Council and Medical Ethics', in *Social Science Perspectives in Medical Ethics*, ed. George Weisz (Dordrecht: Kluwer, 1990), 175.

44 Robert A. Nye, 'The Legacy of Masculine Codes of Honor and the Admission of Women to the Medical Profession in the Nineteenth Century', in *Women Physicians and the Cultures of Medicine*, ed. Ellen S. More et al. (Baltimore, MD: Johns Hopkins University Press, 2008), 147.

45 Léon Cassine, *Le Médecin dans la société actuelle* (Saint-Quentin: Baudry, 1896), 63. On this issue generally, see Robert A. Nye, 'Honor Codes and Medical Ethics in Modern France', *Bulletin of the History of Medicine*, 69 (1995): 91–111.

46 Reddy, *The Invisible Code*, 62, 228–38.

47 This account is taken from a letter of Claparède to his mother, April 1858 in 'Lettres de René-Edouard Claparède', ed. Georges de Mosier, *Basler Veröffentlichungen zur Geschichte der Medizen und der Biologie*, 30 (Basel, Schwabe, n.d.), 56–58.

48 Robert A. Nye, 'The Discourses of Practitioners in Nineteenth and Twentieth-Century France', in *The Cambridge World History of Medical Ethics*, 418–26.

49 Baker, 'Britain and the United States', in *The Cambridge World History of Medical Ethics*, 455.

50 Samuel Haber, *The Quest for Authority and Honour in the American Professions, 1750–1900* (Chicago: University of Chicago Press, 1991), 46, 74, 236–37, 300, 348.

51 Reddy, *The Invisible Code*, 65–113.

52 Andrea Mansker, *Sex, Honour, and Citizenship in Early Third Republic France* (Basingstoke and New York: Palgrave Macmillan, 2011), 89–126.

53 See on this issue, Rachel Fuchs, *Contested Paternity: Constructing Families in Modern France* (Baltimore, MD: Johns Hopkins University Press, 2008). Eliza Ferguson has shown how the honour system worked to hold men responsible in cases of domestic violence in *Gender and Justice: Violence, Intimacy, and Community in Fin-de-Siècle France* (Baltimore, MD: Johns Hopkins University Press, 2010).

54 Mansker, *Sex, Honour, and Citizenship in Early Third Republic France*, 193–233. On other efforts to level the playing field in matters of sexual honour, see Elinor Accampo, *Blessed Motherhood, Bitter Fruit: Nelly Roussel and the Politics of Female Pain in Third Republic France* (Baltimore, MD: Johns Hopkins University Press, 2006).

55 Nathan Oman, 'The Honour of Private Law', *Fordham Law Review*, 31 (2011): 44–53.

56 James Q. Whitman, 'Enforcing Civility and Respect: Three Societies', *Yale Law Journal*, 109 (April, 2000): 1372–77.

57 Whitman, 'Enforcing Civility and Respect', 1284.

58 Whitman, 'Enforcing Civility and Respect', 1291–98, 1345–56.

59 Ann Goldberg, *Honour, Politics, and the Law in Imperial Germany, 1871–1914* (Cambridge: Cambridge University Press, 2010), 10, 56.

60 Goldberg, *Honour, Politics, and the Law*, 66–70.

61 Goldberg, *Honour, Politics, and the Law*, 59–64; James Q. Whitman, 'On Nazi Honor and the New European Dignity', in *The Darker Legacies of National*

Socialism and Fascism over Europe and Its Legal Traditions, ed. Christian Joerges, et al. (Oxford and Portland, OR: Hart, 2003), 243–66.

62   Whitman, 'Enforcing Civility and Respect', 1361–66. On the broad influence of aristocratic manners and concepts of mutual respect, see Elizabeth Macknight, *Aristocratic Families in Republican France, 1870–1940* (Manchester: Manchester University Press, 2013), 170–95.

63   Whitman, 'Enforcing Civility and Respect', 1285.

64   Whitman, 'Enforcing Civility and Respect', 1314; Goldberg, *Honour, Politics, and the Law*, 44.

Honour, violence and emotion: An afterword

Carolyn Strange

In 1688 Scottish philosopher and historian David Hume described violence in the name of honour, particularly the duel, as an absurdity that civilization would conquer over time: 'All advances towards reason and good sense are slow and gradual', he proclaimed.[1] Hume's aphorism appeared in his history of England, from the Roman invasion up to the time of the book's publication. During the twentieth century, the historiography of honour-based violence echoed and developed Hume's confident analysis. The rise and fall of duelling in its numerous guises as well as ritual violence carried out by combatants of more humble station over questions of honour have provided the standard plots, with angry men the stock players. The diminution of interpersonal violence over time has also inspired historical studies, most of which contend that civilizing processes reshaped social relations and reduced the intensity of violent impulses. In Western societies, the story goes, honour gradually grew to mean less, and its violent defence came to be seen as gratuitous, absurd. Honour-based violence persisted past the nineteenth century only in the world's less civilized pockets, and among groups whose reason and good sense remained underdeveloped.

The contributors to this volume disturb these narratives – thematically, geographically and historiographically. Foremost, we apply the interpretive tools of historians of emotion, who have developed new ways to understand the past and the individuals who made it. We can use those tools to comprehend the righteous anger of elites responding to the humiliating conquest of the Ming Dynasty, and the prickly confrontations of *sertanejo*s in the backlands of nineteenth-century Brazil without ascribing their violence simply to the sway of cultural codes; rather, their behaviour illustrates how individuals and groups juggled socially inscribed norms and deeply felt emotions under intense political and economic pressure. Analysing emotion historically hinges on the close reading of evidence, often fragmentary, such as the dying speech of an unwed mother, about to be executed for killing the infant who symbolizes her lost honour. The frameworks through which affronts to honour have been registered also vary within and between social groups. In some contexts, such as fin-de-siècle France, a lack of emotional display could be cited as evidence of a victim's dishonourable character, while in others, such as late-Chŏson Korea, the honouring of chaste widow suicide rested on the convincing emotional expression of Confucian virtue. Similarly, on the fringes of empire in convict-era Australia, a diversity of emotional styles and conflicting notions of honour is traceable through Aboriginals', settlers', convicts' and imperial authorities' responses to a dishonourable death. The insights of pioneering anthropologists into the centrality of shame, pride and anger as honour's vital emotional ingredients are affirmed in this collection, although the chapters emphasize a diversity of understandings of honour and a wide range of individual acts of violence in response to it, both self-inflicted and outwardly directed. The limits of the developmental trajectory Hume envisioned and the model of ever-tightening impulse control, associated with Norbert Elias' oeuvre, are evident.

The chronological arrangement of the chapters expressly rejects the convention of regionally and culturally specific approaches by integrating, rather than simply adding, studies of 'other' cultures. Just as the rise of gender history emerged by exploring the interrelations of men's and women's history, and by considering men, no less than women, as gendered subjects, our volume questions the universalist assumptions that have crystallized around the history of the West. Accordingly, we invite readers to consider Confucian beliefs concerning virtue and duty alongside Christian ones, and to appreciate that neither was static. Clearly, the supposed East–West, guilt–shame dichotomies can no longer claim credibility.[2] Nor is any culture static. Deeply embedded religious and cultural understandings of honour are inescapably dynamic and responsive to local and large-scale changes in demographics, political regimes and economic conditions. As the authors document, these shifts have shaped concepts of honour and inclinations towards violence, though not in a single form or direction. The eighth-century Viking ethic of revenge, for example, provided more alternatives to the violent restoration of honour than did the norms of eighteenth-century aristocrats. As this collection underlines, analysing honour-associated violence requires scrutinizing social and temporal specificities, which cultural stereotypes, such as the 'macho' or 'Southern' codes of honour, merely caricature.

The temporal and geographical span of this volume marks a step towards research that will incorporate histories of African, Middle Eastern and Pacific societies to further decentre the West.[3] The cultural, political, social and religious complexities of societies in these regions will introduce a wider repertoire of honour and associated values, and possibly a larger array of associated emotions. Rapidly advancing neurobiological research will challenge historians to collaborate with scientists in order to discern with greater confidence the distinctions and connections between biological and social elements of emotion, as well as its cognitive and psychological dynamics. As this cross-disciplinary research proceeds, it will encourage historians to remove the Eurocentric blinkers that have allowed the history of emotions in Western societies to stand as the history of emotion. Advances in digital humanities scholarship, also likely to be team based, offer new methodological tools suited to mapping and analysing verbal expressions of emotion. The growing corpus of digitized historical documents makes large-scale text mining projects viable, and this new resource will expand the range of questions historians may ask of their evidence, well beyond the scope explored through earlier studies based on hand-compiled lexica.[4] Yet the historian's immersion in primary sources remains vital in the interpretation of clues about emotions associated with the noblest and the cruellest aspects of human behaviour.

Finally, we envision that historical studies of honour-based violence will augment current-day efforts to tackle so-called honour killing. By the beginning of the twenty-first century, feminist and human rights lobbyists successfully elevated this issue onto a global stage, but few critical studies approach the issue historically.[5] Unfortunately, most Western analysts of honour-based violence in countries such as Jordan, Egypt, India and Pakistan, where the practice remains prevalent, attribute the problem to culture or religion. Patriarchal cultures of honour, and their associated emphasis on female chastity, have become targets of reform, prompting authorities from the United Nations to local policing agencies to commit themselves, with varying degrees of sincerity, to stamping out violence in the name of honour. Increasingly, critics charge that these campaigns exoticize and demonize entire cultures and religions, and fail to acknowledge the connections between honour-based violence and patterns of 'domestic' violence, in which feelings of honour and shame frequently arise.[6] Antiviolence campaigns have begun to move from condemnation and punishment towards community-based educational strategies, aimed to realign honour with virtues, such as the protection of the weak and self-sacrifice for the good of others. Nevertheless, efforts to invoke the state's power to punish continue to play a role. In 2011, for instance, Palestinian president Mahmoud Abbas decreed that the penal code be amended to remove leniency provisions for perpetrators of honour-predicated violence. Yet, this amendment did not threaten a timeless practice; rather, the existing Palestinian law was based on the 1960 Jordanian penal code, which itself incorporated elements of Ottoman, French and British as well as Islamic ecclesiastical law.[7] Thus, historical insight has a role to play in support of contemporary struggles for reform. Like late eighteenth-century Cape Town, postcolonial states carry a history of complex imperial conflicts and accommodations into shifting local and geopolitical matrices. The Jordanian Women's Union and similar organizations elsewhere, such as the Indian National Commission of Women, are reshaping values by demanding that women's right to autonomy be enshrined in law and culture locally and around the world.[8] Inspired by these efforts, our final ambition is that collections such as this will inspire further research into the history of individuals and associations that have rendered honour-based violence a thing of the past.

Notes

1   David Hume, *History of England, from the Invasion of Julius Caesar to the Abdication of James the Second, in 1688, Volume One* (Boston: Aldine Publishing, 1852 [1688]), 347.

2   This reading of cultural difference was first defined by anthropologist Ruth Benedict. Ruth Benedict, *The Chrysanthemum and the Sword: Patterns of Japanese Culture* (Boston: Houghton Mifflin, 1946).

3   This ambition prompted the 2008 Umeå University-sponsored conference, 'Cultural History of Emotions in Premodernity'. See http://www.umea-congress.se/emotions2008/programme.pdf (accessed 20 April 2013).

4   For an example of this methodology applied to the study of emotions in history, see Shigehiro Oishi, Jesse Graham, Selin Kesebir, Iolanda Costa Galinha, 'Concepts of Happiness across Time and Cultures', *Personality and Social Psychology Bulletin*, 39, 5 (2013): 559–77.

5   Carolyn Strange, 'Adjusting the Lens of Honour-based Violence: Perspectives from Euro-American History', in *'Honour' Killing and Violence: Theory, Policy and Practice*, ed. Aisha Gill, Carolyn Strange and Karl Roberts (London: Palgrave Macmillan, 2014).

6   Lila Abu-Lughod, *Veiled Sentiments. Honor and Poetry in a Bedouin Society* (Berkeley: University of California Press, 1999); Lynn Welchman and Sara Hossain, ed., *'Honour': Crimes, Paradigms and Violence against Women* (London: Zed Books, 2005).

7   Nadera Shalhoub-Kevorkian, 'Femicide and the Palestinian Criminal Justice System: Seeds of Change in the Context of State Building', *Law and Society Review*, 36, 3 (2002): 577–606; Mazna Hussain, 'Take My Riches, Give Me Justice: A Contextual Analysis of Pakistan's Honor Crimes Legislation', *Harvard Journal of Law & Gender*, 29, 1 (2006): 223–46.

8   The resilience of the belief that honour-based violence is justifiable is analysed in Manuel Eisner and Lana Ghuneim, 'Honor Killing Attitudes amongst Adolescents in Amman', *Aggressive Behaviour*, 39, 5 (2013): 405–17.

INDEX

Note: The locators followed by 'n' refer to note numbers